AN ORIGINAL HARBINGER BOOK   H 060 $2.85   Slightly higher in Canada

CHINA
SINCE 1800

JOHN A. HARRISON

China Since 1800

JOHN A. HARRISON

CHINA
SINCE 1800

AN ORIGINAL HARBINGER BOOK

HARCOURT, BRACE & WORLD, INC.

NEW YORK

To C.T.H.

E F G H I J

ISBN 0-15-616880-4

Library of Congress Catalog Card Number: 66-28625

Printed in the United States of America

The excerpts on pages vi and 52 from Mary C. Wright, *The Last Stand
of Chinese Conservatism: The T'ung Chih Restoration 1862-1874*
(Stanford University Press, 1957), are reprinted by permission
of the publisher. The excerpt on page 7 is from *China in the Sixteenth
Century: The Journals of Matthew Ricci: 1583-1610,* trans. by
Louis J. Gallagher. Copyright 1953 by Random House, Inc.
Reprinted by permission. The excerpt on pages 34-36 from S. Y. Teng,
New Light on the History of the Taiping Rebellion (Harvard University
Press, 1950), is reprinted by permission of the publisher.
The excerpt on pages 55-56 from Walter H. Mallory, *China: Land of Famine*
(American Geographical Society, 1926), is reprinted by permission
of the publisher. The excerpts on pages 129 and 150-51 from T. C. Woo,
The Kuomintang and the Future of the Chinese Revolution
(George Allen and Unwin, Ltd., 1928), are reprinted by permission
of the publisher. The excerpt on pages 200-201 from Mu Fu-sheng,
The Wilting of the Hundred Flowers (Frederick A. Praeger, Inc., 1962),
is reprinted by permission of the publisher. The excerpts on page 214 are
from Dennis J. Doolin's *Communist China: The Politics
of Student Opposition* (Stanford: Hoover Institution, 1964),
pages 33, 38, 61, and 64. Reprinted by permission.

PREFACE

Readers accustomed to hearing of the stately stride of traditional Chinese history will be struck by the great acceleration of change in its modern phase. History had come to expect a kind of solidity and endurance of Chinese values and to count on China's ability to survive. But as we study the nineteenth and twentieth centuries the whole monumental structure of Chinese culture seems to come clattering down. And though it is tempting to look at this as a phenomenon of Chinese history, the fact is that this same upheaval is characteristic of the entire world. In this century the time scales have gone awry, and every civilization is moving ahead of itself. For the West this pace seems normal; for China it is astonishing.

In this volume we shall deal with a period of Chinese history that parallels the entire development of the United States, from the Constitutional Convention of 1789 to the present day; or, in terms of European history, from the opening of the French Revolution. In the West this epoch witnessed the destruction and remodeling of nations, the crumbling of old certainties, and the triumph of ideologies undreamed of in the late eighteenth century. As one traces events in China during the same period, one can, with benefit of hindsight, perceive the hairline cracks in the walls of China that would later thunder apart. But to contemporaries the impending collapse of the sureties on which they rested sounded a warning no louder, perhaps, than the faraway tinkle of wind bells—certainly no louder than the warning sounds at the Court of the Sun King at Versailles, whose inheritance was swept away in much less time than that of his contemporary, Ch'ien Lung, Emperor of China.

The rate and extent of change in China, as viewed through Western eyes, has led to simplisms such as "collapse of China," "shattering of tradition," and "failure of Confucianism." Both

v

Confucianism and tradition did lose their force in time, but the significant transformation occurred around them, in the context of Chinese life. Confucian tradition found itself naked and alone in a world that it never made, despite great efforts to modernize it within traditional frames of authority. The whole environment that contained it slowly imploded.

To the reader coming fresh to Chinese history, it is only fair to quote Professor Mary C. Wright on the study of modern China:

> As the study of modern China is an underdeveloped area of historical scholarship, so the study of economic growth is an underdeveloped area in economics. This being so, comments on the absence of economic growth in nineteenth-century China are doubly hazardous. We have not even rough estimates of the gross national product, much less any means of determining how it was used. We not only know little of shifts in the employment of the labor force, we actually lack reliable general population figures, and there has been no work done on the historical population of China with reference to any feature other than its size. We know neither the total receipts from the various taxes and from various areas, nor the total expenditures of the various government agencies. We lack not only statistical material but descriptive material as well. We do not know precisely how a number of agencies of government functioned, or precisely what many of the terms used in the documents mean.[1]

Students of China are agreed that the dimensions of the subject are enormous and expanding. The postwar surge of interest in China has coincided with the turning of professional historians to intellectual history. This is a rewarding aspect of history, as applied to China, because of the primacy of intellectual constructs in Chinese history. But we must remember that the derivation of such constructs is based on the work of Chinese historians writing for the Chinese educated class; or, in effect, intellectuals writing for and about intellectuals. This research, while fruitful, is not entirely satisfying to those who would like to know more about the round of life, about the people in the

---

[1] Mary C. Wright, *The Last Stand of Chinese Conservatism: The T'ung Chih Restoration 1862-1874* (Stanford: Stanford Univ. Press, 1957), p. 190.

villages and towns, the farms and the markets, not for the sake of curiosity but because these people made the history of China in modern times. Yet these classes, comprising some 80 per cent of the population, appear only occasionally in historical accounts and then as peripheral objects in impersonal records. And since the annals of the poor do not exist, any history of China is incomplete, and the historical imagination must substitute. To paraphrase the English historian Coulton—how much Confucian scholarship would we not give for one townsman's diary or one generation of peasant letters?

This book was written, over a period of five years, to provide Americans with a much-needed short, readable, and accurate history of modern China. The author gratefully acknowledges his obligation to every major scholar and observer of China in the nineteenth and twentieth centuries. An enormous amount of material in a variety of languages has been studied, and, like all authors of general histories, I stand on the shoulders of those who have preceded me.

I especially acknowledge the inspiration derived from the teaching, works, and personal examples of Peter Boodberg, L. Carrington Goodrich, John Fairbank, and Mary C. Wright.

John A. Harrison

University of Miami
Coral Gables, Fla.
February, 1967

CONTENTS

China Since 1800

Introduction

The Discovery of China

THE MISSIONARIES

Europe's discovery of China began in the sixteenth century with
the commercial activities of the Portuguese and the Spanish in
South and Southeast Asia and with the missionary labors of the
new Society of Jesus. The missions were beholden to the secular
government of Portugal, which held as a state secret the charts
of the routes to the East it had pioneered; indeed, in the heyday
of Portuguese power, missionaries could go to the East only in
Portuguese ships.

The Portuguese first came into the Chinese trade at Mallaca,
depot for a great South China–Malaya junk trade. In 1517 two
Portuguese traders, Tomas Pires and Fernao Peres d'Andrade,
managed to make such a favorable impression on the authorities
at Canton that they were given permission to trade off the mouth
of the Pearl River. But almost immediately this privilege was
withdrawn, due to the arrogant demands of the Portuguese, and,
in 1521, trade with them was stopped, and Portuguese ships
were banned from the China coast. The foolhardy arrogance of
the Portuguese stemmed from their experience in India, where
they had become accustomed to dominating a gentle and agreeable people. In China they had expected to find another people

3

and culture to whom they could feel superior, but they soon found they were mistaken.

Because the South China trade was too rich to abandon, the Portuguese continued a furtive and lucrative trade off the many coves and islands of the region. Later, when they had established a base in Kyushu, Japan, they began to act in concert with Chinese and Japanese coastal pirates. Then, in 1544, despite their reputation, the local authorities at Canton permitted them to have a trading post on the island of Macao, provided they kept no firearms there, paid a handsome annual sum to the Viceroy of Kwangtung Province—and also provided that Peking never found out about the deal. It was from this post at Macao that the Jesuit missionaries set out about their work.

The Franciscans, the other great missionary order that labored in East Asia, had the Spanish Philippines as their base. Spain, unable to obtain a foothold in the Spice Islands (Mollucas), turned to the archipelago that Magellan had discovered because they knew that the Chinese traded there. In 1564 Legaspi led a fleet from Mexico to found a Spanish settlement on Cebu Island. Then, in 1571, with the ambition of eventually reaching the coast of China and conquering that country—for these men believed that a handful of Spaniards could conquer all China—the Spanish moved to Manila on Luzon, which became the depot between Spain in America and Spain in the Western Pacific, and where Legaspi became Governor of the Philippine Islands. Trade with China was carefully cultivated, although the Spanish lived in fear that China would descend upon the islands or that the some 20,000 Chinese already living there would throw off this new alien rule—an apprehension that almost came to pass in 1603, when a terrible rising of the Chinese was beaten off with grievous losses on both sides. But trade with China continued. Indeed, Spaniards had been of such assistance to Chinese coastal authorities in eradicating piracy that the authorities of Fukien Province invited them in 1575 to send a mission to China. This was the mission of Fr. de Rada, whose Augustinians stayed one month and returned with 300 volumes of *materia medica,* herbals, and botanical and pharmaceutical works, all far in advance of those of the West. It was the study of these learned works that marks the West's cultural discovery of China.

The Spanish missionaries continued their efforts to get a foothold in China and in 1579 traveled as far as Canton, but Portuguese traders had them imprisoned on spurious charges, and after two months they were expelled. Again, in 1580, Franciscans attempted the trip, but they too were arrested and sent back. Then, in 1585, the Spanish and Portuguese settled their conflicts, which had become world wide; missionary work in China was relinquished to the Jesuits.

The pioneer Jesuit in Asia was St. Francis Xavier, Apostle to the Indies, who had died, thirty years before, on the China coast just after writing to Fr. Perez in Mallaca of his intention to enter China:

> According to the natives of the Country, the risks which we run are two. The first is that, having received his two hundred *cuzados,* our transporter may abandon us on some desert island or cast us into the sea to avoid discovery by the Governor of Canton, and the second, that, if we are taken to Canton and reach the Governor, he will order us to be tortured or thrown into prison. . . . Besides these two risks there are many other more serious ones, not connected with the Chinese . . . for instance, the danger of losing trust in the mercy and power of God because of the perils we may run into on His service. That is a much greater danger than the mischief which all the enemies of God could do to us . . . considering those dangers of the soul . . . we find it is safer and surer to pass through the physical ones, . . . and so, by whatever way, we are determined to go to China. . . . Pray much to God for us because we run the very greatest risk of being made prisoners, but we comfort ourselves with the thought that it is far better to be a captive for the love of God alone than to be free by fleeing the toils and pain of the Cross.[1]

The most remarkable Jesuit missioner was Fr. Matteo Ricci, born in Italy in 1552, who came to the Jesuit House in Macao in 1582. Lest the achievements of Xavier, Ricci, and their followers be dismissed in a world shrunken by the jet engine, let it be noted that not only did Europeans know nothing of China, but no European knew the language. When, in 1565, Fr. Peres, superior of the small Jesuit group at Macao, asked the Chinese for permission to live in Canton, he was refused and advised to first learn Chinese. Yet even with a grasp of the language China seemed a sealed land. When another Macao missionary, Fr. Riberia, left in 1568 he said: "During the three years I was at Macao I did everything possible to penetrate the continent but nothing I could think of was of any avail." [2]

It was Alessandro Valignano, Visitor General to the Indies, who fitted the key to the lock. Arriving in Macao in 1577, he ordered the Jesuits to abandon the idea of Europeanization and to adapt themselves to Chinese culture. Chinese converts were to remain culturally Chinese. "Instead of Portugalising them the missionaries were to 'sinicise' themselves." [3] Fr. Ricci turned to an intensive study of Chinese the year of his arrival and, in 1583, went to Chaoch'ing on the mainland to live with Fr. Ruggiero, who had been permitted to live there for a year. Ricci lived there for six years as priest and scholar, translating from the one language into the other, assembling grammars and vocabularies, and, in general, preparing for the entry of Christianity into the mainstream of Chinese life and thought. In 1589 he and a companion, Fr. d'Almeida, left for Shachow, where, with two Chinese candidates for the Society, they immersed themselves for six years in a study of the Chinese classic writings and took on the dress and habits of Chinese scholars. At the end of this period Ricci was accepted by scholars and officials, and in 1595, invited to Nanchang, he began an apostolate of scholarship.

Living, thinking, talking as a learned Chinese, advancing Christianity not through preaching but through discussion and conversation, he communicated with China through the medium of Chinese learning, respecting it as the Chinese scholars came to respect him. In 1600 he and his small mission were given Imperial permission to reside in Peking itself, and there he gained an immense reputation. Before his death at Peking in 1610, his conversions were small in number, perhaps two thousand, but they were all among the educated class for whom the learning of Europe as well as its religion were exciting. As Ricci wrote:

Whoever may think that ethics, physics and mathematics are not important in the work of the Church, is unacquainted with the taste of the Chinese, who are slow to take a salutary spiritual potion, unless it be seasoned with an intellectual flavoring. It was by means of a knowledge of European science, new to the Chinese, that Father Ricci amazed the entire philosophical world of China; proving the truth of its novelty by sound and logical reasoning. . . . Once this new knowledge became known to a few, it was not long before it found its way into the academies of the learned class. One can gather from this how the reputation of Europe was enhanced, and how they were slow to segregate it as being barbarous, and ashamed to call it such in the future.[4]

The new cosmology and the unified concept of the world that Ricci and his colleagues supplied, while eagerly received, also made them enemies among traditional scholars. After Ricci's day, because of resurgence of Confucian cultural supremacy and centrality, much of this knowledge was discarded. Five years after Ricci's death the enmity aroused by these teachings led to the persecution of eight European Jesuits and six Chinese lay brothers, an action incited by high officials on the Board of Rites and the Board of War. It was a great storm to be directed at so small a number, but the Court, then in the grip of eunuchs and concubines and quaking from the rise of Manchu power in the North, was striking out at all supposed enemies. The harassment of Chinese Christians and of missionaries continued until 1628, when, in a striking reversal of attitude, a number of Chinese Christian scholars were admitted to state offices on the Board of War, the Board of Rites, and other boards of government.

The missions continued, but uneasily, for no one was sure when proscriptions might not recur. Nevertheless, in the sack of Peking, following the fall of the Ming dynasty, the Manchus spared the Dutch Jesuit mathematician and astronomer Fr. Johann Adam Schall von Bell and his followers. Indeed, in 1645 Schall, a remarkable man by any standards—Chinese scholar, Latin scholar, master of European languages, mathematician, astronomer, instrument maker, architect—was raised to President of the Board of Astronomy, a post he had to accept despite the opposition of his own order (the rules of the Society bar eccelesiastical preferment) and the envy of some Chinese scholars. Before the advent of Schall Chinese astronomical calculation had gone awry for years. The Jesuits who were charged with reforming the Chinese calendar found, to their astonishment, that Chinese astronomers were not using the fine old instruments available at Peking; they had lost the art. Instead they relied on computations from old tables. Schall was succeeded by an equally able man, Fr. Verbiest. Verbiest became Vice-President of the Board of Astronomy and Vice-President of the Board of Works and enjoyed a close relationship with the Emperor K'ang Hsi, of whom, on August 1, 1685, he wrote to his superior:

> . . . this Emperor is very fond of all the *belles lettres* and all the sciences; there has been no Emperor for centuries who can compare with him in this. Moreover, even among the Chinese who apply themselves especially to study one will not find one who possesses such a wide knowledge and practice of the various sciences carried up to a certain point. Thus I explained to him the first six books of Euclid twelve years ago, . . . music is being introduced to him by Father Thomas Pereira. . . . The Emperor had expressed a desire a few weeks ago to have our European philosophy printed as well.[5]

After these men the brilliant epoch of missionary work came to an end, the victim of the continuing enmity of Chinese scholars and of conflict among Manila, Rome, and Macao over the role of the missions in China.

By this time there was a greater need for bishops and native clergy in Asia, from Japan to Malaya, than Portugal could supply. In 1633 Rome removed China from the province of the Archbishop of Goa and ordered a seminary established in China. Franciscans from Manila clashed with Jesuits over means and methods of proselytizing, a side issue being concerned with the proper names of God in Chinese, and a fierce argument centered around the question of whether a Christian could practice the Confucian rites of respect for the dead. The Franciscans and Dominicans (i.e., the French and the Spanish) said No, it was idolatry. The Jesuits said Yes, the practice was simply social. In 1704 Rome decided against the Jesuit case, which had the incidental effect of suppressing an inscription written by K'ang Hsi himself for the Catholic Church in Peking. Two years later the Emperor, having reached the conclusion that the interference of Rome was inimical to his power, ordered all missionaries in China to adhere to Ricci's principles of cultural toleration or get out. Although the Jesuits appealed the 1704 decision, it was reconfirmed in 1715 and again in 1742, and thus the Society of Jesus, which had its church in the Imperial capital, with the Emperor of China as its patron, and which had founded a native Catholic Church, saw its achievements crumble away. After K'ang Hsi the missions had no new friends among Chinese rulers.

THE TRADERS

For centuries porcelain (its ingredients a mystery in Europe where it was first, and badly, made in 1575) had come west from the Orient, and then came silk and then the ". . . China drink, called by the Chineans Tcha, by other nations Tay alias Tea." [6]

With the growing commerce in these exports the West came to have a greater interest in China than just for her books or converts. The Dutch were the first to attempt to trade with China through an organized commercial company, the Netherlands-Indies Company, whose ships were forced away from Canton by the Portuguese in 1604 and 1607. A Dutch attempt to storm Macao was repulsed in 1622. Then, in 1624, the Dutch settled in Formosa (it was at that time free of any domination) and began an arduous solicitation of the Chinese, to the point of consenting to be treated as inferior tribute bearers. In 1662 Formosa was taken from the Dutch by adherents of the defeated Ming dynasty. But even though the Dutch helped the victorious Manchus capture the port of Amoy in 1662 they still had no status with Peking. They remained largely clandestine traders until 1715, when they were permitted to build a factory in Canton. This was a very small victory, for in 1685 all the ports had been opened to foreign trade by Imperial order.

The English first arrived on the China coast in 1637 with the voyage of Captain James Weddell, who waited six days for permission to trade, and receiving none, forced his way into Canton harbor, fired on the Chinese forts, and was fired on in return. Thereafter, until 1685, the English traded at Amoy or at Formosa (the latter was still being held by Ming adherents). Then in 1715 the East India Company was permitted to open a factory at Canton. Here at Canton were located not only the factories of the commercial charter companies of Holland and England but also those of the great trading cities of Genoa, Bremen, and Hamburg, among others. The Emperor Ch'ien Lung, successor to K'ang Hsi, chose to make Canton the sole open port in 1757, because it kept these commercial nuisances as far as possible from Peking. As it happened this also suited the foreigners, because Canton was a safe and good port and the largest and richest trading depot in the Empire. By tradition China viewed these people as tributaries to the Chinese sovereign, a concept rejected by Westerners despite their century and a half of experience on the China coast and despite the Anson incident in 1743.

Captain Anson had sailed into Canton, with Spanish prisoners of war on board, to refit. The Chinese refused to allow him to refit because they had no intention of becoming involved in Anglo-Spanish colonial disputes, and the Prefect for the Governor-General of Kwangtung Province told Anson: "For long it has been a strict rule with us that the Bogue was to be regarded as the frontier of China. But now, being at war with another country, instead of quickly passing the Bogue with furled ensigns you flaunt your arms there. This is violent rebellion." [7] Supplies were denied Anson until he surrendered his prisoners to the local authorities, which he did to demonstrate his pacific intent, but from the Chinese point of view this act symbolized a form of tribute and therefore Anson's (and England's) recognition of Chinese sovereignty.

It followed from this incident that the Chinese authorities were to regard English and all other foreigners at Canton as essentially tributaries to China. In 1793 the English government sent Lord McCartney on an official visit. He did get to Peking and was courteously treated, but the Chinese simply refused to discuss trade regulations or the tribute status. Again, in 1816, England sent Lord Amherst as representative to China to attempt to put the trade of the East India Company on a more stable and more official basis and to free it from corrupt local officials. Amherst was instructed to observe the necessary courtesies, but when faced with the kowtow—the ceremonial placing of the forehead on the floor—and additionally rude treatment he refused to attend an audience and came away empty handed.

The foreigners at Canton dealt only with local officials, and they had to penetrate a screen of these to get to the governor of the province, to say nothing of the viceroy of the region, the Imperial Commissioner of the Customs, or the Imperial Commissioner in the province. Thus maritime trade depended, absolutely, upon the favor of certain Chinese officials, who derived a handsome living from it. Since Peking took little note, these men had a free hand with the barbarian traders and squeezed as much as they could from the Canton trade. Leading them was the Imperially appointed Superintendent of the Trade at Canton, who received his share of the duties and the special taxes, as well as 6 per cent on all transactions. In 1720 the merchants of Canton, feeling themselves caught between their own officials and the Westerners, formed a self-protective guild, the Co-hong. But this met with so much opposition from the foreigners, who refused to deal with a monopoly, that the provincial officials dissolved it. Then the officials levied a 10 per cent tax on transactions for their own purses.

For the next thirty-five years foreign traders faced excessive duties, taxes, levies, and regulations. Habituated to free trade and regarding these as unnatural restraints, the foreigners, through the chief trader, the East India Company, sent James Flint to Peking to petition for representation at the capital or an end to the exactions at Canton. Flint got as far as Tientsin, where his petition was delivered to the Court. An Imperial investigation was launched that ended with the dismissal of the Superintendent of the Trade. In retribution the Governor of Kwangtung had Flint jailed, while his Chinese interpreter was beheaded. Flint remained in jail for three years and was then deported. As a result of this incident the Viceroy decreed, in 1760, that the trade would no longer function through individual merchants but that the Co-hong would be reconstituted and would be held responsible, as a corporate body, for each and every foreigner and his trade, and that no foreigner could remain in Canton after his ship had sailed. Thus the Canton officials could now control— and bleed—the trade through the mercantile guild. After 1760, in effect, one monopoly, the Co-hong, dealt with another monopoly, the East India Company. For both sides it was a thoroughly unsatisfactory arrangement for conducting trade, as well as human and international relations.

THE VISION OF CATHAY

Between the missionaries on the one hand and the traders on the other lay the European vision of Cathay. What Europe knew of China began with the reports and translations of the Jesuits, added to by the accounts of returning travelers. The sum of these impressions was that of an empire of enlightened, tolerant philosophers governed by an absolute monarch of stupendous benevolence and justice. By the eighteenth century there came about among the wealthy of Europe a taste for imitating the fabled East. This brought forth rococo decorative art, imitation porcelain, and "moon bridges" in "Chinese" gardens. China tea changed England from a nation of gin drinkers to a nation of tea drinkers. Although to most of the West China stood for fine, fanciful, and exotic things, the ideal vision came through the translations of Confucian texts. The study of these, along with the belief that there was no supernatural religion in China, captured the minds of men such as Leibniz, Voltaire, and the "French Confucius" Quesnay. These men drew inspiration from what they believed to be a perfect and stable moral order for their own patterns of European society, and the imitation of Confucius probably reached its peak when Louis XV took plow in hand at the opening of the spring planting. But in the late eighteenth century this image of China began to fade, and with the discovery of Pompeii, rococo gave way to Roman antiquity as the fashionable cult.

The French Revolution, the rise of Bonaparte, the effects of industrialization, and the colonial wars focused the European mind on its own problems and future, and less and less was heard of China. But what news did emerge, at the beginning of the nineteenth century, came from traders, factors, and employees of the commercial companies. These men were unconcerned with patterns of society, government, and philosophy. They spoke of the harassments and corruptions and the intransigence of the Chinese they knew, and while their audience was small, it was powerful, for they were speaking to their governments and to the European commercial interests. Thus the idealization of Cathay was shifting, at the beginning of the century, from a vision of ineffable Confucius to a picture of grasping merchants and crooked customs officials. Irritation and contempt was replacing admiration and respect.

NOTES

1. J. Broderick, S.J., *The Origins of the Jesuits* (Garden City, N.Y.: Doubleday, 1960), p. 154.
2. G. Dunne, *Generation of Giants* (Notre Dame, Ind.: Univ. of Notre Dame Press, 1962), p. 16.
3. *Ibid.*, p. 19.
4. *China in the Sixteenth Century: The Journals of Matthew Ricci, 1583-1610*, trans. Lewis J. Gallagher (New York: Random House, 1953), p. 326.
5. H. Bernard, "Notes on the Introduction of the Natural Sciences into the Chinese Empire," *Yenching Journal of Social Studies*, III, No. 2 (August, 1941), 234.
6. H. Honor, *Chinoiserie* (London: J. Murray, 1961), p. 427.
7. A. Waley, *Yuan Mei* (New York: Grove Press, 1956), p. 207.

One

The Great Vise
(1796-1870)

THE EXTERNAL PRESSURES

The Conditions of Trade and the Coming of War

From the point of view of Western commercial practices, the Chinese conduct of the trade at Canton was both irregular and humiliating. Foreigners were limited to a single port and, at that port, to transacting business with a single agency designated by the government—the guild of Kwangtung merchants, the Co-hong. The Imperial government regarded this as a natural arrangement that kept the barbarians at arm's length while ensuring that trade would continue to be treated as a tributary matter. The aggravation caused by this ignorance of the equality of nations, in the Western sense, was added to by the depredations of local officials, who charged all the traffic would bear in customs and other fees. No one could complain or seek redress, for the Co-hong acted as a protective screen for the officials. The Co-hong held a monopoly, set the prices, and selected the goods to be traded. However, they had grave responsibilities to their government. They were not permitted to go into debt to the foreigners, which placed a great strain on their resources, and they were obliged to enforce the strict regulations which governed not only the trade of foreigner but their right to live on the Canton waterfront. Westerners were allowed to reside for a time each year in their waterfront warehouses (the remainder of the year they had to retire to Portuguese Macao), where their conduct was severely restricted, even as to the hours when they might take walks. There was nothing the Western merchants could do about these shameful restrictions, for neither they nor their governments had any official status whatsoever, nor could they make an appeal to any Chinese group save the Co-hong. It was to alleviate this situation and to open additional ports, regularize the trade, and establish representation at Peking that the McCartney and Amherst missions had been sent.

The Chinese also had their grievances: the crews of the Western ships were a hard lot, and ashore, after the long voyage to Canton, they brawled and carried on incomprehensible Western feuds. Still, chief responsibility for the unhealthy decline of social and trade relationships at Canton lay in a contemptuous, if traditional, national policy and the exactions of provincial and port authorities. Yet trade itself flourished. The English (who accounted for the greatest number of ships calling at Canton) were taking away cotton cloth, tea, and silk, and bringing in metals, raw cotton, and woolens. And after 1816 they began increasingly to take away silver and bring in opium.

The practice of smoking opium gum (as distinct from the medicinal uses of the seed) was introduced to China by the Dutch from the Indies in the seventeenth century; there are no records prior to this time of Chinese habituation. During the seventeenth and eighteenth centuries, however, the Portuguese imported opium into Macao for resale in China, and the habit grew with astounding speed. In 1729 an imperial edict forbade both the sale and the smoking of opium, this Kwangtung practice being viewed by Peking as a reprehensible and dangerous vice. In 1733, however, the edict notwithstanding, the British administration of Bengal brought the trade in opium within that area (the world center of production and preparation) under the monopoly of the East India Company, and thus the Company became the largest merchant of opium. During the remainder of the eighteenth century there was an increasing flow of contraband opium from Bengal to China. The majority of the carriers were English ships (but not necessarily Company ships), who trans-shipped it to Chinese receiving boats off the Canton coast and then themselves sailed into Canton with honest cargoes. Thus, though it was the Chinese who objected to the opium trade, it is obvious that without the participation of Chinese merchants and officials the smuggling would not have survived.

In the early nineteenth century the Chinese became increasingly worried, not only over the rapid growth of the illicit trade —in 1828 it was estimated that about 90 per cent of the total foreign import trade was in opium—but also over the consequent drain of Chinese silver, for opium was paid for only in silver bullion and coin. The loss of silver specie from Canton is now seen to have been an exaggerated problem, for the total economy of China was easily able to carry the export deficit at Canton. Furthermore, this deficit could have been ended by one resolute stroke had anyone in power chosen to do so. But more important than the alarm felt by the authorities over these matters was the fact that for the first time China and her officialdom had met with an equal culture and, moreover, one that was as firmly righteous in its ways as were the Chinese. Even so, a kind of equity might have been worked out had not the controlling factor on the Western side been removed.

The desire of English merchants at large to enter the China trade led to enormous pressures on the British government to end the monopoly of the East India Company. This was accomplished by Parliament in August, 1833, and in April of the following year trade in Chinese commodities was thrown open to all English merchants. Now, whatever its faults, the Company had forced English merchants to obey the Chinese rules of trade, thereby keeping the peace. But the act of Parliament that ended the monopoly substituted for the Company the office of British Superintendent of the Trade, a move that was to accelerate the situation into crisis; in addition, the same Parliamentary act that created resident Superintendents of the Trade authorized a court of justice in China to try British citizens for crimes committed in Chinese territory. This demonstrated not only an understandable English distaste for the operations of Chinese criminal interrogation and trial but also a magnificent presumption that English criminal and admiralty law would have jurisdiction within the sovereign confines of the Chinese Empire. For their part, the Chinese were astounded not only at the attempt to introduce the practices of an alien code into their state, but at the widely variant penalties. They believed that if Chinese were to be subject to the death penalty for opium smuggling then foreigners accused of the same crime should suffer the same penalty. At any rate, open trade began with an event of significance: the mission of Lord Napier to China.

Lord Napier, appointed First Superintendent of the Trade in Canton, arrived in China in 1833 under instructions to come into direct contact with the Viceroy of Kwangtung, to seek to protect the interests of English trade, and to announce himself as possessing legal and juridical rights over Englishmen in China. When the Viceroy refused to see Napier or even to receive his petition, Napier persisted in his effort, bringing pressure to bear on the Co-hong by rejecting their advice to petition the authorities through them, a procedure the Viceroy had demanded from the Co-hong. The Co-hong, caught between two powerful forces, attempted to save itself and the situation by bringing the English trade to a stop in August, 1833, in response to the Viceroy's order to stop buying and selling.

This crisis ended with Napier's sudden death at Macao in September, 1833, but not before he had publicly accused the Chinese authorities of double dealing. With his death a lull came in the attempt to resolve matters of trade conditions, the commerce in opium, and official representations of nations, but it was to be simply a temporary respite in the clash between two unbending and irreconcilable political systems.

In 1836, London, under great pressure from English merchants in Canton, appointed Charles Elliot as Superintendent of the Trade. Elliot was to have the handicaps of an impossible personal situation (arising from growing activism in London), the ever-increasing hardening of Peking's attitude toward the opium trade, and the inability (due to lack of authority) to exercise any control over independent English traders or over American traders. Trapped between the complaints of English traders and the obduracy of Chinese officials at Canton, on the one hand, and a British Foreign Office, months away by dispatches, on the other, Elliot, to protect the legal trade, had perforce to protect the illegal as well.

On March 10, 1839, Lin Tse-hsu, Viceroy of Hupei and Honan, arrived at Canton. He had been sent as Imperial Commissioner to abolish the opium trade (it had seeped into his northern bailiwick, and he had presented to the Court the most formidable of memorials against it). Bent on an annihilation, without compensation, of this trade, on March 18, he demanded of Captain Elliot that all opium stores in British hands be turned over to him.

> There is a clause in our Code which says that people from countries outside our sphere of influence are subject to the same penalties as the Chinese themselves. Strictly speaking, foreigners who have sold opium are now liable to suffer the death penalty. By a special act of grace you are only being asked to hand over your opium and sign our undertaking never to bring opium again and to accept that if you are caught doing so you will be dealt with according to the law and the whole of your cargo will be confiscated.[1]

Opium stocks were immediately seized from Chinese merchants. Then trade was stopped while the police seized the foreign warehouses, holding the merchants as hostages. The desperate Elliot finally persuaded the English at Canton to turn their entire stocks of opium over to the Chinese authorities, and without compensation. Lin next demanded, before any resumption of trade would be allowed, that foreign traders—and Elliot—sign a bond renouncing the drug traffic, under pain of death. Americans and other foreigners signed, tongue in cheek, and resumed the profitable trade. Elliot was unable and unwilling to enter into such a bond. He and his government held the view that it was up to the government of China to enforce Chinese law, and until Peking took such measures there existed a prescriptive right of trade. While not in any degree favorable to a trade in opium as such, both Elliot and his government were aware that the government of British India was largely maintained through exportation of Indian opium to China.

Lin was convinced that the Superintendent of the Trade was

deliberately protecting smugglers, particularly the great merchant firms of Jardine and of Dent, and he was further embittered in November, 1839, by an exchange of shots between two British frigates and his war junks at Canton. In December, 1839, Peking granted him an Imperial edict permanently forbidding English trade and expelling English ships from Chinese waters. This precipitous act was answered by Elliot's ordering all English ships to boycott Canton (under the circumstances a ridiculous order); by the Governor-General of India declaring war on China (January 31, 1840); and, most importantly, by the dispatch from India of a British expeditionary force. The force was to safeguard the lives and properties of Englishmen, secure indemnities for outrages and wrongs, and arrange for the exchange of envoys between China and England.

On June 21, 1840, twenty men-of-war and transports carrying British and Indian troops arrived off Canton to blockade that port. The commander, Commodore Bremer, began to move northward along the China coast toward Taku, to demand representation on behalf of his government. The Court of Peking refused to negotiate at any place save Canton, so the British force returned there, seizing as hostage Chusan Island off the mouth of the Yangtze River. The discussions at Canton in the winter of 1840 and the early part of 1841 were fruitless. The Chinese agents refused to pay compensation for the opium seized, to guarantee the debts of the Co-hong, or to treat the English on an equal basis. Peking was as determined not to negotiate as London was to force her conditions on China.

In January, 1841, Commissioner Lin was removed to the post of Governor-General of Kwangtung-Kwangsi and was replaced by the Manchu officials Ch'i-shan and I'li-pu. On January 21, under duress, Ch'i-shan concluded a convention at Chuenpi that conceded all the English wanted—cession of the island of Hong Kong to the Crown, resumption of trade, indemnities, and the principle of equality of nations. However, since London thought the indemnity too small and Peking had never intended Ch'i-shan to do anything but "negotiate," both sides repudiated the agreement as unsatisfactory, and the war, if it can be called that, was resumed. The British occupied the city of Canton and "ran-

somed" it for 6,000,000 pounds, happy to withdraw their handful of troops from the center of a vast and increasingly hostile
population.

Evidently the course of events since 1839 had been as unpalatable to the Cantonese traders as it was to the English, for Lin's
actions had hurt the entire Kwangtung trade, and he had not
been popular in the city he had come to protect:

> There was at this time much more indignation against the
> Government's opium policy than against the foreigners. It was
> not until May 1841, when English troops looted and raped in
> the villages north of Canton, that hatred of the English began.[2]

In this same month Peking seems to have become aware that its
officials had not, for years, been telling the truth about the situation at Canton. Viewing the English resumption of hostilities with
horror and chagrin (for during the summer of 1841, Bremer took
Ningpo and Amoy and now controlled the China coast), and
discovering that the opium trade had not been officially sup-
pressed, the Emperor dismissed Lin in disgrace. In August,
1841, Elliot was replaced by the able Henry Pottinger. Meanwhile, in June, Bremer had taken Shanghai; in August, Nanking
was also taken. Now, for the Chinese, there was nowhere to
hide and nothing to do.

The Treaty System

Ignorance and arrogance had permitted a local problem to become a national disaster—indeed a permanent disaster, for
China's surrender was to take the form of unequal written commitments. Upon the advice to Peking of the new Commissioner,
Ch'i-ying, serious negotiations began at Nanking. Ch'i-ying and
I'li-pu, who had studied the demands made by the foreigners,
reported to Peking that while the barbarians were undoubtedly
rapacious, they only wanted trade, and unless this was assented
to, it was possible that all China south of the Yangtze might be
lost. On August 29, 1842, the Treaty of Nanking opened Canton,
Amoy, Foochow, Ningpo, and Shanghai for trade. The wild
island of Hong Kong was ceded to the English, who pledged to
make it a free and open port. The Co-hong system was abolished,

and it was agreed that a system of "fair and regular" tariffs would be established. For China the only gain was the provision against the smuggling of opium.

The most important clause of the treaty lay in Article VIII:

> Should the Emperor hereafter from any cause whatever be pleased to grant additional privileges or immunities to any of the subjects or citizens of such foreign countries, the same privileges and immunities will be extended to and enjoyed by British subjects.

Since all subsequent treaties between China and foreigners contained a similar "most favored nation" clause, China became placed in a most peculiar situation among the nations of the world. Her obligations to any particular nation could never be ascertained in the treaties with that nation, but only by totting up the sum total of her obligations to all nations. Internationally, China became a legal pauper, living on the good will of the treaty nations. The war of 1841-42 contained the seeds of a kind of cultural, economic, and political destruction unknown in any previous war in Chinese history.

London was now satisfied. Palmerston said:

> There is no doubt that this event, which will form an epoch in the progress of the civilisation of the human races, must be attended with important advantages to the commercial interests of England.[3]

Both sides had to accept their share of blame for the war. Both sides had had grievances, and both sides had become irreconcilable in their views. However, on the larger issue of the conflict of national interests, it must be asked whether, despite their legitimate complaints, the Westerners had the right to demand that China conform her policies and procedures, commercial and diplomatic, to those of another civilization. Yet this question is based on subsequent history. At the time the Chinese regarded the treaty as a temporary measure, the English, as the establishment of normal practices.

The Nanking Treaty was followed, within two years, by two treaties of exceptional importance. In October, 1843, Pottinger and Ch'i-ying arranged the first one (the Treaty of the Bogue), to set in order the matter of detailed trade regulations and to clarify certain vague provisions of the Nanking Treaty. The tariff on imports and exports was set at an average of 5 per cent *ad valorum* (with the exception of tea, which was taxed at 10 per cent). This was a moderate rate for the time, but the principle that permitted China to establish its customs duties only through the consent of another nation was also to deprive her of control of an important part of her revenues. The Treaty of the Bogue also reinforced the most-favored-nation principle. Furthermore, it provided for English merchants and their families to reside peacefully in the treaty ports, and for this purpose land was to be set aside, marking the inception of the foreign concession and the International Settlement.

The second pioneering treaty was the American Treaty of Wanghia (1844). Indeed, it and not the British treaty became the model for succeeding foreign treaties. Six weeks after the Treaty of Nanking, Commodore Kearney arrived in China to secure commercial rights for United States citizens. Kearney accomplished nothing: Peking refused to allow the Viceroy at Canton to deal with him, and the Americans in China, then enjoying the rights gotten by the English and fearing that if Congress pressed too hard they might lose the advantages they had, wanted Kearney to go home. But Congress wanted these de facto rights to be placed on a treaty basis. In February, 1844, Caleb Cushing, agent for the Congress, arrived at Macao. Despite the almost total ignorance of Peking regarding the United States, Cushing's path to a treaty was easy, for the way had long been paved by Ch'i-ying, now Viceroy at Canton, and I'li-pu, who was managing foreign affairs at Peking. They had agreed in 1843 that if trade rights were denied to any foreigners now that the English had them, there was a good possibility that other Western nations, all of whom, they believed, had helped England to arm and prepare for the war, would force China into a war, and that China could not afford. They were also convinced that part of the trouble had lain in the extortions imposed by local officials and the Co-hong, and in the failure of Peking to take direct charge early on. They came to the conclusion that a fresh look and attitude had to come into Peking's foreign policy. The key statement is found in a memorial dated June 18, 1843: "When a system is worn out it should be changed." [4]

Therefore, when Cushing arrived Ch'i-ying was willing to negotiate whatever treaty Cushing had in mind—as long as Cushing did not persist in trying to get to Peking. The United States Treaty of Wanghia contained the most-favored-nation clause and a clearer statement of extraterritoriality than did the Nanking Treaty. Also, importantly, it provided that the treaty could be revised at the end of twelve years.

The affair was over. The Chinese felt they had concluded a nasty bit of business. Now that the barbarians had their desired commercial privileges they would live and let live. In a sense, the treaties merely set up a truce between two civilizations still ignorant of one another. China was not conversant with the Western practices, and, to her, most-favored-nation treatment meant, in common sense terms, equal privileges of trade. No superior commercial rights or foreign loans or territorial acquisitions were even dreamed of. The Westerners knew of China only through the distorting mirror of the treaty ports, particularly the Cantonese. It was not until later in the century that the West was to rediscover China: Expert linguists, qualified scholars, and just curious Westerners began digging into all aspects of China's life and history; Henry Yule visited places where no European had been since Marco Polo's days; Legge commenced a lifetime's work, making the first Confucian translations since the seventeenth-century Jesuits; Maspero and Chavannes applied the canons of Western scholarship to Chinese studies; and men like Meadows and Williams began an analysis of Chinese government and society. It was Peking that was to blame for holding even scholarship at arm's length.

From 1842 to 1854 the conduct of relations was left to the viceroys of the treaty port provinces (Fukien, Chekiang, Kiangsu, Kwangtung, Kiangsi, Anhui, Chihli). In front of the viceroys was a screen of prefectural intendants, provincial governors, and port controllers, and in front of these was a hedge of lesser officials. Behind all of them was, of course, the Grand Council. While Westerners, though ignorant about China, were eager to learn, the Chinese officials remained fixed in their ignorance about the

West. "Their first tendency, naturally, was to force the new wine into old casks." [5] The old cask was the ancient and regular means of handling barbarians and "barbarians are by nature inscrutable." [6] It was to be a while before new and discerning officials discarded the old casks.

Meanwhile, during the decade following the treaties, the pressures of the West increased. The open ports thrived, Hong Kong developed as a great port and colony, Westerners acquired land at Shanghai. But neither Peking nor the Western powers were happy with what was essentially a truce. There was continual friction and bickering at Canton, the Chinese being especially irritated by the continued illegal trade in opium. Hong Kong became the greatest opium depot in the world, and from the stores there the drug was trans-shipped either to havens established by Chinese on the coast or to receiving hulks anchored outside China's territorial limits. From the hulks fast cutters ran the chests of opium to merchants on land. British authorities at Shanghai and Canton did not permit any ships to come into the port whose manifest showed opium, but there was nothing the Western consuls could do about the connivance of high Chinese officials, whose financial interests in the drug business overrode their duty to enforce Imperial edicts.

A second cause for legitimate Chinese protest was the "pig trade"—the commerce in Chinese emigrants to work in the fields and mines and on the railroads of the United States, Australia, Cuba, and Peru. The emigration of Chinese had always been illegal without a permit, although myriads of Chinese through the centuries had migrated at will to Southeast Asia. When the Imperial government had the contract emigrant trade investigated in 1847 it became evident that, while both free and contract emigration to Australia and to the United States were conducted under honorable conditions, the "pig trade" to the tropics was a horror. The agents in China received a fee for each coolie placed on a ship, which eventually led to forced recruiting, that is, kidnapping. Once aboard the ships for Peru or Cuba:

> The conditions of the emigrants on the voyage may best be expressed by the phrase constantly found in official reports and books of the period, that the coolie ships were "floating hells."

Even the modest space of twelve square feet—2 ft. x 6 ft.—
allowed by the Hongkong ordinance, was adhered to only in a
few cases, and in general the space accorded was only eight
square feet in slow sailing vessels. These twice traversed the
breadth of the tropics in the passage of 168 days to Cuba and
did not leave the tropics on the voyage of 120 days to Peru.
The mortality was great—from fourteen per cent to forty-five
per cent died on many of the emigrant ships.[7]

A third condition giving rise to trouble for China in this period
was the prevalence of piracy on the South China Sea, which
was so bad in the 1840's and 1850's that the whole China coast
was dominated by a loose confederation of pirates who demanded protection money from Chinese merchant vessels. The
situation was complicated by the Portuguese, who were not a
treaty power and who, in traditional pursuit of a policy of corruption in Asia, began to issue "protection" passes to Chinese
junks and, for a fee, convoy Chinese ships along the coast. This
high-level piracy got so bad that Chinese shippers preferred to
have pirates protect them against the Portuguese. Indeed, in
1857 the Chinese pirates met and badly defeated a Portuguese
squadron at Ningpo. Yet the ravishment of coastal shipping,
which a weak government was powerless to prevent, could not
go on without serious impairment of the entire maritime trade.
Therefore in 1847 the British Navy, with the consent of the
Chinese authorities, began operations to suppress piracy. This
was not finally achieved for many years, but it offers one of the
few examples of international cooperation with China in the
nineteenth century.

Additionally, there was a great deal of violence in Canton,
some of it started through irresponsible actions. In July, 1846, an
Englishman, angered by the cries of a street hawker, seized and
caned him. A bloody riot resulted, directed by a mob of natives
against Westerners. On other occasions seamen on shore leave
started fights that sometimes resulted in murder. Such distur-
bances were deplored by Western governments and their representatives, as expressed in this statement by Lord Palmerston:

It cannot be tolerated that British subjects should indulge toward
the people of China in acts of violence or contumely which they

would not venture to practise toward the humblest and meanest
individual in their own country.[8]

That Westerners were quite often contemptuous and even
violent in their relations with the Chinese—especially the merchants—is without doubt. But their attitude can be explained
largely by the fact that Canton, where they could rightfully live
under treaty provisions, was bitterly hostile to them, frequently
denied them their rights, and subjected them to the continual
threat of bodily harm by individuals or mob action. Repeated
efforts of Western representatives to approach the government at
Peking (now engaged in the attempt to quell a full-fledged
rebellion in South and Central China) were implacably refused.
Until 1852 the able and diligent Ch'i-ying, Viceroy at Canton,
tried his best in the situation. But he was succeeded in that year
by Yeh Ming-ch'en, who was granted full powers to deal with
the foreigners. Yeh was bitterly antiforeign—so much so that he
refused even to see foreign representatives. The appointment of
such a man represented the settled policy of Peking to have
nothing to do with the foreigners at the treaty ports, and this
attitude contributed greatly to another series of disasters for
China.

The Western powers, especially the British, French, and Americans, were agreed that the existing diplomatic, commercial, and
human relationships could not endure. There were three main
things they desired to see established: (1) The right of foreigners to trade and to reside in the interior of China; (2) control
of the distasteful opium trade by legalizing it; (3) the right of
foreign representatives to reside in Peking. But they were, of
course, unable even to secure appointments with Viceroy Yeh,
with whom the northern authorities insisted they deal.

In 1856 a final series of incidents, together with continued
stubbornness on both sides, brought the need for treaty revision
to a head. The incidents began in October, when the Arrow, a
Chinese-owned boat with a Chinese crew and British master,
registered in Hong Kong and flying the British flag, was boarded
by Chinese officials in Canton harbor; the crew was seized, and
the British flag hauled down. The Chinese authorities claimed

that the *Arrow* and her crew had been engaged in piracy and were entitled to neither British registration nor the protection of the British flag. The British demanded an apology and redress. This was refused. Then the British sent an ultimatum to Viceroy Yeh demanding that he accede to the rules of international law governing such cases. The crew was returned to British hands, but no apology was offered. At this point the British commenced naval action, and in the last days of October they took the forts of Canton. Yeh declared this action to be warlike, and the Cantonese, unprepared to face armed troops, retaliated in December by burning down foreign factories.

Throughout 1856 and into 1857 a savage kind of warfare continued at Canton. The trouble was that the Second Anglo-Chinese War at Canton (there was no trouble elsewhere) began to expand to include Russia, France, and the United States. The Russians, who had no intention of taking coercive measures against their old treaty allies, nevertheless desired to make use of the situation to gain rectification of trade across the Central Asian borders and control of the Amur Valley. The French had no concern with Britain's troubles at Canton, but one of their Catholic missionaries, Father Chapdelaine, had been brutally and judicially murdered in 1856 by authorities in Kwangsi Province, where the French were not protected by treaty. The French wanted reparations and guarantees of future protection. Both Russia and France wanted to join England in seeking treaty revision, and they requested the United States, as a treaty power, to join them. The United States refused to join, but it did send its first envoy extraordinary to China, Mr. William Reed. Reed arrived in 1857, confident he could make his way to Peking. He received the same icy refusals and insulting treatment as others before him, and he wrote back: "The powers of Western civilization must insist on what they know to be their rights and give up the dream of dealing with China as a power to which any ordinary rules apply." [9]

So within twelve years of the first treaties the Western nations and China drifted into a useless war, and in December, 1857, a joint Anglo-French force took the city of Canton. After six years of stalling, Viceroy Yeh could no longer avoid a face-to-face con-

frontation with the victors. He was seized and sent to Calcutta
as a prisoner. While he has been accused of the basic responsibility for the war of 1857, and while it is true that a show of
common sense on his part would have forestalled any excuse
for force, an examination of his papers reveals that he always
acted in accord with orders from Peking.

Once in possession of Canton, the powers sent a joint note to
Peking requesting revision of the treaties. The note was returned
with the information that Peking was not responsible for Viceroy
Yeh's actions, that a new viceroy was being sent to Canton and
that the foreigners should deal with him there! The Anglo-
French force, with the Russians and Americans as observers,
proceeded north, took the forts at Taku in May, 1857, and arrived at Tientsin. Peking now agreed to negotiate.

By late June, 1858, the four powers concerned had each nego-
tiated a treaty, whose most significant provisions, combined, were:
(1) To open ten more ports for trade, which included Taiwan
and, most importantly, four great river ports in the Yangtze Valley (Nanking, Hankow, Kiukiang, and Chinkiang), (2) to enable
nationals of the treaty powers to reside in Peking itself; (3) to
permit warships to enter, anchor in, and patrol any port where
merchantmen were allowed; (4) to permit foreigners to go into
the interior of China, trade there, and reside there (this included the right of missionaries to practice their faiths and to
proselytize); (5) to legalize the sale of opium, thereby bringing
it under official controls. There were, of course, other provisions,
most-favored-nation clauses, and indemnities, but the overall
effect of this second round of war and treaties was to open the
interior of China.

Ratification was to take place in Peking itself, but the Manchu
Court, deeply humiliated by the prospect of signing under threat
of force, were resolved that the event should never take place
in the capital. The allies had gone back to Shanghai from Tientsin to await the arrival of Chinese agents to lead them to Peking.
When the Chinese came, the allies refused to ratify the treaties
anywhere but the agreed-upon place. The British and French
then took their forces back to Taku, whose defenses had been
strengthened in the interval. The allies had been warned not to

proceed, and the Anglo-French fleet was unable to force the river entrance. The irreconcilables within the Court were determined to hold out. Yet, "if China be considered the party which was throwing down the gauntlet, it must be admitted that England was stretching forth both hands to receive it." [10]

In 1860 the Anglo-French forces forced the Taku defenses, went ashore, and seized the city of Tientsin. While they fought their way to Peking, the Emperor fled to Manchuria. In October, 1860, four years after the obduracy of Peking and of Viceroy Yeh had provoked this war of revision, the Allies entered the capital of China. Angered by their difficulties and convinced of the treasonable nature of the government of China, both because of the Taku incident and because of the deliberate violation of a flag of truce during their march from Tientsin to Peking (and the murder of twenty allied captives), the French and British first looted the great Summer Palace just north of Peking and then, to strike at the pride of the Emperor, burned to the ground this gorgeous site of some two hundred buildings, one of the architectural masterpieces of the world. This unnecessary act of revenge, never forgotten or forgiven by the Chinese, was carried out under the order of the British representative, Lord Elgin, whose name is somewhat better known in the West for the Elgin marbles.

The treaties were finally ratified, and, as a consequence of the delay, a number of further concessions were demanded of China. The British were leased Kowloon, across from Hong Kong, and were paid a very substantial additional indemnity, while the French obtained retrocession for the Catholic Church of lands and buildings seized from the Jesuits. Furthermore, the French inserted, illegally, into the Chinese text of their treaty, a clause permitting their missionaries to buy and lease land in the interior.

The Treaties of 1858 and 1860 were clearly unequal treaties. In sum, they deprived China of sovereignty over her navigable waters, over foreigners in China (by permitting consular jurisdiction), and over her tariffs (by providing for their alteration through mutual agreement). They cost, in indemnities, far more than the Manchus could afford, and the diversion of income to pay claims had a weakening effect on the civil and military abilities of the dynasty. In the process, the ineffective and, indeed, archaic nature of the Court and central government was revealed, dramatizing the need for a change in power. Most significant of all, the Anglo-French expedition of 1858-60 had brought Western might into the heart of China for the first time.

THE INTERNAL PRESSURES

Dynastic Decline

In 1796 Ch'ien Lung's retirement and a White Lotus rebellion marked the apex of Ch'ing dynasty power and the beginning of its decline, for the revolt of that year was the first of a series of destructive rebellions that plagued the remaining life of the regime. Paradoxically enough, it was the highly articulated centralization achieved by the Ch'ing that was a cause both of the rebellions and of the paralysis in foreign relations so puzzling to Westerners. The central government controlled every one of its officials. None were empowered to make more than routine decisions, and even these were made in conformity with a comprehensive book of rules and regulations. In general, Ch'ing officials on the scene were extensions of the will of the Grand Council. Even the operating budgets of the smallest districts were set down by Peking. It was a beautifully worked-out chain of command in which all actions taken along the way (appointments, removals, punishments, rewards, and fiscal, legal, or administrative acts) were initiated or approved by a board at Peking under the supervision of the Grand Council. However, the encompassing will at Peking had to feed on information passed along the chain, and the fact is, increasingly in the nineteenth century, it had either false information (as from Commissioner Lin) or no information at all. For it became the practice of officials to keep silent in order to maintain their tenure of office, and this was encouraged by high officials who did not wish to see the Emperor disturbed. To some extent this situation represented dynastic fatigue, the penalty for overcentralization, and a weakening of the civil service through the increasing practice of selling posts; and, to a large extent, it represented the growing degeneration of the financial health of the government and the people. At the root of the economic ailment was a disproportion between population and arable land. From the mid-eighteenth to the mid-nineteenth century, the population of China, as recorded in the Veritable Records of the Ch'ing dynasty, rose from 143,000,000 to 430,000,000. Indeed the entire nineteenth century is marked by increases in population despite wars and disasters, a decrease in the amount of land under cultivation, and an accumulation of lands in the hands of fewer and fewer landlords, with a consequent decline in the average level of subsistence. There was little the government could do about the dispossessed of the nineteenth century, who formed a steadily growing marginal population with no gainful employment. Peking always made a conscientious effort to seek a balance between protecting the rights of the landlords in their ownerships and rents and assisting the helpless. But the entire system of land ownership was unequal to start with, and it was a Manchu principle that this was a condition of life, a concept illustrated by a section from an edict of 1729:

> Those scholars and common people who possess property and are wealthy [have come to this condition] either as a result of the accumulation made by their fathers or grandfathers, or through their own labor and enterprise. All these are *liang-min* [good subjects] of the realm. Those who are *hsiang-shen* [gentry in their native communities] and possess surplus wealth either inherit it from former generations or derive it from their own official salaries and remunerations. All these are *liang-li* [good officials] of the state. The state therefore cherishes and protects all the gentry, scholars, and common people whose families are well-to-do.[11]

It was, then, impossible, given such conditions and thinking, to protect the distressed from the encroachments of the privileged. This not-unusual situation was aggravated in the mid-nineteenth century by the inexorable pressure of population on a static land and food supply. Female infanticide became common among the poor as a means of keeping the family alive. Even the rich became poor, while the poor became desperate. In

Europe in the nineteenth century (and earlier) the same phenomenon of rapid growth of population occurred, but there technology gave subsistence to the masses who migrated to or were born in the new cities. In China technological stagnation prevented this amelioration, as did the growing foreign control of manufactures. For example, after 1860 the low tariff set by treaty on English cotton textiles nearly drove domestic cotton textiles off the Chinese market.

An immediate consequence of the population problem in the first half of the nineteenth century was a decrease in tax revenues and impoverishment of the government. The whole tax system was geared to conditions of peace and depended on the land tax. Prior to 1840 extraordinary conditions of war or other emergencies could be met through the expenditure of accumulated surpluses, which were renewed when normal times were restored. But by the 1840's not only were the surpluses exhausted, but there no longer was a standard economy to return to. In the period 1850-70 civil wars and rebellions, campaigns of attrition and scorched earth, reduced cities to rubble and the countryside to a wilderness. In the 1870's, and especially in 1877-78, a dreadful drought and famine struck Shansi, Shensi, Hopei, and Honan. While all of these disasters reduced the population, they also ruined land and made the collection of taxes an impossibility in vast areas.

It has been demonstrated that the land tax, which until 1849 supplied 75 per cent of the revenue of the central government, was, by 1885, furnishing only 38-39 per cent of the total. Unable to increase the land tax (partly because an increase would have been intolerable, and partly because the old assessments, having been fixed unalterably by Imperial fiat in the eighteenth century, were still being followed) the government, in 1850, desperate for money, turned to the taxation of trade. This was the *likin*, which, first collected in Kiangsu in 1853, spread from province to province throughout China during the nineteenth century and became a substantial source of revenue. It was an internal customs or transport tax levied on goods as they were moved from producer to retailer. It was really a continuous inventory tax placed on the same stock of goods as it moved through the channels of trade. Like most emergency taxes, the likin became permanent, and, while it supplied revenue, it also crippled trade. For it led to a general price increase, the undervaluation of inventories, the stagnation of commerce, and widespread corruption among those who tried to evade it.

Corruption was another factor in the economic malaise of the Ch'ing. One of the most notorious official examples was the mismanagement of the Yellow River dike system. The government, at least after 1820, could not afford the enormous sums needed to maintain the river's dikes. Even routine repairs on the dikes cost millions of taels, and much of this was converted to private use. Nor could culpable officials be removed without danger of increasing the flood disasters. This sort of malpractice, which left the dikes prey to rising waters, became common as administrative efficiency declined. Other examples of corruption were: forced crop payments, the pocketing of bribes, fraudulent land registrations (productive land registered as waste land), illegal imposts, the unjust allocation of assessments, the juggling of rates of exchange, and the increasing immunities of the landlords. The police officials in the districts were unable to cope with either these matters or the consequent economic dislocations. Local communities were forced to organize to protect themselves against both nature and officialdom, taxing themselves and finding their own leadership. Every Chinese government since the Han era was familiar with the phenomena of hunger, rioting, and banditry consequent on natural disaster and human greed. But it had always been their hope to forestall rebellion. By the mid-nineteenth century the Ch'ing could have no such hope.

Revolution and Civil War

The three successors to Ch'ien Lung each had bad luck with nature, foreigners, officials, and their own people, and none of them had the capacity to deal with any of the resulting misfortunes. The first, Emperor Chia-ching (1796-99), was Emperor only in name; as long as his "retired" father was active, he was not consulted, he had no power, he remained a patient ceremonial figurehead. At his father's death he took over an empire whose administration had become slipshod, whose population had doubled during his father's lifetime, and three of whose provinces were close to revolt. His reign saw the expensive pacifications of Hupeh and Szechuan (1799-1803) and of Chihli (1813), and extraordinary floods on the Yellow River. His successor and second son, Tao-kuang (1821-50), inherited a depleted treasury, a costly war in Central Asia and a population of 400,000,000. He was a friendly, addlepated, and ignorant man who wanted to do something for his country, and had the fates and his officials not gotten him into the Opium War he might have had a reign unmarked by anything worse than bad floods. As it was, the Opium War accentuated the growing bankruptcy and the general distress. In his will Tao-kuang, "aware of his shortcomings . . . ordered that no tablet lauding his achievements be erected at his tomb—he did not wish to provoke yet more criticism from future generations." [12] Neither Chia-ching nor Tao-kuang ever moved decisively to put down unrest, and their basic solutions to financial difficulties were frugality and the excessive sale of civil service offices.

It was Tao-kuang's son, Hsien-feng (1850-61), who, falling heir to the unequal treaties, the weakening administration, and a disordered population, was faced with the climax of one of the most destructive civil upheavals in history, the Taiping rebellion. No better view of the situation can be given than by citing parts of a memorial addressed to the Emperor by Tseng Kuo-fan on February 7, 1852. The memorial itself is a lucid and authoritative digest of the condition of China as seen by a very high and wise official through whose hands had passed statements and reports without number from every province and locality in the Empire.

> . . . The virtuous will of the sage emperor cannot reach the people and the distress among the people cannot appeal to the emperor. Your minister ventures to mention them one by one.
>   *The first is that the silver price is too high so it is difficult to pay taxes.* . . . In former days a tael of silver was worth one thousand cash; then a picul (= 133 pounds) of rice could get three taels of silver. Nowadays one tael of silver is worth two thousand cash and one picul of rice only gets one tael and a half

of silver. In former days to sell three *tou* or pecks (1 peck =
1/10 of a picul) of rice could pay the land tax for one *mou* (ca.
1/6 of an acre) and still have something left. Nowadays to sell
six *tou* or pecks of rice to pay the land tax for one *mou* is still not
enough. The Court naturally keeps the regular amount of the
annual tax but the small people actually have to pay twice the
tax. . . . Those who have no power to pay are innumerable.
The officers in the counties and districts exhaust their full
strength to urge them to pay . . . soldiers and government
servants are sent over the houses and their blood and flesh are
spreading in disorder. Are all these actions of cruel officers? No,
because if they do not do so, when it is time to check their
achievement they cannot collect 70 per cent of the required
amount and they fear impeachment which usually costs them
thousands of taels and leaves trouble to their descendants. Therefore, before 1835 the full amount of tax in Kiangsu was paid.
From 1836 to the present (1852) every year is reported a season
of dearth and every year people have to be excused entirely or
delayed from paying taxes. . . . Therefore, there is a method of
chieh-ch'uan which is an advanced collection at the time of the
spring to levy the tax of the coming spring, or in this year to
check the tax certificate of the coming year. When the small
people do not respond, then the tax is slightly reduced in order
to make them come. The more advanced the collection is, the
larger the deficiency is. The succeeding official has nothing to
collect, so even a very good functionary has no means to keep
his integrity; for a covetous official, he secures a further pretext
for treating the people as his fish and meat. . . . Since the
soaring of the price of silver, the people's paying of tax becomes
more difficult and the officials urging and reprimanding likewise
become more cruel. Sometimes if the proper family cannot pay,
then the rich members of the same clan are arrested, hand-cuffed
and charged to pay on their behalf. Sometimes they even hand-
cuff their relatives and imprison their neighbors. The people
hate and resist and so form into big cases of rioting such as in
Lei-yang and Ch'ung-yang of Hunan and Kwangtung, respec-
tively. . . . It is also caused by the doubling of the silver price,
the extra collection of the tax by officials and the illegal punishment by government soldiers and servants. People are really in
the condition of being unable to live day by day. That is one of
what your minister calls distress among the people.

Secondly, the thieves and bandits are too numerous and it is difficult for good people to live peacefully. . . . Recently it is heard that the bandits' power has become more severe. They plunder and rape people in the daylight and kidnap the people for ransom. People cannot help but appeal to the officials. When the officials go in to arrest, an announcement is proclaimed in advance and till the government [forces] reaches the spot the local gentry usually tell a lie that the bandits have fled. Sometimes it is trickily said that the bandit is killed by putting another prisoner to death in order to substitute the case and yet actually the bandit does not die. When the case of plunder is not cleared up, the lost articles are not returned and the family of the suffering host is already bankrupt, he has to swallow his voice, sip his own tears and has no more strength to reappeal. Even if he does, and fortunately soldiers are dispatched to meet together and to arrest the bandits, nevertheless the soldiers in ordinary times all have connections with the bandits and at the very time they will set the latter free after getting a bribe and leave no footstep to trace. Sometimes, on the contrary, they take the pretext of calling them bandits to frighten the foolish villagers and forcing them to pay a heavy bribery. Otherwise, they will be burned and they will be tied up with fetters. . . . Today the bad soldiers and harmful government employees who foster bandits and set bandits free appear everywhere. This is another one of what your minister calls distress among the people.

The third one is that the unjustified imprisonments are too many, so it is difficult for people to redress their grievances. . . . When one family has a long-pending case ten families become bankrupt. When one person is falsely accused a hundred persons will be involved in his sufferings. There is frequently a tiny, small case which is not concluded for years. The right and wrong are turned upside down and the accused become old and die in prison which makes one's hair stand on end upon hearing it. This is again another one of what your minister calls distress among the people.[13]

The titular head of the great civil war set off by these conditions cited by Tseng Kuo-fan was a Kwangtung man, Hung Hsiu-ch'uan, who, having four times failed his examinations, underwent a nervous crisis, during which visions told him he was the younger son of God. His self-pronouncement as a younger brother to Jesus Christ, together with statements concerning the ideals of his movement, led Westerners to see it as a "Christian" revolution. However the "Christian" influence on the early leaders was nothing more than a distortion of Protestant fundamentalism, fragmentarily known at that time from early missionary tracts and a poor Chinese translation of the Bible. The movement's religious drive was more Judaic than Christian, for it was centered on the Mosaic code, monotheism, and iconoclasm. The first two of the Ten Celestial Commands were:

THE FIRST COMMAND
Thou Shalt Honour and Worship the Great God

Remark—The great God is the universal Father of all men, in every nation under heaven. Every man is produced and nourished by him; every man is also protected by him; every man ought, therefore, morning and evening, to honour and worship him, with acknowledgments of his goodness. It is a common saying, that Heaven produces, nourishes, and protects men. Also, that being provided with food we must not deceive Heaven. Therefore, whoever does not worship the great God breaks the commands of Heaven.

THE SECOND COMMAND
Thou Shalt Not Worship Corrupt Spirits [Gods]

Remark—The great God says, Thou shalt have no other spirits [gods] beside me. Therefore all besides the great God are corrupt spirits [gods], deceiving and destroying mankind; they must on no account be worshipped; whoever worships the whole class of corrupt spirits [gods] offends against the commands of Heaven.[14]

But if the Taiping leaders around Hung were religiously influenced, the influence was as much Taoist as Pentateuchal—Taoist in its secrecy, organization, and abstract anarchism; Pentateuchal in its social code. It was clearly not Confucian.

Hung gathered around him an anti-Manchu religious-military group (The God Worshippers) who by 1850 had control of Kwangsi, and in that year Hung proclaimed himself the T'ien Wang (Heavenly King) of the Taiping T'ien-kuo (Heavenly Kingdom of the Great Peace). Once the weakness of the Imperial forces became evident, followers came swarming in, not only the believers but entire units of secret societies and bandits. Hung led his army north to the Yangtze, taking Nanking in 1853. It was the government's policy to avoid pitched battles (because it lost them) and to try to pen the rebels within their captured cities. The Taiping forces were well led and organized; they had great determination and morale; and, in the beginning, they had better relations with the countryside than did the government. Masses of Chinese joined the rebels, although not all, for the Taiping war was no more a general peasant war than it was a "Christian" revolution.

The Taiping appeal is a measure of the spectrum of disaffection in China, for it called to the Chinese on many grounds: to all Chinese against the Manchus; to scholars without office or the hopes of purchasing any; to merchants and town dwellers who paid heavy taxes and inflated prices; to the villages in which the government could maintain neither order nor justice. For the peasant, the Taiping had their agrarian reforms of 1853. This law, proclaimed for their conquered territory, gave every man, woman, and child a share of the land. Every twenty-five families formed a self-governing group, with their own fields, storehouse, church, and elders. The unit kept what grain it needed and turned the rest over to the government for distribution to the needy. Taxes were light. The law was not a practicable measure—the Taipings never organized their conquests—but it was genuine. It could not be made to operate in occupied territory, but even a declaration of the ancient right of peasant ownership was compelling. The Taipings neither appealed to nor won over the landed class, the officials, or the educated Confucians. By throwing overboard traditional Confucian reforms, and by projecting solutions to China's massive problems through nationalism, equalitarianism, agrarian communalism, and radical social restructuring (especially in improving the status of women and the administration of justice), they alienated the entire Chinese ruling group. And what sympathy they might have gained was lost in the turbulence of their role.

They also began to lose foreign sympathy. The Westerners, disenchanted with the Manchus, had originally been taken with the rebellion, and missionaries, especially, were well disposed toward the "Christians." A number of official contacts were made, with a view toward offering help and even giving recognition to the movement, but the Taipings, intensely nationalistic, disdained Western assistance, save on equal terms. While they offered to trade freely with Western powers, they refused to continue the unequal arrangements, the most flagrant of which, in Taiping eyes, was that Chinese vessels could fly foreign flags and thus carry opium with immunity.

But these negotiations were all in the early years before the tide turned. In October, 1853, the Taiping armies reached Tientsin but fell short of their destination, Peking. They were slowed by heavy floods and were turned back on the northern plains by Imperial cavalry. In 1853-56 the Yangtze territory, from Hankow to Kiukiang, was the main theater of war, and by 1856 the Taiping movement was beginning to ebb. Corruption, nepotism, the attrition of leadership, the failure to carry out promised reforms, the loss of zeal by the masses, and simple war weariness all took their toll.

Then, too, beginning in 1854, a new kind of army had been formed to face the rebels. Peking had discovered how worthless the Manchu banner armies had become. It had been forced to resort to siege warfare, thus permitting the Taiping forces to maneuver. What was needed was a robust militia. Happily, a number of good local militia bodies were in existence, illegally, for their own protection. It was upon such forces that, beginning in 1854, a reluctant but helpless government permitted local authorities to build regional and provincial armies of defense. The most famous model was the Hunan Braves (the Hsiang Army), organized by Tseng Kuo-fan. Drawn from reliable village men, these new-style forces were carefully trained and indoctrinated, well led, regularly fed and paid. Ultimately they were the means of quelling the rebellion. Tseng's basic strategy was to concentrate the rebels in areas he had selected, interdict them, and then strike them an overwhelming blow. Meanwhile, in recovered areas, he bent all energies to restoration of normal life, refusing to allow his army to live off the land.

In 1860-61, a foolish Taiping attempt to take Shanghai brought against them a strange, mixed force of British and French troops (a sort of foreign legion, paid for by the Shanghai international community) and some Imperial Chinese forces led by British officers, given leaves of absence for that purpose. The year 1860 was a most peculiar time for the foreigners to be assisting the Manchus, for, while they fought the anti-Manchu rebels outside Shanghai, the Allied troops were fighting their way from Tientsin to Peking, where they sacked and burned the Summer Palace. By 1862 the West had come to realize that it was unlikely that the Taiping rebels would win, and that, if they should, it would mean the end of trade and settlement on Western terms. Led by the British, the treaty powers now consistently backed the Manchus, who until 1862 had only the support of the Hunan Braves. In 1862 Tseng Kuo-fan organized the Anhui Army to retake Kiangsu and Anhui and protect Shanghai, the rich port upon which the Army was dependent. It was the first Chinese force to use Western rifles and cannon and to be taught by Western instructors. These new model armies, led by Tseng Kuo-fan, Tso Tsung-t'ang, and Li Hung-chang, carried the fight throughout the Yangtze Valley. By March, 1864, the remaining Taiping forces were besieged in Nanking. By July, the Heavenly King was dead, his capital taken, his army slaughtered, his followers dispersed, and his high colleagues executed out of hand, despite their surrender under guarantees.

This was not the end of rebellion in China. More than a decade earlier, in 1851 and 1852, floods and famine in the Huai Valley had caused an uprising, at first not associated with the Taiping movement, although later it was to cooperate with it. This was the Nien rebellion, led by the White Lotus Society. It was put down in 1853, but it reorganized and rose again in 1856, centering in Anhui Province and spilling over in Honan, Kiangsu, and Shantung. The Nien used guerrilla warfare tactics far advanced for their time, and the government suffered a crushing defeat in the long campaign against them (1856-65). At this point, the government called for the services of Tseng Kuo-fan, creator of armies. He carefully won over the support of the local peasants and incorporated them into his new Army of the Huai, which was a regional army that had done well against the Taipings. By a process of contraction, he (and later Li Hung-chang) forced the Nien rebels into an ever more constricted territory, and by 1868 the Nien movement was strangled to death.

The Moslems of China had always been unhappy with Manchu rule, and in 1862 a Moslem group in Shensi rebelled. The rebellion spread to all the Moslems of Shensi and Kansu. Peking, its hands full with the Taiping and Nien revolts and a minor Moslem irruption in Yunnan, could not concentrate on the Northwest until 1868, when Tso Tsung-t'ang arrived in Sian to take charge of the government forces. As a military man he was bold but not rash, seeking scope but never hasty in detail. It took him four difficult years to suppress the Moslem revolt in the great reaches of Western China, during which there were grave financial difficulties and international repercussions. In the first place the Court was unable to deliver enough money to Tso Tsung-t'ang to support his troops, so he turned to borrowing money from foreign firms, such as Jardine, Matheson, and the Hong Kong and Shanghai Banking Corporations. These were short-term loans at high rates of interest, approved by the Court and secured by the bonds of various provinces, from whose tax collections the bonds were to be redeemed (had the tax collections come in in time, Tso would not have had to turn to commercial sources). The provincial bonds were, in turn, guaranteed by the customs service revenues.

Meanwhile, China came to the verge of war with Russia. The Moslem rebellion almost tore Sinkiang loose. The Moslem rebels, led by Yakub Beg, self-proclaimed "King of Kashgaria," who was a pawn of the British in their great game with Russia for control of Central Asia, took the cities and garrisons of Sinkiang and the Ili and Tarim Valleys. Russia could not tolerate any independent adventurer's control of the Ili region, where the passes led into Russian Turkestan. With the Chinese control smashed by the Moslem revolt and the shadow of England in the background, the important Balkash and Semipalatinsk areas of Russia were now threatened. Therefore, in 1871 Russia began a unilateral pacification and occupation of Kuldja and Ili. In the 1850's and 1860's Russia had encircled the Kazakh Steppe with a chain of forts and had taken Tashkent, Samarkand, and Kokand. In 1873 they took Khiva. They had depended upon the stability of Chinese Turkestan for protection on the east, but the Moslem rebellion now threatened to set up an independent tribal state along the eastern flank of Russia, supported by the British. This worried the Chinese, who did not want Russia spilling into their part of Central Asia, but they were too busy with the Moslems in Kansu to do anything about it.

When he had pacified Kansu, Tso Tsung-t'ang regrouped his forces and slowly built supply bases at Lanchow and Suchow, preparatory to moving an army along the old bloody oasis road north of the T'ien Shan. From Kansu, which he first had to rebuild, repopulate, and resow, he moved an army westward eight hundred miles, most of which was desert. To do this, he had to supply himself through local resources, against the opposition of a Court that was getting increasingly doubtful about a contest with Russia over the Ili passes. In 1876 he was ready with the best led, organized, and equipped army China had had since the early days of Ch'ien Lung. The pivotal center of Kashgar fell to his forces in December, 1877. From this point on, the negotiations over the Ili were conducted under the shadow of a Russo-Chinese war in Sinkiang and Amuria, but by February, 1881, the Treaty of St. Petersburg restored control of the Ili region to China.

The rebellions had ended long before this treaty. In 1873 China was pacified. But the twenty years' war brought incalculable human destruction and a ravaging of cities and countryside. The Yangtze Valley was left desolate and a good deal of the Northwest and parts of the North and the Southwest of China were destroyed.

> Ruined cities and desolated towns and heaps of rubble still mark their path from Kiangsi to Tientsin, a distance of 2000 miles . . . wild beasts roam at large over the land . . . and make dens in the deserted towns. . . . The pheasant's whir resounds where the hum of busy populations had ceased and weeds and jungles cover the land.[15]

The organization and success of the new model armies changed the power relationships between Peking and the provinces for good. In 1860 a desperate Court had made the leaders of the anti-Taiping armies the administrative heads of the provinces they were defending. Thus, when the peace came, the most powerful armed forces in China were under the command of and personally loyal to the viceroys and governors who had raised, trained, supported, and led them, and who retained control of their local and provincial taxes to keep their forces. Since they already had administrative control of their areas, this meant that the military, the administrative, and the fiscal resources of the provinces were all now in the hands of power-ful regional civil servants, thus marking the end of the old tra-ditional division of powers. Even when the armies were dis-banded the men remained loyal in spirit to their old commanders, and, even with disbandment the leaders retained their adminis-trative and fiscal controls. Peking could never again exercise full control over the provinces.

Looking back at the civil wars and foreign wars of the mid-nineteenth century, it seems incredible that any state or govern-ment could have recovered from destruction of such widespread magnitude over such a period of time, and indeed the London *Economist* in 1863 held China to be in a state of decomposition.

> China is fast succumbing beneath those toils of European in-fluence by which it has so long been threatened. The latest news . . . shows that the Empire is dissolving at a rate that we could hardly have anticipated on the first contact with European am-bitions. We have always maintained that the resolution taken by the Foreign Office to loan military and naval power to the Im-perialists in China would be a powerful impulse urging the Em-pire there in the same direction in which India has gradually slid under European dominion. . . . China is becoming, as India became in the last century, a prey to contending foreigners,— French, English, and American. The Chinese are falling into the same subordinate position as the native troops of India,—making admirable soldiers when disciplined and led by Europeans, but a mere crowd of craven-hearted Orientals when they are not stiffened by the distinct purposes and guided by the originating intellect of the West. . . . Finally, the foreigners, *even on the same side*, are beginning to quarrel amongst themselves. We find the Franco-Chinese officers holding back prize-money from Anglo-Chinese officers, and much, though not hitherto serious,

wrangling and coldness, and incapacity for cooperation, resulting therefrom. . . . The English, the French, the Americans, and the Russians will all be at work before long, forming temporary alliances and carrying the Chinese with them into their mutual animosities. Instead of setting up the Imperial authority in concert, there can be no doubt that we have substituted for the struggle between the Taepings and the Imperialists the struggles between very many distinct parties, led by Western science and backed by Western courage. . . . The wickedness of which mere adventurers, with full command of Western science and no predilections for Western morality, are capable among an inferior race of malleable Orientals, will probably soon receive valuable illustration in China, as it did in India. We would not willingly have it said that they were acting under any sanction from the English Government.[16]

Yet simultaneously the inner toughness of the system and the excellence of some of the Confucian statesmen were making a great contribution toward strengthening and modernizing China.

NOTES

1. A. Waley, *The Opium War Through Chinese Eyes* (New York: Macmillan, 1958), p. 37.

2. *Ibid.*, p. 88.

3. John K. Fairbank, *Trade and Diplomacy on the China Coast, 1842-1854* (Cambridge, Mass.: Harvard Univ. Press, 1953), p. 83.

4. Earl Swisher, *China's Management of the American Barbarians* (New Haven: Far Eastern Association, 1953), p. 109.

5. *Ibid.*, p. 43.

6. *Ibid.*, p. 47.

7. H. B. Morse and H. F. MacNair, *Far Eastern International Relations* (Boston: Houghton Mifflin, 1931), pp. 263-64.

8. Lord Palmerston to Sir J. F. Davis, January 25, 1847, in *Papers relative to the riot at Canton in July 1846 presented to the House of Commons in 1847*, p. 89, and cited in H. B. Morse, *The International Relations of the Chinese Empire* (3 vols.; London: Longmans, Green, 1910-1918), I (1910), 384.

9. Reed to the Secretary of State as cited in J. W. Foster, *American Diplomacy in the Orient*, Appendix S.

10. Morse and MacNair, *op. cit.*, p. 217.

11. K. C. Hsiao, *Rural China: Imperial Control in the Nineteenth Century* (Seattle: Univ. of Washington Press, 1960), p. 387.

12. A. W. Hummel, ed., *Eminent Chinese of the Ch'ing Period* (Washington, D.C.: Govt. Printing Office, 1943), I, 575.

13. S. Y. Teng, *New Light on the History of the Taiping Rebellion* (Cambridge, Mass.: Harvard Univ. Press, 1950), pp. 44-46.

14. Augustus Lindley, *Ti-Ping Tien-Kwoh: The History of the Ti-Ping Revolution* (2 vols.; London: Day and Son, 1866), Appendix A, "Religious publications written by the T'ien Wang Hung Hsiu-ch'uan," pp. 823-24.

15. S. Wells Williams, *The Middle Kingdom* (2 vols.; New York: Scribner's, 1895), II, 623.

16. *The Economist* (London), October 31, 1863.

Two

The Struggle for
Traditional Principles of
Authority and Stability
(1860-1900)

"SELF-STRENGTHENING"

After 1861 . . . the vermilion pen
was wielded by the hidden hand.
—V. Purcell, *The Boxer Uprising*[1]

Since 1842 there had been a hopeful and moderate element in government and, at the Court, men who were not intransigent about foreigners and who believed that they could, with some reasonable adjustments, save the situation. This flexible element received its chance in 1861 when the weak and debauched Emperor Hsien Feng died. Under the leadership of Prince Kung, younger brother of the deceased Emperor, and the two Dowagers Regnant (the Consort and the Mother of the Heir) power was taken from the most corrupt and reactionary elements. The Western representatives regarded this changeover with benevolence. Apprehensive of the dangers for them of the collapse of the Manchu dynasty, they were now resolved to let China find her way to civilization without intervention. Thus began the T'ung Chih Restoration, the next-to-last stand of Chinese conservatism, which lasted officially until 1874 but which did not fade out until sometime just before 1895, under the manifold pressures of reaction, a new imperialism, the death of its leaders, and the general impossibility of attaining its goals.

The Dowager Empress

The Restoration was led and directed by some exceptional civil servants of great moral and intellectual stature: in addition to Prince Kung, there were Li Hung-chang, Tso Tsung-t'ang, Wen Hsiang, and Tseng Kuo-fan. They were a generation of historically minded and patriotic men who held a serene faith in Confucianism and hence in the possibilities of a beneficial change within that order. There seems to have been no doubt in their minds that there existed substantial precedent for a regeneration. We now realize that they were seeking a state of order and stability according to traditional postulates of Chinese life and society no longer self-evident; yet for almost twenty years the government progressed in the making and administration of foreign policy, the adoption of certain Western industrial techniques, and the invigoration of education. All Chinese officialdom was not, of course, unanimous on the need for reform, certainly not with barbarian methods, but for a generation, at least, the reform movement had the support of the highest officials and for fifteen years, fitfully, of the throne.

Had not the Court and the Imperial power slipped into the grasp of the favorites of a clever, vengeful, and increasingly ambitious woman, then perhaps the history of China after 1856 might have been different. For unless one knows something about the Dowager Empress of China, her position and power, much that occurs between 1874 and 1908 cannot be understood. The Empress Hsiao-ch'in, better known as the Dowager Empress Tz'u Hsi, began her official life in 1851 as a seventeen-year-old minor concubine of the Emperor Hsien Feng. Her future and that of China was decided by a throw of the genetic dice, for in 1856 she bore the Emperor a child, his only son and hence the

heir. When the Emperor died, his will ordered that, for their
official action, the Board of Regents for the five-year-old heir seek
the consent of the two Dowager Empresses. For several months
a bitter struggle took place between the two women and the
eight-man Board of Regents. With the help of Prince Kung, the
uncle of the child heir, the Regents were destroyed, and the
power passed to Prince Kung and the two women. Since Tz'u
Hsi was ambitious and skillful and the Consort was not, and
since Prince Kung's position depended upon the former, she came
to dominate the inner life of the palace. She staffed the palace,
the Court, and the state services with men loyal to her, and,
screening herself behind Confucian principles, she became, as
early as 1865, the greatest source of power in China.

It has always seemed incredible to outsiders that China at
this point in its history could fall under such disastrous leadership—not because Tz'u Hsi was a woman, but because she was
conservative, stubborn, ignorant, intensely self-willed, and a
shrewd manipulator of men and events.

> In the ancestral and family law of the Ch'ing dynasty there was
> no precedent for having an empress dowager manage court affairs
> . . . family law was absolutely disregarded in allowing the two
> empresses to become so powerful; this was a momentous change
> in the political history of the Ch'ing dynasty. . . . After the
> Heavenly Kingdom of the Great Peace had been successfully de-
> stroyed, the scholar-official class, whitewashing all court troubles,
> eulogized the T'ung-chih period (1862-1874) as one of the na-
> tional revival. They praised the sacred virtue of the two empress
> dowagers. They disregarded the fact that one leg of the dragon
> throne had been broken. They did not foresee the ruinous fate
> of the four hundred million Chinese as the subjects of the former
> concubine Yehonala.[2]

The regency ended in 1873 when Emperor T'ung Chih assumed his majority, but he was still under the domination of his
mother and her favorites. Then, in 1875, under mysterious circumstances, he suddenly died, and within three months his preg-
nant wife committed suicide. Under the rules of Imperial succession a mature relative of the Emperor's generation should
have taken the throne, but the Great Council, meeting in a

capital controlled by Tz'u Hsi's troops, was forced to accede to her wish that the throne go to her own nephew, a three-year-old boy. The day following the meeting, he was proclaimed the Emperor Kuang Hsu. Thus Tz'u Hsi once again became Regent, and not until her death in 1908 was she to be unseated.

Her effect on China was not a simple matter of personal good or evil. She could not have been other than she was. She simply exercised enormous power in a society whose central leadership groups were highly conservative and benefited from supporting her. Her greatest personal asset was her self-confidence, which enabled her always to control herself and those around her.

During the 1860's and 1870's her influence was behind the Restorers, who, to place China on a competitive footing, thought it feasible to incorporate within the traditional framework Western techniques in armaments, industry, and communications. Their way was to seek out promising young men, train them in Western languages, educate some abroad, have others read good translations of basic Western technical works, and then proceed, with this cadre, to create armament manufactures, communications, and, in general, sufficient industry to ensure the safety of China.

Foreign Affairs

The initial step toward achieving modernization was to revise the methods of dealing with foreigners, every accustomed way having failed. In early 1861 Prince Kung proposed a new foreign agency. To be called the Tsungli Yamen, it was motivated fundamentally by the treaty powers, tired of being fobbed off on lesser officials for a generation, for prior to 1858 all of China's treaties had been signed by Imperial commissioners at Canton. In 1860 the treaty powers had demonstrated their dissatisfaction through force. The proposal for the agency was approved, but neither the Dowager nor the Grand Council were happy about the autonomy of such an office and required the new Tsungli Yamen to function through the hidebound Board of Rites. The members were housed in cramped and cheerless quarters, and they labored under the stigma that attached to those, even to a Prince, who parlayed with barbarians. It was the leading, but not the only, government body dealing with foreign affairs, and its strength came from the ableness of its men. Until 1884 it was led by Prince Kung, "the only man in the empire of whom the ambitious Tz'u Hsi was afraid," [3] although after 1875 she slowly stole his power away. The agency performed well and bravely, although harassed by antiforeignism among Chinese, a xenophobic Court, a jealous Grand Council, and shoals of perpetually dissatisfied foreigners. It was much more than a Foreign Office. It became the focal point for modernization. It sent students abroad, arranged for schools to be established in languages and in sciences, and pressed for railroads, telegraphs, and technical services.

Education

Tseng Kuo-fan took the lead in modernization. He had become thoroughly converted to the need for arms, was conversant with the technology from which they sprang, and, though Confucian, saw no essential conflict between technical modernization and ethics. He was the most remarkable official of the nineteenth century, being a first-rate scholar and war commander, the very model of a tough, incorruptible leader. He despised his unprincipled colleagues and believed that hard work, honesty, and frugality were necessary in official practices if China were to survive. Had he not spent the better part of his life in military actions against rebellions, he might well have forced through substantial institutional changes.

Another forceful exponent of industrial modernization for China was Yung Wing, who had been educated in the United States, graduating from Yale in 1854. One of his views on the subject is expressed in the following statement, which he made in 1865:

I said that as I was not an expert in the matter, my opinions or suggestions might not be worth much, but nevertheless from my personal observations in the United States and from a common-sense point of view, I would say that a machine shop in the present state of China should be of general and fundamental character and not one for specific purposes. In other words I told them they ought to have a machine shop that would be able to create or reproduce other machine shops of the same character as itself; each and all of these should be able to turn out specific machinery for the manufacture of specific things. In plain words, they would have to have general and fundamental machinery in order to turn out specific machinery. A machine shop consisting of lathes of different kinds and sizes, planers, and drills would be able to turn out machinery for making guns, engines, agricultural implements, clocks, etc. In a large country like China, I told them, they would need many primary or fundamental machine shops, but that after they had one (and a first-class one at that) they could make it the mother shop for reproducing others—better and improved.[4]

In 1865 he—along with $500,000 worth of Yankee machinery—helped Tseng Kuo-fan found the Kiangnan Arsenal, near Shanghai. Associated with the arsenal was a technical school whose students, when trained, were to replace the foreign experts Tseng depended upon. The students studied both in English and through Chinese translations of Western works, made by the arsenal's own translators. Kiangnan was only one of a number of arsenals, machine shops, and technical schools set up during the next twenty years, and it represented, in miniature, the hopes, triumphs, and failures of the Restorers. It was designed to train men in matters regarded as essential to the security of the state, the Empire, and the civilization.

It was at Kiangnan that the struggle began over the full implications of westernization, with a growing recognition of the need for an entirely new kind of education. The proponent of Western culture was Yung Wing, and as a result of his influence 120 young men were sent to the United States (along with Confucian tutors) at a great cost. They arrived in groups during the 1870's to go to secondary schools, boarding with local families, while preparing to enter Yale College, then a small but respectable school for boys of good family in New Haven, Connecticut. The success of these young men was unpalatable to conservative officials at home, who had always distrusted the idea, and their misgivings proved justified when an investigation showed the youths living, dressing, talking, and acting like Americans rather than Confucian scholars. The chance to end this experiment came with the outbreak of violence against Chinese in the Western United States and with the United States' unilateral abrogation of her treaty of 1868 with China. To the charge that their young men were being decultured in America, the officials now added that Americans were racists, hostile to Chinese. Therefore, in 1881, the Chinese educational missions to the United States were withdrawn. The officials then made it clear that while foreign techniques were desirable, they did not replace a Chinese education, and young men who chose to be trained in the arsenals or other types of Western schools would not find a position within the traditional system. Even the most advanced officials, such as Tseng and Li Hung-chang, stated they desired modernization only within the Confucian ethic and learning.

The Confucians of this period saw the world in terms of moral principles and thought ultimate solutions lay in the persistent cultivation of the superior man:

> As to why men are unequal, it is not that Heaven endowed men [differently] and made them unequal; it is simply that men have made themselves unequal. If Heaven had endowed men [differently] and thereby created inequality, it would be shameful [for China, but] though it was shameful, there would be nothing we could do about it. Since man himself creates the inequality, it is still more shameful [for China]. But though it is shameful, there is something we can do about it. If one is ashamed, there is nothing better than self-strengthening.
>
> Now this so-called inequality [between China and the West] is a very real inequality. It is profitless to be angry about it; it is impossible to gloss over it; it is useless to talk it away.
>
> Of late, China's accumulated experience and skill have not been applied. The proper course lies in truly understanding the points of inequality. How is it that they are small, yet strong; that we are large, yet weak. We must seek the means of attaining equality; we will find that it still simply rests with man.[5]

The leaders of the "self-strengthening" movement were no less dedicated to these principles than their conservative colleagues, yet they remained convinced that the way to strength was to be found in using the arts of barbarians against the barbarians. But

they never understood the intellectual and emotional transformations of the young men they trained. For many years it was considered disgraceful for a Chinese to work for or with foreigners.
Such men, whether employed by foreign firms or governments
or by the Chinese government itself, were in a no man's land.
Yet they were the first among the Chinese to see that the power
of Europe was founded on a commercial economy sprung from
technology and protected by military force. The more perceptive
also came to understand the role of Western political institutions
and of nationalism in Western power, and they saw that Confucian ethics could not accommodate the institutional changes
needed for strength—that is, a primacy to trade, an end to the
classical examination system, the limitation of autocracy, and
the initiation of forms of local self-government. Unlike their
superiors, the "self-strengtheners," these young men understood
that Western power sprang from more than arms, that it rested
on institutions. They thus came to think that reform in China
should begin with institutional change. These youths were caught
in the tensions of re-examining the validity of the entire tradition. They were a generation ahead of their time.

Industrialization

The economy could barely support the costs of the arsenals,
shipyards, technical schools, mines, and the military and naval
establishments. For one thing, the quasi-autonomous provincial
leaders withheld a large part of the Imperial tax revenues. Great
efforts were made to improve and stabilize the agrarian economy
by lightening the land tax, levying maximum taxes on other
sectors of the economy, and practicing strict economy in government. Full industrialization—the mechanization of production
and trade—was forestalled, partly because of a shrewd conviction that this would benefit foreigners more than Chinese. China
was already losing her domestic market to imports, and there
existed no Chinese entrepreneurial class that could compete with
the treaty-protected Westerners at their own game. The only
Chinese to enjoy the fruits of progress were the compradors (the
most westernized group in China) and a certain few of the
officials, who regarded modernization on a personal level, as a

perquisite of their status, rather than in terms of the national economy.

The first railroad in China was a ten-mile stretch between Shanghai and Woosung on the Yangtze, built in 1876 with British capital and the implied consent of the local officials. Fearful of any encroachment on its sovereignty, the Chinese government bought it in 1877, tore it up, and moved it to Formosa to let it rot. However, within a few years the development of mining and shipping would require another railway.

In 1872, Li Hung-chang, together with a few officials and merchants, had formed the China Merchants Steam Navigation Company, a private venture under official patronage. Li owned a large part of the stock, and his influence was enough to secure substantial government business at high rates for the firm. The company became wealthy enough to buy out the American-owned Shanghai Steam Navigation Company. In 1878, the same group opened the coal mines at Kaiping, seventy-one miles north of Tientsin, in order to supply coal for their steamships. This met with the approval of Peking, since it promised the coal supply for the projected modern Chinese navy.

The mines and the ships had to be connected by a railway. But, following the Shanghai-Woosung experiment, there was already intense opposition at the Court. So the group built not a railroad but a tramway, while the locomotive that hauled coal the seven miles of its length (the *Rocket of China*) was put together secretly by an English engineer. This little line was the genesis of the Peking-Tientsin line, built in 1886-98.

Thus the first large industrial enterprises in modern China, in shipping, mining, and railroads, were privately owned and controlled by high officials, though dependent upon government patronage. Even so, in the case of the railroad (and of the later telegraph line), the scheme had to be presented, not as a normal and desirable advance in transportation, but in terms of future military benefits.

Modernization during the period of "self-strengthening" was carried on by a small number of dedicated men against considerable odds, somewhat haphazardly, and, in not a few instances, for purely personal gain. The movement failed in its final objective, which was to make China strong. Not even the ablest man ever questioned the base upon which any reforms would rest—the administrative system of China, and especially the thousands of minor officials, unconcerned with the future of China, much less reforms. The point is that by this time traditional beliefs, hopes, and assumptions had become frayed beyond repair. In particular the official-educated class had ceased to possess the firm image of themselves that permitted them to carry on with assurance and self-respect. Too many uncertainties were arising from the defects of tradition. The author of the most illuminating study of this period [6] concludes that what failed was the Confucian system itself and that no individual or group was responsible. Yet to assert that an entire system of life and society was a failure is to beg the question. The real pressures that collapsed the system bore not upon its values but upon its manifestations. What the West attacked was not what the conservatives defended. The West thrust against the body and not the spirit. So a question arises parallel to that raised by the Opium War (Does one civilization have the right to ask another to conform to it?). In the failure of "self-strengthening" the question is: Must China have adopted modern Western things and ideas? The answer is Yes if she wanted to survive as anything more than a dependent client state; but No if it were a matter of assumed obligation to the civilization of the modern Western world. Yet, despite the varying assessments of the era, the wisest judgment may well be that of Li Hung-chang, made in 1876, that China's weakness lay in her poverty, for impersonal nature was taking a hand. In 1876, there were terrible floods in Kwangtung, Fukien, Chekiang, and Kiangsi, accompanied by locust plagues. In the same year drought struck Honan, Shensi, and Shansi. Hunger and death came for millions. The following year was no better:

In November, 1877, the aspect of affairs was simply terrible. The autumn crops over the whole of Shansi and the greater part of Chihli, Honan, and Shensi had failed. . . . Tientsin was inundated with supplies from every available port. The Bund was piled mountain high with grain, the Government storehouses were full, all the boats were impressed for the conveyance of supplies toward Shansi and the Hochien districts of Chihli. Carts and wagons were all taken up and the cumbersome machinery of the Chinese Government was strained to the utmost to meet the enormous peril which stared it in the face. During the winter and spring of 1877-78, the most frightful disorder reigned supreme along the route to Shansi. Hwailu-hsien, the starting point, was filled with officials and traders all intent on getting their convoys over the pass. Fugitives, beggars, and thieves absolutely swarmed. The officials were powerless to create any sort of order among the mountains. The track was completely worn out, and until a new one was made a dead block ensued. Camels, oxen, mules, and donkeys were hurried along in the wildest confusion, and so many perished or were killed by the desperate people in the hills, for the sake of their flesh, that the transit could only be carried on by the banded vigilance of the interested owners of grain, assisted by the train bands, or militia, which had been hastily got together, some of whom were armed with breechloaders. . . . Night traveling was out of the question. The way was marked by the carcasses or skeletons of men and beasts, and the wolves, dogs, and foxes soon put an end to the sufferings of any wretch who lay down to recover from or die of his sickness in those terrible defiles. . . . Broken carts, scattered grain bags, dying men and animals so frequently stopped the way that it was often necessary to prevent for days together the entry of convoys on the one side, in order to let the trains from the other come over. No idea of employing the starving people to make a new, or improving the old road ever presented itself to the authorities; and passengers, thankful for their escape from the dangers of the journey, were lost in wonder that the enormous traffic was possible.[7]

It is then perhaps more accurate to study the failure to modernize in the light of the intricate balance between Chinese society and the Chinese economy. The nineteenth century was an economy of balanced poverty wherein unusual natural calamities or wars destroyed surpluses, tilted the balance, and forced men to begin again. The general economy consisted of a number of subeconomies. There was the traditional agricultural economy, which can be broken into types according to crops and marketing traditions. There was the commercial economy of the treaty ports, which varied from port to port. There was the government sector involving defense, reclamation, and relief, which had to be maintained in some balance with each other. It must also be remembered that unemployment was always a factor in China. Therefore, modernization in the sense of the industrialization of production could aggravate this factor, and entire districts could be put out of work. In many instances rejection of machines was based on nothing more than a wise desire to maintain the local peace. Given all these economic conditions it is then doubtful whether the most dedicated efforts could have succeeded.

The middle and later years of the nineteenth century had brought to China almost more hardship than could be borne. Yet it is astonishing to contemplate that her worst trials still lay ahead.

THE NEW IMPERIALISM

During the 1880's all Africa was divided like a birthday cake, and the islands of the Pacific parceled out, among the capitals of Europe. This activity, the New Imperialism, so unlike the accepted commercial expansion of previous generations, came rapidly and with grave consequence for all concerned. Its causes and its effects—among other things, it gave birth to modern colonialism—are still the objects of intense and sometimes passionate examination, and power, greed, and idealism have all been cited as the fundamental driving forces. Certainly, as it operated on China after 1869, the economic motivation does not seem sufficient to have warranted embroiling whole nations in war. Although a handful of firms benefited, the material results, over a long span of time, proved unprofitable to nations; many areas of the New Imperialism were marginally profitable at best. Power and prestige fueled the imperial engine, and both arose from European politics, which now had a world-wide arena in which to play out its ancient feuds and pretenses.

The New Imperialism was supported by a growing mystique of national superiority not too alien in its cultural aspects from China's own ancient attitudes toward its barbarian neighbors.

If any one generalization may stand, however, it is that British imperialism was based upon a sense of superiority, upon a conviction of a superior political code, on access to a superior view of some Higher Being, on a superior way of life. Idealists and realists alike sought to spread what they felt in their hearts was superior, to spread their institutions *because* they were superior and therefore not only easy to spread but a positive good for those to whom they were applied—or a positive way to preserve the power and prestige of England, itself worth preserving at all costs because superior. The argument was circular, closed, complete. The British strategist, with no thought of God, could advocate annexation of a crucial peninsula because it controlled a strait that must, in turn, be controlled by the British Navy if the British were to prosper; the missionary, with thought only of God, could advocate annexation so that "pagans" might obtain the protection of a Christian nation, a nation superior because Christian.[8]

It was this conviction of cultural superiority that gave rise to the grave problems of Westerners in China, for after 1870 every part of Chinese society was caught up in the New Imperialism. For the next thirty years old territorial claims were taken from her, inviolate colonies of outsiders settled in her midst, her financial sources came under foreign supervision, and the very fundamentals of her culture and national integrity came under attack. The reaction of Chinese and Westerners to each other eventually exceeded the bounds of rational controls.

Missionaries and Colonists

The most delicate, intricate, and passionate relationships rose from the most visible human adjuncts of imperialism—missionaries and foreign settlements. With the signing of the Treaties of Tientsin, missionaries were permitted to travel anywhere in China and to acquire property for mission homes, schools, and churches. Neither the Protestant nor the Roman Catholic missionaries of this time were like the Jesuit missionaries of the sixteenth century. On the other hand, neither China nor the West nor, indeed, Christianity were what they had been in the sixteenth century. The tolerance arising from national strength in the late Ming and early Manchu periods had been swept away after 1842 in the tide of antiforeignism in the South of China, exacerbated by the suppression of the great Taiping Rebellion with its "Christian" overtones. Difficult as Jesuit accommodation with the gentry had proved earlier, it was to be insuperable for the nineteenth-century Protestant and Catholic missions. Gentry officials, who were the local political and cultural arbiters, were now on the defensive, contemptuous and hateful of foreigners and their traditions. Their greatest power was in the smaller communities, which was exactly where the missionaries began to move after 1860. For years they had failed to make converts in the great cities and they were full of the hope that they could bring their message to simple villagers.

The missionaries were good and zealous men. A few such as Timothy Richard and W. A. P. Martin were exceptional Chinese scholars and admirers of Chinese culture, but the great Western missionary movement of their time followed the flag and was very much dependent upon the commercial expansion of nations. Then, too, missionaries were caught up in the pride of their own heritage, and the dominant note of their enterprise was not theological but cultural. They were going to civilize the Chinese. As Arthur Smith wrote in 1894:

> What China needs is righteousness, and in order to attain it, it is absolutely necessary that she have a knowledge of God and a new conception of man, as well as of the relation of man with God. . . . The manifold needs of China we find, then, to be a single imperative need. It will be met permanently, completely, only by Christian civilisation.[9]

Indeed, some missionaries became more articulate champions of the material advantages of the West than did their commercial and diplomatic colleagues. It is not surprising, then, that missionaries, in Chinese eyes, were undistinguishable from any of the other Western agents who were destroying China, and in the swelling wave of antiforeignism it was the missionaries who were the most exposed and most defenseless of the Westerners in China, often suffering horribly.

The nineteenth century is full of riots and incidents against the missions, some minor and some, like the 1870 Tientsin massacre, appalling. This incident, provoked by false and malicious rumors, fanned by the gentry, involved the atrocious murders of fifty-seven Christians, including ten French nuns, two French priests, the French consul, and thirty Chinese Christians. For each incident China paid—with indemnities, executions, and banishments—and with each payment antiforeign and antimission sentiment grew.

What the Chinese specifically resented about the missions was the alienation of Chinese Christians, and the extraordinary rights —exemption from taxes and legal obligations—demanded by the missions for themselves and their converts. Further, they called upon the Chinese and their own authorities to enforce these demands. In a country where land and land titles were almost sacred, it was inevitable that disputes often arose over the right guaranteed to missions by treaty to buy land and erect buildings. The Roman Catholic Church laid claim to properties once held by it in the seventeenth and eighteenth centuries, and, despite the incongruity of such a claim, Chinese occupants were forced to yield without question and without compensation. Riots resulted, during which the Chinese government, obligated to protect the missions from physical harm, often abdicated its police powers. At least they permitted and even encouraged calumnious stories to be spread about Christians, and it was widely believed that the most atrocious kinds of things happened in the missions—that simple medications provided by their dispensaries were potions designed to steal the wits and souls of men, that children in their orphanages were kidnapped and used for awful purposes, that bodies in their hospitals were dismembered, that immorality was part and parcel of their private church services and of Christianity in general. The government and the gentry knew better, but those Chinese who came to the missions in the interior were often not only the lowest elements within the population but also the most disaffected. A government involved in a life-and-death struggle with rebellion was not likely to regard with favor what they believed to be a sanctuary for their enemies, rebels, outlaws, or the mean people in general.

Beyond this, the Chinese resented the missionaries acting in

China as they would not have been permitted to act in their own countries. They were, with few exceptions, completely intolerant of Chinese religions and customs, consigned unregenerate Confucianists and Buddhists to hellfire, and were seen to be working toward substituting an alien civilization for one that the Chinese believed worked quite well.

The missions also suffered for events and acts that were not their fault and that they themselves deplored. In Kwangtung, the most antiforeign of the provinces, they inherited the hatreds engendered by long exposure to Westerners, and in 1883 they took the brunt of riots in Canton. In Hunan they inherited the legacy of bitterness against the "Christian" Taipings. They were even disdained by their own national authorities, who, continually seeking to restrain mission activities, were unaware that they themselves were objects of the antiforeign feeling. But, fundamentally, the missionaries suffered from being regarded by the Chinese as political agents whose avowed aim was to build a new Chinese life on Western models. Not until after the turn of the century did the picture change. Then, a new generation of missionaries was welcomed, but for the prestige of Western education and its technical skills.

The Foreign Settlement

Concurrent with the spread of missions were the growing settlements of foreigners in the open ports, of which the Shanghai International Settlement was the great example. Like all such settlements, that of Shanghai was a piece of land, originally under Chinese sovereignty, set aside so that foreigners might live and do business there. It had started and grown as a segregated European colony, but the Taiping rebellion brought to Shanghai a flood of Chinese refugees, many of them wealthy, increasing the population to city size and creating a settlement of mixed nationalities. When the Yangtze was opened up by the treaties of 1860, Shanghai became a great port. But the government of China was too weak to exercise police power over the Chinese nationals resident in this new metropolis. Thus arose problems concerning the jurisdiction and control of the Chinese in the settlement, problems that were not settled until 1927.

Both foreigners and Chinese had justifiable grievances, but the greatest irritant to the Chinese was the fact that Westerners regarded these parcels of Chinese national soil as parcels of their own national territory.

Despite good law, good government, and Shanghai's role as a sanctuary (it was a place of complete safety for antidynastic elements or those persecuted by the government), the idea that it and all such colonies were not under Chinese control angered even those who sought refuge in them. They were the centers of foreign financial and mercantile controls exercised on China from the outside, and since they were entirely commercial in character, except for the missionaries, they gave the Chinese an unbalanced concept of Western life and purposes.

There was little if any community of interest between the missions and other Westerners in the settlements. The missionaries did have a contempt for a corrupt China, but they lived and worked among the Chinese to save them from their own decay. The treaty-port Westerners lived behind stockades in their own social hierarchy, isolated completely from China. Unlike the missionaries, they rarely bothered to learn the language, to come to grips with Chinese civilization, or even to know any Chinese save their servants. The missionaries regarded them almost as bitterly as did the Chinese, for to the religious, Shanghai was a Babylon whose excesses and indifference only complicated the work of God. Essentially, the missions and the settlements represented another failure of communication between China and the West.

The Imperial Maritime Customs

Not all Western-inspired or Western-dominated organizations were inimical to China, as can be seen in the operation of maritime customs after 1863. When the Taipings occupied Shanghai in 1853, the collection of the customs and enforcement of customs procedures was undertaken by a committee of foreign merchants, who proved so honest and efficient that they were permitted to continue even after the defeat of the Taipings. Thus there emerged the great Imperial Maritime Customs service, which, by 1858, had its authority extended to all Chinese trading ports. It was predominantly Chinese in personnel but was supervised and executed by a predominantly English international civil service, headed by an inspector-general who, in turn, was responsible to the Tsungli Yamen. The inspector-general, from 1863 until his retirement in 1904, was Sir Robert Hart, the most exceptional foreigner ever to serve in China, as can be seen by his instructions:

Inspectorate General of Customs
Peking, 21st June, 1864

In the first place, it is to be distinctly and constantly kept in mind, that the Inspectorate of Customs is a Chinese and not a Foreign Service, and that, as such, it is the duty of each of its members to conduct himself towards Chinese people as well as officials in such a way as to avoid all cause of offence and ill-feeling. Whatever other Foreigners resident in this country may deem themselves entitled to do, whether from their position or fancied superiority to the Chinese, or in the way of showing their superior enlightenment by riding rough-shod over prejudices and by evincing a general contempt for customs differing from their own, it is to be expected from those who take the pay and who are the servants of the Chinese Government, that they, at least, will so act as to neither offend susceptibilities, nor excite jealousies, suspicion, and dislike.[10]

A singularly able executive officer, he was, for generations, the trusted adviser to the Tsungli Yamen.

The Imperial Maritime Customs, in its way, kept the government solvent. Apart from collecting customs scrupulously (to the disconcertion of both Chinese and foreign traders), it kept China out of foreign lenders' hands by providing security, in bond issues or domestic loans obtained by the government through the agency of international banks in China, such as the Hong Kong and Shanghai Banking Corporation. Peking was neither the borrower nor the guarantor. It simply ordered the provincial authorities to issue bonds and the customs service to guarantee them. This arrangement, started in 1868 with the loan to support Tso Tsung-t'ang's Moslem campaign, kept Peking clear of indebtedness until 1895. The Maritime Customs service was also a training school for young Westerners in Chinese and for young

Chinese in the English language and ways. During the tenure of Sir Robert Hart, it was the greatest stabilizing force between China and the West.

THE LOSS OF THE BUFFER EMPIRE

For almost one thousand years Chinese governments had, at great cost, attempted to preserve the security and integrity of the Central Kingdom by maintaining, around its periphery, a ring of vassal buffer states and regions: Annam, Burma, Tibet, Mongolia, Turkestan, and Korea. Within twenty years (1875-95) most of this carefully accumulated sovereignty was to be stripped away.

The South

It was an ambition of the British and the French to rid themselves of the traditional Chinese influence in their new colonies in Burma and Indochina and, at the same time, to tap the South China trade (Yunnan, Kweichow, Szechuan) for the benefit of these new lands. In the First Anglo-Burmese War (1824-26), the British had taken Rangoon and the Burmese areas bordering British Assam. In the Second Anglo-Burmese War (1852), England had come into control of all Lower Burma. But the Burmese continued to resist and relied on China for help. In 1868, for the purpose of reaching an agreement with China and opening the Yunnan trade, the British sent an exploratory expedition over the difficult and dangerous Burma-Yunnan border, followed by a second expedition in 1874, during which Augustus Margary of the consular services was killed by bandits. Although this occurred in restless tribal territory over which China exercised no effective control, England treated the incident as an act of war and demanded indemnities, punishment, and British rights to explore in Yunnan. Sir Thomas Wade, representing the British in Peking, was more interested in exploiting the incident as a lever for general treaty revision than in gaining satisfaction for Margary's death. In March, 1875, he impatiently threatened to break relations with China if his demands were not met. Surprised at the demands but helpless, in August, 1875, the Chinese government delegated Li Hung-chang to meet with him at Chefoo. After a stormy conference that lasted from July to September, 1876, terms were set up whereby China renounced her sovereignty over Burma, a Burma-Chinese trade was established, and a railway and commercial penetration of the Southwest was projected. Also, eleven ports of the Yangtze River were opened to call, thus making that river accessible for foreign vessels all the way to Chungking. In 1885-86, the Third Anglo-Burmese War gave England control of all Burma, and the consequent annexation of Burma as a colony of the Crown was formally recognized by China.

In part, the British haste to annex northern Burma was triggered by their fear that the French would tap South China first. The French had been politically and militarily active in Indochina since the 1780's. They were most desirous of seizing Annam and Tonkin and of controlling the Red River, which carried trade to and from South China.

Of all the Chinese vassal states, with the exception of Korea, Annam was the most Sinicized. She had ancient connections with China and, in the nineteenth century, was a tribute-bearing state whose northern frontiers, although not well demarked, sometimes lay within direct Chinese jurisdiction. Between 1858 and 1864 a joint Franco-Spanish war against the Emperor of Annam resulted in the French getting Saigon and its surrounding area (Cochin-China); and in 1863 Cambodia was taken under French protection. In 1873-74 a French force moved up the Red River to open Hanoi despite great losses, and concurrently the Treaty of Saigon forced the Emperor of Annam to declare his loyalty to Paris rather than to Peking. The Chinese protested France's unilateral action toward a state that was still sending tribute missions to China, but to no avail, because France had grandiose schemes of empire in Indochina.

In 1882 the Tonkinese rose against the French and, with the help of the Black Flags—Chinese irregulars in Annamese service —destroyed their garrison. The French retook Hanoi and moved toward the Chinese border. Peking had informed Paris that if the French took the border towns, it would mean war. The French proceeded to take these from Imperial Chinese forces in

1883-84 and in 1883 made both Annam and Tonkin protectorates. Helplessly, the Chinese withdrew their border garrisons and signed, in 1884, the Li-Fournier agreement, whereby France was to respect the border while China was to open the entire frontier to trade. But after an outbreak of fighting the same year, China declared war. France made no formal declaration, but her naval forces attacked Hainan and Formosa without notice, patrolled the Chinese coast to intercept and destroy grain shipments to Peking, and even considered naval action against Port Arthur. On land, in Annam, Chinese regular forces, along with the irregular Black Flags, routed a French army at Langson on the border (1885). With victory in her hands (the main French forces had been killed or dispersed, the Chinese held Tonkin, and the government in France resigned because of the defeat), the Dowager, appalled at the costs of the war, ordered her army to stop its pursuit and open peace negotiations.

Despite her position, in 1885 China lost by the subsequent Tientsin Convention, which ratified and amplified the earlier Li-Fournier agreement. Under its terms China recognized the French protectorate over Annam and Tonkin, lost control of the frontier, and opened it to the French trade. In 1887, the French joined Cambodia, Annam, Tonkin, and the Cochin-China area in the Indo-Chinese Union and, in 1893, made Laos a protectorate. Not until the turn of the twentieth century had she pacified the interior.

In the catalogue of grievances that China accumulated during the nineteenth century, none seemed so real to her as the Tonkin case, for throughout the French acted as if China (or indeed any Asian state) had no rights that a European power was bound to respect.

The West

While China retained control in Central Asia, her protectorate over Tibet, established by K'ang Hsi and Ch'ien Lung, ran up against British policy in the Himalayas. The British hoped to protect the mountain frontiers of India against the warlike Gurkhas and Bhutanese of the Himalayas, and also to open the Himalayan trade routes from India to Central Asia and China.

The Gurkha War of 1814-16 had brought England into a close relationship with Tibet, and she was uneasy that an unfriendly Tibet was under Chinese control. British trade with Tibet was small, but British prestige in India was at stake, unless they could stabilize the Himalayan frontier.

Then, in the 1860's, the British began to see that a foothold in Tibet would enable them to keep trade from the interior of China flowing across the passes into India, while they shipped great quantities of British Indian tea back across the borders into Tibet and China. For twenty years the Indian government, under prodding from London, attempted to get a British mission into Lhasa. But by 1886 it became apparent that, even with Chinese assent, the Tibetans themselves would have nothing to do with England. Indeed, far from welcoming a British mission, the Tibetan government in 1886 claimed and then fortified the mountain state of Sikkim, which the British had declared a protectorate in 1861. In 1888 the British forces pushed Tibet out of Sikkim and, two years later, recognizing Chinese rights, entered into negotiations with China to establish an Indian-Tibetan market at Yatung. An agreement was reached that included a definition of the frontier between Tibet and Sikkim. However, the Tibetans refused to recognize the demarcation, and the Chinese were powerless to enforce it.

It became evident to England in the 1890's that there was no real Chinese power in Tibet, and it was feared that the Russians, moving in from Central Asia, might become the most influential power in that theocracy. Russia had several advantages. She was already established at the passes into western Tibet, and she had under her benevolent jurisdiction great numbers of Mongol Buddhist tribes who looked to the Dalai Lama for their spiritual guidance. By 1902 the British Foreign Office was convinced that Russo-Chinese-Tibetan moves or treaties were in motion, designed to unsettle the Indian frontier along the Himalayas. To counter the Russians, in 1904 the British dispatched the Younghusband expedition, the first Western penetration of Tibet. Younghusband succeeded in procuring the Convention of Lhasa, which demolished the fiction of Chinese authority over Tibet, for it permitted a permanent British agent at Gyantse and, in effect, a British occupation of the Chumbi River Valley. Yet, the British continued to recognize, through agreement with China in 1906, the concept of Chinese sovereignty in Tibet.

Actually, the Lhasa Convention was to strengthen China in Tibet, for subsequent Tibetan drives for complete independence provoked anti-Chinese uprisings, which in turn led, in 1908-10, to the Chinese occupation of eastern Tibet and incorporation of this territory into China. Independence came to Tibet only with the Chinese revolution of 1911. The end of the Manchu dynasty led to the expulsion of the Chinese from Tibet in 1912 and the recognition of Tibet as an independent state by England in 1914, an independence unrecognized by subsequent Chinese governments.

But now, with the western frontiers in dispute and the southern ones lost, a great danger arose in the Northeast.

Korea and the Sino-Japanese War

The ancient kingdom of Korea, under great Chinese cultural influence and political control since the Han period, was almost mortally stricken in the Japanese invasion of 1592-98. In 1637 the highly conservative Korean court isolated the country to protect it from foreign influences except for China, to whom she yielded like a vassal. She maintained stringent control over her borders and coasts, forbade the import of books considered dangerous, and made subject to death all foreigners who violated her seclusion. Despite the great respect for China, the annual tribute missions, and the permeation of Confucian culture into all phases of Korean life—or perhaps because of them—the Korean court became more and more withdrawn and conservative during the succeeding centuries.

In the late nineteenth-century world of imperialism, Korea, lying helplessly between two powers, Russia and Japan, and viewed by each as a necessary adjunct to its empire, was to place an insuperable burden upon China's relations with the West. For, as Peking learned to become increasingly flexible in her own foreign policy, she was charged with the protection of Korea, which was becoming increasingly inflexible. In 1876, the new Restoration government of Japan, with the acquiescence of

China, signed the Treaty of Kangwha with Korea, in which Japan recognized Korea as a sovereign independent state and established a Japanese Resident at Seoul, the only foreign representation, save Chinese, in centuries.

For the next eighteen years an undercover struggle went on between China and Japan for control of the Korean government. This was exaggerated within Korea by the rise of two powerfully opposed factions at court. The one, seeking to retain isolation and conservatism, turned to China. The other, seeking a modernization of Korea along Japanese lines, turned to Japan. In 1884 both powers intervened with troops to further the causes of their adherents and were on the edge of hostilities when they decided to arbitrate their differences. This was accomplished by the Li-Ito Convention (1885), wherein both countries agreed to withdraw their troops from Korea and to refrain from sending troops again without notification.

Nevertheless, for ten more years China and Japan, acting through their agents at Seoul, jockeyed for power, while the schism between the conservative and the reform factions at court became even more deep and affected Korean daily life. The Japanese proved far more aggressive in Korean affairs than China, and soon anti-Japanese resentment began to build up among all factions. Meanwhile, the Russians and the British, both of whom had interests in Korea, became worried about the effect of a Japanese hegemony.

The Chinese Resident at Seoul, Yuan Shih-k'ai, was playing a dangerous power game with no power to back him. The struggle for Korea became the most dangerous game in which China could participate, because, as she became ever more deeply involved, she was becoming militarily impotent. During the Taiping war Peking had lost essential control of both the standing army and the regional and provincial reserves. A series of semiprivate armies, commanded by governors and governors-general, had been recruited to save the dynasty. After the rebellion some of these armies were disbanded, but some of them were nationalized, that is, put under the Board of War. Their tested commanders became high civil officials while untested civil officials became commanding officers. Thus, at one stroke, the finest armed forces in China were radically weakened, for it proved practically impossible to make good officers of the untried civilians and socially impossible to make experienced officers from men of the peasant class. In addition, the attempt to create a sound national army from these former regional forces was doomed because Peking could not support a modern army. She could not manufacture sufficient modern arms and ammunition, and what she could supply were improperly used by untrained officers. Both socially and economically, military reforms were beyond reach at a time when China desperately needed a competent army.

There were also grave administrative weaknesses. By the eve of the Sino-Japanese war China had a rather peculiar dual military system. Under Imperial control were the Disciplined Forces, which were a part of the old Green Standard or National Army, which had been reorganized to protect Peking. Under partial Imperial control were the Defense Armies, which were organized from the militia forces of the Taiping wars. The types of forces at the disposal of the government ran from the Western Border Forces, led by Tatar governors and armed with spears and bows and arrows, to the Northern Army, formed by Li Hung-chang in 1888 for Chihli province, armed with rifles and using Western methods of drill and organization.

The armies that fought Japan in 1894-95 were totally unfit for modern warfare—poorly armed, for the most part incompetently led, and with no medical, communications, or logistics facilities; it was this that led to such mocking evaluations of the Chinese as fighters as the one that follows:

> Serving under such conditions, scorned by his own society, it is not surprising that the Chinese "brave" appeared to be little more than the caricature of a soldier. The typical Chinese enlisted man had little resemblance to his Western counterpart. His uniform consisted of baggy trousers and a brightly colored, but ill-fitting jacket, topped by a turban or conical bamboo hat. This unmilitary appearance was often accentuated by the addition of a fan and umbrella. The weapons which this neglected son of Mars was expected to carry into battle might include a matchlock, gingal, spear, sword or bow, but in rare instances he was

armed with a modern breech-loading rifle. In some cases there was a bull's-eye on the front of his jacket, which was suggestive of the fact that he was cannon fodder. On the back of his blouse he might display the character for courage, the location of which some thought was also suggestive. Underfed, housed in a dirty, inadequate hut, debilitated by enforced idleness he might well be addicted to gambling and opium. It is amazing that such underpaid, poorly led, and ill-trained men could call forth during the next few decades not only scorn and derision, but also dire predictions of a yellow peril. Few could then evaluate the true potential of Chinese soldiers, for their real military characteristics would not become apparent until they were well trained, equipped, and led.[11]

As to the navy of China, the 36,000,000 taels accumulated for its construction and maintenance had been taken by the Dowager for her own pleasures. Outgunned and outmaneuvered, it fought just one day off the Yalu River and never fought again.

By July, 1894, the situation was most favorable to Japan. The Korean government had been "reorganized" on July 23 by the Japanese, operating in the shadow of their military garrison in Seoul; Japan had promised Russia that no matter what happened Russian interests would be respected, and the same guarantee was given to British trade concerns. Although the Tsungli Yamen insisted that China was and would remain sovereign over Korea, China was unprepared for the role. She had no policy for peace or war. Japan, on the other hand, was ready for a war and had clear-cut ambitions to dominate Korea and to advance its own destiny as supreme arbiter of Eastern Asia.

On July 25, the Chinese troop transport *Kaoshing*, leased from a British company and flying the Union Jack, was sunk without warning by the Japanese destroyer *Naniwa*. Japan sent England apologies and compensation. Then General Oshima moved his troops south from Seoul to cut off Chinese forces at Asan, where, on July 30, he met and destroyed them. Two days later Japan declared war on China. On August 26 the Korean government authorized the Japanese to expel all Chinese forces from Korea and to set up an independent Korea. The following month the Chinese army in the North at Pyongyang was crushed, and two Japanese armies set out to invade China, the one moving into Manchuria, the other to Port Arthur—China's greatest fortress, whose defenses had cost 16,000,000 taels. On September 17 a naval battle was fought off the mouth of the Yalu River, but the Chinese retreated to Weihaiwei, leaving Japan master of the sea.

In the midst of these disasters the Dowager ordered Li Hungchang to seek mediation. When the European powers whom he consulted failed to agree on the substance of mediation, the United States offered assistance. The Japanese refused mediation. China then offered peace on the basis of an indemnity to Japan and the absolute independence of Korea. The Japanese, in occupation of all southern Manchuria, including the important Liaotung area, would agree only to meet and talk with Chinese envoys at Hiroshima. She was delaying for good reasons: She desired to seize as much territory as possible prior to any peace; she was not sure what the reaction of European powers might be to her demands, and within her government there was a dispute as to how great the demands should be. Extremists were pressing for terms that would give Japan most of Manchuria and parts of Chihli and Shantung Provinces, but a compromise was reached in which it was agreed that Japan would seek (1) an indemnity, (2) the independence of Korea (as a sop to the Western powers), (3) the cession of Formosa and the Liaotung areas, and (4) Japan's admittance to most-favored-nation status in China.

The preliminary peace talks took place at Hiroshima, and the Japanese continued to stall on points of protocol while they consolidated their conquests on the continent. The Western powers, increasingly uneasy over the Japanese foothold on the continent, advised her, delicately, to temper her demands. At the risk of European intervention, the Japanese government decided to proceed with their original demands. In March, 1895, a peace conference opened at Shimonoseki, without an armistice. The Japanese would agree to one only if its army controlled the Peking area, as an evidence of Chinese good faith.

The extraordinary privileges in China that Japan listed among its terms included not only everything the Western treaty powers enjoyed but also the opening of the Yangtze and the West River systems in their entirety to Japanese trade and residence, the establishment of Japanese warehouses and industry in China, and the free importation of Japanese goods. Li Hung-chang (who had been wounded at Shimonoseki by a Japanese patriot on March 24, 1895) protested. The Japanese modified some of the demands but presented the new draft as an ultimatum. An imposed peace was signed at Shimonoseki on April 17, 1895.

Now in occupation of Formosa and Liaotung, Japan dominated the South China Sea, the Yellow Sea, Manchuria, and North China. She had the right to undersell Chinese goods in China and to import industrial machinery into China. The huge indemnity of 230,000,000 taels was the climax of her drive for modern power, for it enabled her to go on the gold standard, cover her national deficit, expand her army and navy, and become a modern industrial and military state. For China, the indemnity hastened national bankruptcy, forced her to extend special privileges to foreigners to raise the money, and broke the Chinese domestic market for Chinese goods.

On April 23, 1895, came the blow that many highly placed Japanese had warned would come unless Japan moderated her demands. Germany, Russia, and France bluntly told Japan to disgorge the Liaotung. Their ostensible reason was that the presence of Japan so close to Peking threatened the integrity of the Chinese government; the real reason was their fear that Japan would outgain and outsell them in Northeast Asia. Of the three intervening powers, Russia had a powerful navy and army in the area and was prepared to use it. Japan, unable to sustain another war, yielded the Liaotung to China, for an additional 30,000,000 taels indemnity.

The war and the retrocession may well have been the most decisive single events in the modern history of China and Japan. The war established Japan on the continent of Asia, bringing her face to face with Russia and the West. The forced retrocession humiliated her and gave her an implacable desire for revenge. For China it was not only the end of empire (Korea was gone, and Manchuria would follow within a decade), it was the end of her integrity as a state. The drives for empire that had cut away her own buffer empire in the South and the North would now be directed at China herself.

SQUEEZING AND CUTTING THE MELON

Financial Imperialism

After Shimonoseki Napoleon Bonaparte's "sleeping giant" was now more nearly a decaying corpse. For generations the West had treated the China it knew with a certain circumspection, mindful of its size and population, and respectful of its history, never daring to believe that its power was not, in the last analysis, commensurate with its mass. Now its weaknesses were revealed. Its armies were poorly trained and armed, its commanders corrupt and cowardly; it had been soundly beaten in a short campaign by other Asiatics and stripped of its last defenses. The respect it had commanded turned to contempt, and with the same equanimity with which the Powers had divided Africa, they now contemplated China. The initial step was not territorial control but economic domination, with Russia, France, and Germany each demanding as compensation for their intervention great economic concessions.

Peking had paid for the conduct of the Sino-Japanese War, such as it was, by a series of loans: a three-million-pound loan, secured by the customs revenues; a one-million-pound German loan, secured by the salt taxes of Kiangsu Province, with a second mortgage on the customs; and a one-million-pound English loan, secured by a mortgage on the customs. All three of these loans were made with private banking corporations, each under the auspices of its government, and each loan was secured, of course, by the government of China. Until these loans of 1894-95 China had borrowed very little from abroad and had paid that off rapidly. But the corruption of her officials, the costs of the war, and the enormous indemnity threw her into the hands of the moneylenders. Her credit was good because in the past it had always been good; she was meeting current expenses out of current revenue and hence was able to pledge the future. The rapid liquidation of the 23,000,000 pounds sterling promised to Japan at Shimonoseki could only be gotten by borrowing it abroad. Peiping turned first to a private agent, the Hong Kong and Shanghai Banking Corporation, selected at the urging of Sir Robert Hart of the Imperial Maritime Customs, who thought it best for China to use an honest agent to secure loans at a reasonable interest. The security was the universal recognition of Hart's splendid reputation as controller of the Maritime Customs. However, this idea was soon abandoned, for the interest and commissions from such a large loan were so magnificent that every banking group and syndicate of any size, backed by its government in one way or another, sought to participate.

The Russians got there first on the grounds of their old friendship with China and claims of being more politically disinterested than other foreigners. In 1895 a Franco-Russian syndicate lent China 15,800,000 pounds, for a thirty-six-year period at 4 per cent interest, plus charges and commissions, to be secured by customs revenues, and the security was in turn guaranteed by the Russian government (although essentially by French taxpayers). A year later a German-English group lent 16,000,000 pounds for a period of thirty-six years. This loan was also secured by future customs receipts, and rapid amortization or prior redemption was forbidden by its terms. In 1898 a syndicate of the Hong Kong and Shanghai Banking Corporation with the Deutsche-Asiatische Bank advanced 16,000,000 pounds for a period of forty-five years. This was secured not only by pledges on the customs receipts but also by revenues from the likin, or internal transit taxes.

The sum total of these loans enabled China to pay off the Shimonoseki indemnities. They were also the beginning of China's national debt, and had the effect of placing the revenues of China almost totally in foreign control. From that time onward, for at least a quarter of a century, the government, without much success, was forced to look beyond the Imperial Maritime Customs for capital to operate the government, for even the provincial taxes were in some measure pledged to the indemnity loans.

It was the terms of the loans that proved so damaging, being uniformly unfavorable to the borrower in ways that would not have been permitted within the most irresponsible of Western countries. The agents for the loans, the banking groups, were not obliged to render statements of account to the government of China, nor were they in any way obliged to the bondholders for default in payments. Payments on the debt were generally made by the government of China to the banking agents well in advance of the time due, and the agents used the money for their own profit before repaying bondholders. There was no time limit set on redemption of bonds. China could neither repay the loans in advance nor renegotiate the loans at a more advantageous rate of interest. Thus, it is no mere generalization to say that imperialism in the late nineteenth century was responsible for wrecking the internal economy of China.

The Seizure of Territory

Beginning in 1897 the major powers became fearful that China, weak, helpless, in debt, and torn by internal dissensions, would fall apart into constituent areas and provinces without each power falling heir to what it considered its rightful slice of the "melon"—a euphemism that the Chinese themselves perceptively originated. The German Emperor led the way. William II, who had a passion for empire building, had already proposed, three years before, the German seizure of Formosa. The Kaiser, who had come off second best in Africa, was also seeking an opportunity for Germany to assert herself in East Asia in a manner equal to England, Russia, France, and Japan. The opportunity came in 1897. Two German missionaries, Fathers Henle and Nies, were killed in a bandit raid on a small town in Shantung. This was neither an antiforeign nor an anti-Christian act, as the Germans were to claim, for Chinese were also killed and every Chinese house in town sacked. But within two weeks of the murder, a German naval force was landed to seize the heights surrounding Kiaochow, and the Chinese were challenged to fight or to offer apologies, compensation, and the Shantung area— an unparalleled use of force in international relations. China appealed to the treaty powers for mediation, but Russia and France backed Germany while England stood aloof. So in March, 1898, China was forced to sign a convention with Germany that gave Germany control of the Kaiochow area for ninety-nine years, and thus all of Shantung became an area of predominant German interest. Within three days of the signing of this convention, Russia demanded the lease, for twenty-five years, of Port Arthur and Dairen, plus the right to build a railroad that would connect Harbin with Dairen. (Russia had already secured, secretly, in 1896, the right to build a railroad across Manchuria from the Mongol frontier to Vladivostok.) China signed. Next, the French demanded the right to mine in South China, the rectification of the China-Annam border in favor of Annam, and the right to extend the Annam railway into China. China signed.

The British, not to be outdone, requested first a lease on Weihaiwei to run as long as the Russians held Port Arthur, and, secondly, in order to make Hong Kong more secure, a ninety-nine-year lease on the mainland of Kowloon. China signed. The French, who had so far satisfied themselves with mining and railroad concessions, now sought their recompense in a ninety-nine-year lease on Kwangchowan. Once more, China signed.

It is admittedly poor historiography to judge past events by contemporary morals, but by any standards these actions were extortionate. They were followed, in the waning years of the nineteenth century, by a competition for privileges and advantages. By the end of the century there were concessions for 6,000 miles of railways to be built at a cost to China of almost 80,000,000 pounds, secured by first mortgages on the railways and rights of way. In addition, the Inland Waters Steam Navigation Act of 1898, forced on the Chinese, gave foreign flag vessels practically sovereign rights on the great waterways of the West and Yangtze Rivers. The interior of China, heretofore barred to the foreigner, now stood in pawn.

"The fact is," said Sir Robert Hart in 1899, "everybody's for exploiting China. . . ." [12] And in the same year, "Poor China: even yet they'll not wake up to the necessity for real reform. They can be hammered and hectored into giving up anything, but no advice,—no warning—will rouse them to strengthening their backbone or sharpening their claws." [13]

REFORM AND REACTION

The last sixteen years of the Ch'ing dynasty were marked by the speed with which both planned and unplanned events converged to end the traditional state. Yet, through all, the ancient principles of authority, however futile, were regarded by the dynasty as immutable and inviolable. When driven to moderate change, it was never prepared to concede one jot of its prerogatives. After China sustained its worst defeat in almost a quarter of a millennium, the dynasty sought refuge in reaction, and then, jarred by the violence of events, moved toward reform with both hands outstretched—the one giving, the other taking away. It chose always the course that would guarantee its own survival. Three totally unconnected events in 1895 give an indication of the choice of action open to the dynasty at that time. In February the official Hu Yu-fen urged the creation of a modern, centrally directed army. In March a small revolutionary group, on its way to overthrowing the dynasty, failed to seize Canton. In May the scholars, led by K'ang Yu-wei, urged a thorough modernization of education, industry, agriculture, and administration, under supervision of the dynasty.

Contrary to Hart's opinion, there were Chinese seeking ways to strengthen spines and sharpen claws. The educated agreed that China needed desperately to protect herself. But these Chinese were not agreed on the method of protection. Some thought that the protection should be limited to a reformed military structure sufficient to produce a force that could halt the demands. Others wanted reforms so deep as to alter institutions beyond recognition. In addition, there was no agreement as to whether the search for strength should include the preservation of the Manchu dynasty. This fundamental disagreement on objectives fatally inhibited the kind of surgical change that China seems to have needed. The most significant leaders during the years when choice still seemed possible were: Chang Chih-tung, the last of the great Confucian officials, who believed that to strengthen China was to uphold the dynasty and tradition; K'ang Yu-wei, scholar and visionary; his disciple, Liang Ch'i-ch'ao, scholar and journalist, who believed that radical modernization was in the true Chinese tradition; and Sun Yat-sen, medical doctor and agitator, who sought to make China strong by ending both the dynasty and tradition.

The most obvious need after the Sino-Japanese War was for military reorganization. Chang Chih-tung (1837-1909), at that time Governor-General of Nanking, pressed the throne for such reforms. He was in an excellent position to do so. A first-class scholar who had always taken an optimistic view of China's strength and prospects, he had been for years a favorite of the Dowager. Since 1882 he had governed, successively, Shansi, Kwangtung-Kwangsi, Hupeh-Honan, and Nanking. In each of his posts he showed enormous energy and vision in reform, and introduced modernization and honest administration. While at Canton he fought the French incursions from Annam with vigor and established arsenals, schools, and a mint. At Wuchang he pressed for railroads, reformed the provincial troops, and founded China's greatest industrial enterprise, the Hanyeping coal and iron complex. Now, at the end of the Japanese war, he memorialized the throne for modern military academies. This was refused. The throne knew that to start such institutions would be to admit publicly the corruption, incompetence, and nepotism of the officer corps of the various armed forces, as well as the failures of the arsenals. Chang was permitted, however, to organize two brigades, using specially selected recruits and German officers, who would serve not merely as instructors but as functioning officers, until Chinese were trained to take their place. These two brigades, the Self-Strengthening Army and the Newly Created Army, were essentially provincial (Hupeh-Honan) forces, and by 1898 were, along with the new Tenacious Army of Chihli Province, the only reasonably modern military units in China. Military modernization seemed to stop with this. Reorganization was minimal in other provincial forces and within the National Army, and China was still essentially without defense. But a start had been made toward elevating the respectability of the military profession, for the new brigades recruited literate men and honest and efficient Chinese officers, gave them discipline, paid them, and trained them in Western organization and techniques. These three armies also comprised, through their officers, the most Western-trained and Western-oriented segment of Chinese officials, and because of this, as well as more practical reasons, they became the seedbed of modern warlordism in China. For, when all else had failed and it came about that no one could rule China without an army, the only functioning army in China was the Northern Army, centered around the three new brigades and commanded by the Viceroy of Chihli.

The Hundred Days

In 1895, a substantial number of scholars from most of the provinces of China had petitioned the throne to reject the treaty with Japan. The organizer of this petition was K'ang Yu-wei (1858-1927), a notable scholar whose principles of reform reached far beyond the modernization of his country. He was that rarest of creatures, a Chinese Utopian. His intensive study of Chinese and Western thought had led him to a concept of human unity wherein he viewed all humanity as one in its suffering and its essential goodness. He believed that human institutions were perfectible and that one compassionate world for all was possible, and with great erudition he interpreted the original teachings of Confucius, not the textual perversions of the post-Han schools, to support his evolutionary views. Progressive Confucianism, he thought, could show the world the path to human brotherhood.

K'ang Yu-wei was from Kwangtung, the force bed that produced the shakers and movers of Chinese life. He had taken first place in the Imperial exams of 1895, but since officials objected to his well-known heterodox view on Confucius, he was downgraded and ultimately refused an official position. Regarded as China's greatest scholar by many, he had, in the 1890's, become the organizer of reform societies and the leader of a large group of able young scholars. After the Sino-Japanese War he urged broad changes for China's government based on the Japanese model of constitutional monarchy, but his recommendations were ignored until the German seizure of Shantung in 1897, when such panic reached the Court itself that the Dowager Empress lost power.

The Dowager Empress was a woman whose grasp of affairs

beyond those of her family and clan was minimal, and whose dominant aim in life was the acquisition of money and power. The locus of her power still lay in the immovably senior position she held as the consort of a dead emperor and as the mother of emperors, and in her superb opinion of herself. As late as 1900 she could say to her first lady-in-waiting:

> Do you know I have often thought that I am the most clever woman that ever lived and others cannot compare with me. . . . Now look at me. I have 400,000,000 people, all dependent on my judgement. Although I have the Grand Council to consult with, they only look after the different appointments, but anything of an important nature I must decide by myself. What does the Emperor know? [14]

In the scale of Chinese bureaucracy her position was higher than that of the Emperor Kuang Hsu, whose reign had begun when he was a child. The Dowager acted as Regent until 1889, after which she stepped aside, but she still wielded enormous influence through her niece, who was the wife of the young Emperor and, of course, through the Chinese-Manchu bureaucracy, which was her creation over the decades.

The Emperor Kuang Hsu (Tsai-t'ien, 1871-1908) was a nephew of the Empress who had been adopted by her as her son. In 1875, through the Empress's schemes, he had been placed on the throne, in violation of the dynastic laws of succession, because the old woman needed someone she could manipulate. But he grew up to be a man of character and ideas, a believer in reforms, and he was increasingly in conflict with the Dowager over the state of China. In 1898 he nerved himself to break with her for, as K'ang Yu-wei said:

> If he sat idly by and allowed her to go on in the old way, the country, piece by piece, should be all gone and the empire lost. Rather than lose his empire like those of the Chin and the Ming dynasties and become a byword of disgrace for all future generations he would risk the dangers of reform. If he succeeded, then he would get power into his own hands and save his country. If he failed, he would greatly open the minds of the people and prepare them for the future, and then perhaps, preserve a remnant of China. . . . It was death or victory. . . .

He saw his country about to sink in the earth, about to be
buried in ruins, about to burst like an egg, about to mortify,
about to be torn to shreds, about to become like India or Anam
or Burmah—a dependent of another power.[15]

It is known that the Emperor had read memorials of K'ang Yu-
wei, but exactly how the two came to meet is unknown. It was
generally thought that Weng T'ung-ho, a member of the Privy
Council and Tutor to the Emperor (an honorary position that
gave him direct access at any time to the throne), brought the
two together in early 1898, because he saw reform as the only
way of saving the dynasty. However, this seems contradictory,
since Weng was an opponent of such moderate reformers as Li
Hung-chang and Chang Chih-tung, as well as of K'ang's works
on Confucius. Furthermore, he was dismissed from his post as
Tutor the day before K'ang and the Emperor met.

After the meeting, in June, 1898, the Emperor issued the first
of a flood of edicts calling for a top-to-bottom reform of Chinese
institutions, and for exactly one hundred days thereafter there
followed a spate of appointments, demotions, orders, and
changes, which in theory were to remake China. Although these
paper reforms were criticized as ill advised and hasty, the action
of two immature men, there is not a single edict that was not
valid and that, in one form or another, was not later executed
under other auspices. The haste, too, was necessary. With the
exception of the guarded sympathy of a few powerful men like
Chang Chih-tung, the reforming group, from the Emperor down,
had very powerful opposition. Nor was there any organized body
within the Chinese government through whom the Emperor
could work, or was there any possibility of his forming any.
Therefore all changes had to be initiated by the Emperor.

The chief accomplishments intended by the Emperor during
this period were a reorganization of the entire administrative
system, the liberalizing of laws permitting subjects to memo-
rialize the Emperor, and, above all, the promulgation of educational reforms, including a national university, provincial and
prefectural schools, technical schools, military schools, and medical schools. But the opposition grew, and on September 13, 1898,
the poor young man wrote to his friends:

In view of the present difficult situation, I have found that only reform can save China, and that reforms can only be achieved through the discharge of the conservative and ignorant ministers and the appointment of the intelligent and brave scholars. Her Graceful Majesty the Empress Dowager, however, did not agree. I have tried again and again to persuade her, only to find her Majesty more angry. You K'ang Yu-wei, Yang Jui, Kin Hsu, and T'ang Ssu-t'ung should deliberate immediately to find some way to save me. With extreme worries and earnest hopes. The Emperor.[16]

On the next day, September 14, the entire Manchu class of pensioners were informed that they could go to work, and an annual budgetary system was projected that would have ruined every official in the Empire whose accounts were subject to audit.

The only help the scholar-reformers could give to the Emperor was to muster force against the Dowager and her supporters, and for this they turned to their friend the governor and army commander, Yuan Shih-k'ai. On September 19 Yuan Shih-k'ai agreed to protect the reformers from any countermeasures by the Dowager and the aroused bureaucracy. He then betrayed the reformers to Jung Lu, Commander-in-Chief of the Northern Army at Tientsin, who in turn informed the Empress of the plans to keep her neutralized. On September 22, the Dowager ordered the Emperor into her presence, compelled him to publicly acknowledge his incompetence, and then reinstated herself with the brief announcement, "The Emperor being ill, the Dowager Empress has resumed the regency."

The Emperor spent the remainder of his life in close confinement within the Forbidden City, and his nephew, Pu-yi, was named Heir Apparent. Thus the Empress demonstrated not only her hatred of reform but also of China. Yet she was the tool of the entire bureaucratic system.

The conservatives turned to her not because she possessed consummate qualities of statesmanship and leadership, not because they regarded her as the embodiment of wisdom and prudent statecraft; but because by inducing her to place herself at the head of militant conservatism, they would be able to annihilate the reform movement under cover of what in China would pass

for orderly constitutional procedure . . . to invoke the aid of
the one personage in China who could claim the constitutional
(and what was in China more important) the ethical right to
overrule the Emperor.[17]

Had there not been a Dowager, it would have been necessary for
the bureaucracy to invent one. Nor could the conservatives alone
be blamed. The elimination by decree of the entire civil service
system and the substitution of a new system of education, examination, and appointment won over to the extreme conservatives thousands of traditionally educated men who regarded civil
service posts as sinecures for those of their background.

Furthermore, in 1898, most of the moderate conservatives were
heartened by the backing of Chang Chih-tung, who told them
in his *Exhortation to Learning* that reforms were desirable but
that they should be slow, moderate, evolutionary, and consistently in the Chinese tradition. With the statement "Chinese
learning for fundamentals, Western learning for practical application," he urged a syncretism that would combine the material
advantages of the West with the cultural advantages of China.
It may have been Chang's reminder that China still had something to offer that tied moderates and conservatives together in
that year. While appreciating certain benefits of the West, none
were prepared to dispense with China, her history, her ethics,
her tradition—in sum, all that meant Chinese culture.

In viewing the dramatic years 1894-98, we must remember
how many educated Chinese were caught, in the modern jargon,
in the tensions of choice. Like Liang Ch'i-ch'ao, the disciple of
K'ang Yu-wei, who with his master had to flee the country in
1898 (six other eminent reformers were executed by the Dowager), they saw not merely the possibilities of two worlds but the
impossibility of totally denying their own. No Chinese had ever
before had to make such choices. In the full sweep of the history
of Chinese civilization up to the 1890's, such disasters as had
come had merely intensified belief in the stability and ultimate
values of the system. True, from the Han through the Manchus,
there had been many significant adaptations and changes, but
they had always been within the tradition. Now it seemed as if

men were being forced by the march of events to abandon every-thing that made them Chinese.

What men like Liang Ch'i-ch'ao wanted was a reformed Chinese tradition, for to abandon Chinese tradition altogether would have signaled the failure of the entire Confucian ethic. Liang believed that true Confucianism made compatible both Chinese civilization and the fruits of the Western world. Confucianism meant constitutionalism, reform, industry, and, above all, progress, "and once the iron network has been spread over the length and breadth of the Middle Kingdom, there will be no more halting in the march of progress. . . ." [18] Patriotism and pride in China, combined with the nineteenth-century Western doctrine of progress, formed the objectives toward which these men moved.

Liang was to be, for almost twenty years, the most widely read and respected of the reformers. He represented those whose distaste for violence and radical reform would keep them apart from the rising revolutionary movement as well as those who admired the West yet understood it too well to be single-minded about innovation. Liang, a far more widely educated man than K'ang, tried to reconcile the classical culture with the times but eventually had to face the fact that the classics were not relevant. His understandable commitment to Chinese thought and culture drove him to rationalize Chinese weaknesses and, indeed, Chinese history, pointing out that all the workable and desirable things in the West came late and at enormous human cost. In effect, the Western superiority, he said, was a materialistic one only, whose value was ephemeral for Chinese culture; China, with its non-material objectives, would recover its stability. This dichotomy was a forced one, motivated by his distrust of the rising revolutionary movement and was not to come until years later. In a brief span of years, ending in September, 1898, the school of K'ang Yu-wei lost its chances to regenerate China.

It now remained for the conservatives to salvage what they could. The opinion of the Dowager (who had immediately re-voked the reforms) was that China could survive if left alone, and to be left alone required strength. If China could muster sufficient force to say No again and again to the barbarians, the old system would work. Thus, army reorganization was the one reform pressed by the conservatives all through 1898.

The Boxer Movement

In September, 1898, the control of all military forces in the North was given to the Manchu Viceroy and favorite, Jung Lu, and this army was ordered to be trained and armed in accordance with the latest methods. While this was primarily a paper reform, it gave the Court enough confidence to face up to a European power in 1899, when the Italians demanded that Sanmen Bay be ceded to Italy as a naval station. Chinese forces in Chekiang Province were ordered to resist any Italian attempt at a landing, and Italy withdrew her demand. This was encouraging, and therefore, in November, 1899, an edict was circulated to every province in China ordering the authorities to resist to the end foreign aggression. "Never shall the word 'peace' fall from the mouths of our high officials nor should they harbour it for a moment in their breasts." [19]

Unfortunately the new toughness of spine had to be paid for by squeezing money out of provinces already impoverished, especially in the Yangtze region, which suffered from floods and famine. In addition, it was the time of the loss of Weihaiwei, Liaotung, and Kowloon, and foreigners engaged in commerce and missionary work were aggressively active in certain areas of China. As a result of these two factors, an increasing hatred was building up among the Chinese against both the foreigners and a dynasty that could not protect them. In the midst of this national emotion there began to be evidence of the activities of the I Ho Chuan (The Righteous Harmony Fists, who came to be called "The Boxers" by Westerners because part of their ritual was a boxing-like dance in which the aid of spiritual powers was sought to give physical immunity), a quite old society that had been dormant for years but became active again in 1898, particularly in the disaffected and hard-hit provinces of Chihli and Shantung. Various Boxer risings were put down by the government in 1898, but they arose again in 1899 and 1900, and in these latter years it became evident that some powerful personage at Peking was advising moderation in suppressing this antiforeign, anti-Christian movement, which was now being joined by other secret groups. Yet the complicity of the government in the rapidly mounting violence of I Ho Chuan can be overemphasized by historians, for, although Peking refused to put the movement down, it nevertheless continued to use its police power to protect foreigners in China.

In May, 1900, the I Ho Chuan groups began to move on Peking, and it became obvious that this was a full-fledged rebellion. Despite the protests of the foreign legations and of responsible Chinese officials, the Court remained aloof. The Dowager was making use of the movement for her own ends. Where provincial officials, such as Governor Yuan Shih-k'ai in Shantung, realized that the murder of foreigners would bring a terrible retaliation, they acted to crush the movement. The powerful southern officials agreed with the foreign consuls at Shanghai to keep the southern and central provinces at peace, but in other areas, such as Shansi, where the conservative Manchu Yu Hsien hated foreigners, the Boxers were permitted a free hand to kill and pillage.

On June 13, 1900, the Boxers seized the city of Peking. Two days earlier an expedition had left Tientsin under the British Admiral Seymour to succor the large number of foreigners in the capital. The I Ho Chuan, along with a considerable number of other Chinese, cut communications between Tientsin and Peking and, after a sharp engagement, threw Seymour back. Regarding this aborted expedition as an act of war against China, an emboldened Court, on June 21, declared war on the foreign powers. By that act the Court declared its allegiance with the I Ho Chuan, for now government troops participated shoulder to shoulder with the rebels in the attacks on the legations in Peking. Almost at once the Court realized it was caught in an impossible situation, and it spent the summer of 1900 waging war with one hand and offering peace with the other. Thus thousands of Boxers and government troops failed, despite sustained assaults, to take the legations compounds in Peking, which were manned by a mere 533 defenders.

In mid-August an international relief expedition reached Peking from Tientsin, stormed the gates of the city, took it, relieved the siege of the legations, and began a systematic sacking of the city. Meanwhile the Dowager and the Court fled westward to the ancient capital of Sian, leaving the aged Li Hung-chang to pick up the pieces. The Western peace was Draconian and hardly calculated to assure the Chinese, who made no pretense of not having started the mess. Peking—its palaces and homes—were looted thoroughly, not only by the expeditionary force, but by every foreigner in the city.

The peace demands of January, 1901, were these: the dispatch of a special Chinese delegation to Berlin to apologize for the murder of the German ambassador to China and a delegation to Tokyo to apologize for the murder of a Japanese consular official; the cession of the Legation Quarter in Peking to the foreigners (a demand comparable to making a part of Washington, D.C., forever foreign soil); exclusion from the civil service of candidates from any one of forty-five cities where there had been violence; execution of four high officials (the death penalty had actually been demanded for twelve, but several were permitted to commit suicide, while others were banished); foreign garrison and control of the route from Tientsin to Peking; and finally, the levying of a great indemnity, of which almost half went to Russia and Germany.

This was the cost of what had been a miscalculated but genuine union of the Court and the Chinese people against foreigners. The excesses of the Chinese were matched by the excessive punitive demands of the West. One nation that left no doubt that its motivation was primarily revenge was Germany, the Kaiser stating to his troops that no quarter was to be given or prisoners taken, so that the name of Germany would become known in such a manner in China that no Chinese would ever again dare to look askance at a German. It was now obvious even to the Dowager that reform was needed, but the really obvious thing to a great many Chinese was the fact that reaction was dead; thus the way to revolution was becoming clear in the Chinese mind.

NOTES

1. New York: Cambridge Univ. Press, 1963, p. 10.
2. C. N. Li, *The Political History of China,* trans. and ed. S. Y. Teng and J. Ingalls (Princeton: Van Nostrand, 1956), pp. 90-91.
3. S. Meng, *The Tsungli Yamen* (Cambridge, Mass.: Harvard Univ. Press, 1962), p. 51.
4. Gideon Chen, *Tseng Kuo-fan* (Peiping: Yenching Univ. Press, 1935), p. 44.
5. Mary C. Wright, *The Last Stand of Chinese Conservatism: The T'ung Chih Restoration 1862-1874* (Stanford: Stanford Univ. Press, 1957), p. 65.
6. *Ibid.*
7. Walter H. Mallory, *China: Land of Famine* (New York: American Geographical Society, 1926), pp. 29-30.
8. *European Problem Studies: British Imperialism,* ed. Robin W. Winks (New York: Holt, Rinehart and Winston, 1963), p. 3.
9. Arthur H. Smith, *Chinese Characteristics* (2nd ed.; New York: Revell, 1894), p. 330.
10. H. F. MacNair, *Modern Chinese History—Selected Readings* (Shanghai: Commercial Press, 1927), p. 384.
11. Ralph L. Powell, *The Rise of Chinese Military Power, 1895-1912* (Princeton, N.J.: Princeton Univ. Press, 1955), p. 31.
12. S. Wright, *Hart and the Chinese Customs* (Belfast: Mullan, 1950), p. 711.
13. *Ibid.*
14. Princess Der Ling, *Two Years in the Forbidden City* (New York: Dodd, Mead, 1924), p. 277.
15. K'ang Yu-wei, "The Reform of China," *Contemporary Review,* LXXVI (August, 1899), 181-83.
16. Chester Tan, *The Boxer Catastrophe* (New York: Columbia Univ. Press, 1955), p. 22.
17. R. F. Johnston, *Twilight in the Forbidden City* (London: Appleton-Century, 1934), pp. 32-33.
18. Fung Yee, "A Chinese View of Railways in China," *The Nineteenth Century,* XXVII (1890), 226.
19. Tan, *op. cit.,* p. 32.

Three

The Chinese Revolution Begins
(1901-28)

REFORM AND REVOLUTION

The Conservative Reformers

The Boxer Settlement and the post-Boxer treaty revisions were punitive and designed to gain added privileges and advantages for the major powers. The Shimonoseki Treaty had yielded to Japan the right to undertake manufactures in the treaty ports, and since, under most-favored-nation clauses, this had brought a great amount of foreign capital into combination with cheap Chinese labor, an industrial system was emerging that dominated the domestic Chinese market. The financial situation was already desperate. The Boxer indemnity, based on what the powers thought China could pay, was set at 450,000,000 taels ($330,900,000)—an incredible amount. This was only the principal, and if China chose to pay it in installments, as she would have to do, there was an interest of 4 per cent per year on the unpaid balance. The Imperial Customs receipts (those not already under hypothecation), the Native Customs (every native tax except the likin), and the salt monopoly were reserved as security. Finally, the indemnities were to be paid in gold, although China, who had very little gold, was denied the right to charge customs in that metal. All in all, the indemnity came to almost one billion taels ($600,000,000 to $700,000,000).

In the face of this situation the Dowager stated that China would adapt to the best methods and systems that obtained in foreign countries. Between 1901 and the year of her death, 1908, she decreed a series of changes that were to affect the army, foreign affairs, education, finance, and political structure. The grand old men who had been with her during her reign were by now dead, and the man she now depended upon most was the governor and army commander Yuan Shih-k'ai (1859-1916).

This son of a Honan farmer (adopted by one of the wealthy members of the Yuan clan) had done poorly in his classical studies and had taken, for lack of anything better, a post as a junior officer in Korea in 1882. He managed, in that confused country, to climb to control of the Korean armed forces, and in 1885 he was made the Chinese Commissioner of Trade at Seoul or, in effect, the Chinese Resident in Korea. As Imperial Resident in Seoul he was largely responsible for the ineptitudes of policy that brought China to her ruin in Korea in 1895, but he was shrewd enough to sense the coming disaster and to retire for reasons of "poor health" in 1894.

When it was decided to raise and train a new army under the German military advisor Von Hannekan, Yuan Shih-k'ai, who, even though he had been in control of the Korean armed forces, had never fought a battle or led an army, was given command, because all Chinese generals had been thoroughly discredited by the Sino-Japanese War. He took over the New Army in December, 1895, and turned out to be a careful administrator, a severe disciplinarian, an honest commander, and a man to watch. In an unsuccessful attempt to win him over, Emperor Kuang Hsu made Yuan Vice-President of the Board of War, after which favor Yuan returned to Tientsin to betray the Emperor's reforms to the Dowager. During the Boxer Rebellion, he cleaned the rebels out of his province of Shantung and maintained quiet. By the end of the rebellion he was a powerful man, for, while four of the five divisions of the New Army had been destroyed by the Allies, he had kept the sixth intact in Shantung.

In 1901 Li Hung-chang, on his deathbed, recommended that

Yuan become Viceroy of Chihli. This was a most important post, for from Tientsin that viceroy supervised the defense and economy of North China. Yuan did a skillful job of serving the Dowager, and in his Northern Army he created a group loyal to him. He made enemies, of course, one of them being Prince Ch'un, brother to the Emperor whom Yuan had betrayed. When the Dowager died, on November 15, 1908, Prince Ch'un became Regent, and in January, 1909, he forced Yuan, who had been Senior Guardian to the Heir Apparent (Pu-yi, the nephew of Kuang Hsu), to retire from office.

Constitutional reforms, announced in September, 1908, had been pending since 1905-06, when missions sent abroad to study Western government recommended a constitutional monarchy. The announcement was followed by the drafting of a constitution based on the Japanese model. The projected constitution, together with the administrative changes actually effected, were designed to centralize government more highly than ever before, to preserve the dynasty in perpetuity, and to provide a front for the Imperial power. There was to be a modified parliament. The Regent promised there would be a formal constitution in 1918, and in 1909 he advanced this to 1914. In October, 1910, a Provisional National Assembly met, half of whose members had been selected by provincial assemblies first convened in 1906 and the other half by the throne. It was powerless but turbulent, and it pressed for a parliament in 1913. For its temerity it was dissolved, after functioning only three months, but it was reconvened in October, 1911, just in time to preside over a revolution.

The previous April, the first cabinet in Chinese history had met. Of its twelve ministers, four were Chinese and eight were Manchu, and of the eight Manchus five were members of the royal family. This parliamentary-constitutional farce alienated the monarchial reformers who, although bitterly disappointed, had stuck with the throne to the end. It had been apparent for at least a decade that there was hope or promise neither in the dynasty nor in limited reforms. The appalling failure of the Manchus left the way open for revolutionary ideas and actions.

The Revolutionary Movements

Although the various reformers, holding no brief for the Manchus, would have accepted a change in the dynasty, they all held on to one basic belief—that a monarchial institution was the necessary manifestation of things Chinese. It was this belief, as much as anything, that prevented the westernizing, moderate reformers from cooperating with the gathering antidynastic and antimonarchial revolutionary movement. So deep was the gulf after 1898 that not only did K'ang Yu-wei and Liang Ch'i-ch'ao fail to work with the revolutionary groups who shared their exile, but an actual hostility arose between the two movements, due a good deal to personal, social, and cultural differences. In general, the scholarly reformers felt superiority and distrust toward the Western-oriented and educated revolutionaries. K'ang Yu-wei in particular came to despise the leader of the revolutionary movement as an illiterate (that is, not a classical scholar and degree-holder) and as a braggart. The name of this leader was Sun Yat-sen.

SUN YAT-SEN

There was almost every point of difference between Sun and K'ang, save for their place of origin (both were Kwangtung men). Sun (1866-1925) was born into a family of poor farmers. He received a good traditional education, left incomplete when, in 1879, he was sent to Honolulu, where his brother kept a small store. There he studied in an Anglican school. In 1883 he returned to China, a young deracinated man of seventeen; an apostate to things Chinese; a man who openly mocked the tradition-bound life of his ancestral village. In 1884 he left home for Hong Kong to attend Queens College, and here, with his entry into medicine and Christianity (neither of which, however, he seems to have taken very seriously), he severed his cultural ties with the old China. He graduated as a doctor of medicine in 1892, practiced for two years in Macao and Hong Kong, and then, in 1894, gave up medicine for revolution.

From then on till the end of his life, he was a revolutionary. He wrote, talked, and lived the republican revolution, always on the move, sometimes a hunted man, raising money, making himself the symbol of a new kind of China. How this was so is not immediately apparent. He was not a theoretician, for it is still difficult to discern exactly what his concepts meant. He was not a fighter, for men such as Huang Hsing bore the brunt of action. He was not an organizer, for he could only tolerate being a leader. He was not an astute politician, for he made some dreadful errors in political judgment. He hedged and compromised. He suffered the ignominy of not being in China when the revolution came, and he died before it became a success.

So, by objective standards of leadership his later apotheosis by both the Chinese Nationalists and the Chinese Communists is difficult to understand until one realizes that his sanguinity about the ideals of the revolution, his endless driving dedication, and the force of his personality held the revolution together time and again when it seemed near failure. One of China's greatest tragedies was his premature death, for after that the Chinese revolution became hopelessly partisan. His own greatest asset was his faith—in himself, in China, and in the West, which, he was sure, would rally to the support of a new, a republican China. Had he understood his own people and the West better, he would have been saved the disillusionment of his later years, and perhaps China would have been saved something, too. For this disillusionment, plus his increasing distrust of other leaders, led him to the concept of single-party control, which has cursed China since his death.

THE HSING CHUNG HUI

In 1894 Sun left Hong Kong for Hawaii, and there, in November of the same year, he founded the Hsing Chung Hui (Revive China Society) with twenty small Chinese shopkeepers and workers. The members pledged themselves to expel the Manchus, recover China, and establish a republic. The first China branch of the society was founded in Hong Kong in 1895 by Sun. In March, 1895, this infant group chose to overthrow the Ch'ing by capturing the city of Canton, and when the plot was discovered, Sun fled China, not to return until December, 1911. He lived in England and Canada and in 1897 went to Japan, where, along with an increasing number of Chinese students and exiles, he was welcomed by the government. Japan was, officially and unofficially, pressing for a kind of Pan-Asianism, wherein Japan would gather the Asian peoples under her banner and lead them to freedom from imperialistic humiliation.

In 1900, Sun and his friends planned to seize a port on the coast where the Japanese could land arms for a revolt that would detach Kwangtung and Kwangsi from the Empire. The promised Japanese help did not come, however, and Sun fled to Macao. There, since his coleaders had either been executed or forced into hiding, Sun emerged as undisputed leader of the Hsing Chung Hui. But despite Japanese interest and overseas help, it remained a small group with few members among the large Chinese population in Japan and few in China—and those few were in Kwangtung. The Leader was the leader of very little in 1900.

THE T'UNG MENG HUI

When Sun returned to Japan in 1905 after travel throughout Europe, the Chinese students there had increased both in numbers and in revolutionary sentiment, and they were impatient for action. They had found a popular leader in the Hunanese Huang Hsing. Huang and Sun met to see if the various Chinese revolutionary groups could not unite toward a common goal, and as a result of their efforts a coalition group was formed on September 9, 1905—the T'ung Meng Hui, known in English as either the United League or the Covenant Society.

This was a true revolutionary group. It called not only for an end to all dynasties and for the establishment of a republic but also for an "equalization of rights," drafted by Hu Han-min, the gist of which was that the state authority should see that the land was used well and equitably held by those who worked it. Sun considered the land problem fundamental, but nowhere had it been clearly defined or any specific solution advanced. The approach to this ancient problem was a confused blend of the well-field system, Wang Mang's nationalization, Wang An-

shih's reforms, Henry George's Single Tax, and European socialism.

The question of land reform led to a final break between reformers and revolutionaries after 1905. The central issue was
whether or not an equitable land program would lead to a social
revolution. Whereas the revolutionaries pressed first for economic
and hence social reform, the reformers maintained that equity
would follow only from the right political changes; chaos would
come of any attempt at social and economic revolution. They
pinned their faith on industrial modernization rather than agricultural changes, and it might be said that they were evolutionists.
The T'ung Meng Hui believed in a break with the established
order; the reformers perceived that the broken pieces would
have to be swept up, which might prove impossible.

The T'ung Meng Hui had no opportunity to put its ideas into
practice. It was a "party" only in the sense that it was a broad
union of small revolutionary groups. Although it had a leader in
Sun Yat-sen, there was a constant contest of other powerful
personalities at the center (Wang Ching-wei, Hu Han-min,
Huang Hsing). It was dominated by students who had studied
in Japan and the West, but it was almost totally dependent upon
the support of Chinese living overseas—in Rangoon, Batavia,
Singapore, Hanoi, Honolulu, San Francisco; Sun was constantly
traveling to raise money. Between 1907 and 1911 the T'ung
Meng Hui, despite its lack of a real organization in China, attempted eight armed revolts in Southeast China in an effort to
capture the provinces of Kwangtung, Kwangsi, or Yunnan for
a base of operations. Though most of the revolts were led in
person by Huang Hsing, none of them succeeded, largely because the T'ung Meng Hui had no force of its own but depended upon the cooperation of local secret societies and peasants. Its only successes came in its penetration of New Army
units in Central and South China and in winning increasing
numbers of Chinese to the idea of a republic.

The October, 1911, Revolt

When the successful revolution finally came, it was triggered
not by the revolutionary groups, which, indeed, barely had time

to become a part of the overthrow, but by a dispute over who was to build and control the railway system in China. Between 1895 and 1906 some three thousand miles of railroads had been built, with borrowed capital, by the Imperial Railroad Administration. As a result of fraudulent activities by certain foreign contractors, especially the American-China Development Company and local gentry, a "rights recovery" movement had started, designed to buy out foreign enterprise and enable Chinese capital to build or control the roads. To accomplish this a number of provincial corporations were formed, which depended upon local tax levies, private subscriptions, and private loans for their financing.

In May, 1911, Peking decided to nationalize all the railroads of China, partly to avoid the consequences of a large number of autonomous provincial railroads, and partly to ease the pressure from foreign capital. There was great resistance to the proposal, especially from Szechuan Province, where the government's plan to buy out the provincial corporation was regarded as cheating the taxpayers, whose payment of special levies had formed the public subscription to the provincial loan. In addition, the government refused to reimburse the provincial corporation for "unaccountable" funds. (Of the $16,700,000 that was raised in Szechuan, some $6,000,000 had simply disappeared.) Despite public anger and a tax strike in Chengtu, the provincial capital, dynastic officials ignored the demand that Peking fully reimburse the Szechuanese or abandon the plan for nationalization. During the summer of 1911 the anger grew in Szechuan, and when the leaders of the protest were arrested the furor began to develop into armed movement directed against the dynasty. Officials at Peking urged a reversal of nationalization and full reimbursement, but political intrigues at the capital led only to temporizing measures.

In early October an insurrection broke out in Szechuan. The T'ung Meng Hui, deciding to take advantage of this, planned an uprising in the Yangtze Valley for October 16. But on October 9, due to mishandling of explosives, there was a premature bomb explosion in their headquarters in Hankow. Lest they be taken by the Imperial police, they were forced to act, but the initiative was taken out of their hands the following day, when a regiment mutinied at Wuchang, across the river, setting off a chain of mutinies. The province of Hupeh was seized on October 22 by New Army soldiers, and in the absence of a T'ung Meng Hui leader they conferred leadership on the reluctant brigade commander, Li Yuan-hung.

With a full-fledged revolt now spreading through all of the Yangtze provinces, the dynasty made Yuan Shih-k'ai Governor-General of Hunan and Hupeh Provinces to "suppress bandits." Yuan was not to be so easily used by those who had deposed him from power. Before moving against the rebels he demanded that a responsible cabinet form of government be inaugurated by 1912, that the revolutionary groups be legalized, and that he be given full military power. He was setting himself up as broker between the dynasty and the revolution, and his intended commission—whoever won—was to be power for himself. It was impossible to refuse him: the South was seemingly lost, and just north of Peking a dissident division was poised to move on the capital. On October 27, 1911, Yuan's demands were met, and he was given full command of the military forces of China. He thereupon brought his Northern Army into play, and by November 27 had retaken Hankow and Hangyang.

On October 26 the National Assembly had impeached the high officials responsible for the railroad situation, and on November 14 Peking reversed itself and ordered railroad reforms. It was much too late. By mid-November all of the provinces save Manchuria, Chihli, Shantung, and Honan had declared their independence of the Manchu government and their allegiance to a provisional republic. By early December there were, in effect, two governments in China: the Manchu government at Peking, still nominally in power and controlled by Yuan Shih-k'ai, who was now Premier of the Provisional Parliament and head of the Northern Army; and the provisional republican government at Nanking, with no army and no money. The bumbling Regent, the young Dowager, and the six-year-old Emperor did not count.

The revolutionaries had set up their own provisional government in Hankow, but, when it became apparent very early that leaders of all shades of opinion were willing to join the overthrow of the Manchus, a peace conference was held in the International Settlement at Shanghai on November 15. This secret conference, complex because of the number of factions represented, had two main objectives. The revolutionaries wanted Yuan to overthrow the dynasty and to take the Presidency of China. Yuan wanted to be President, but needed the support of the southern revolutionaries. The secret meetings of December 19 and 20 ended with an agreement that peace would be restored, the Manchus made to abdicate, a republic established, and the person who first overthrew the Manchu dynasty would become President—meaning, of course, Yuan.

The Abdication

On December 4, 1911, the provisional republican government moved to Nanking. Two days later, the Regent Prince Ch'un retired, and the Dowager gave Yuan Shih-k'ai absolute power to deal with the situation. His agents then met in Shanghai with the agents of the Nanking government. The original plans of the T'ung Meng Hui had called for the military conquest of the Manchus and then the slow building of a constitutional government. But Sun Yat-sen, head of the T'ung Meng Hui and the man who could have provided the provisional government with a popular leader, had been in Denver, Colorado, when the revolt started and was not to arrive in China until December 25. On December 3, the provisional republican government had called for an immediate federal constitutional government with a strong executive. The fact that the provisional government entered into negotiations with Yuan Shih-k'ai as a quite powerless mélange of revolutionaries, reformers, and provincial officials, and that this group was in no sense representative, was to have a great bearing on the future of China.

The negotiators agreed on two main points: one, that the Manchus were to abdicate, and two, that Yuan Shih-k'ai was to be the chief executive of the new republic. But on December 29 the problem of the Presidency was complicated when Sun Yat-sen was elected by the votes of sixteen of the seventeen provinces represented at Nanking. Aware of Yuan's position and ambitions, Sun announced on January 15, 1912, that he would

yield the Presidency to Yuan as soon as the Manchus had abdicated, providing that the new President obeyed the constitution and that the seat of government remained in Nanking. He
believed the constitution was strong enough to control an ambitious man, and he was opposed to shifting the seat of the republic
to North China, the center of Yuan's military power. From
January 21 to February 12 Yuan placed enormous pressures on
the Manchus to abdicate, and on the latter date they did so,
stating:

> It is clear that the minds of the majority of the people are in
> favor of the establishment of a republican form of government
> . . . the universal desire clearly expressed the Will of Heaven,
> and it is not for us to oppose the disapproval of the millions of
> the people merely for the sake of the privileges and power of a
> single House.[1]

Under the agreement the young Emperor continued to live in
Peking with his dynastic title and a favorable income. Then all
power was vested in Yuan Shih-k'ai:

> Let Yuan Shih-k'ai organize with full powers a provisional Re-
> publican government, and confer with the Republican army as
> to the methods of union, thus assuring peace to the people and
> tranquility to the Empire, and forming one Great Republic of
> China.[2]

Thus the Mandate of Heaven passed to Yuan Shih-k'ai. He
brought with him to his office a legacy of ability, ambition, and
distrust; a quarter of a million troops in the North; and the
support of eighteen of the twenty-two provincial governors. On
March 10, 1912, he was inaugurated President of the Republic
(at Peking) and controlled the posts of Minister of Army, Navy,
and Interior. On March 11 the provisional constitution of the
republic was promulgated. It was a good constitution, but it had
not been designed to withstand a civil war.

THE FIGHT FOR A GOVERNMENT

The Coup d'État *of Yuan Shih-k'ai*

In March, 1912, the fate of a Chinese republic was vested in the
hands of a Provisional President known to view the policies of

the republican revolutionaries with distaste, his hand-picked Premier, and a cabinet dominated by his trusted military commanders. The power of the President was limited by the provisional constitution, which located the fundamental state power in a cabinet responsible to an elected Parliament. Recognizing the Provisional President for the autocrat he was and conscious of the military force at his command, his opponents put their hopes in their abilities to control events by controlling the Parliament to be elected in the winter of 1912 and convened in April, 1913. To this end, in August, 1912, the T'ung Meng Hui transformed itself into an open political party called the Kuomintang. This was done against the advice of some of its leading members, who, sensing that the unborn republic might well be a military imperium, urged the T'ung Meng Hui to remain a secret and conspiratorial organization prepared to fight, in a revolutionary manner, for the life of the Republic.

The Kuomintang was only one of a number of political parties formed. Most of them were small, but the Progressive Party, formed in 1913, was substantial. It represented that large number of Chinese who were satisfied with the abdication and prepared to support Yuan Shih-k'ai in the struggle for national strength. They were not interested in the matter of representative government; they were anti-Kuomintang; and in some ways they saw more clearly than Sun Yat-sen and Huang Hsing that the end of monarchial principles created deeper problems than could be solved by railway or industrial modernization and a greater vacuum than could be filled by a Western political form. The Kuomintang itself lost members once the dynasty fell: those who believed that the sole objective of the T'ung Meng Hui had been accomplished and that therefore there was no further need for an organization. Thus, except for a minority, the pro-Western and republican idealism of the revolutionaries, never powerful, became submerged in party politics almost at once. Yet the political parties in 1912-13 are unimportant, for not a single one had any popular support nor, indeed, sought roots in the people. The politics of the First Republic were played out between the military captains and the revolutionaries. It was to be fifteen years before a Chinese political party would seek to base itself among the Chinese people.

Sun, looking only to the modernization of China, withdrew from politics and departed for Japan, leaving the Kuomintang in the hands of its new head, Sung Chiao-jen. Secure in his plurality (in the large and unwieldy First Parliament, which met in April, 1913, the Kuomintang held 269 of the 596 seats in the House and 122 of the 274 seats in the Senate), Sung Chiao-jen himself set off for Peking, believing the Kuomintang could control Parliament, and thus Yuan Shih-k'ai. He was shot down in the Shanghai railway station—a warning from Yuan Shih-k'ai that no opposition would be tolerated. But the final break between the contenders came, the same spring, over a matter of finances.

The Provisional Republic had started with an empty purse. Tax remissions from the provinces had stopped with the October revolution, and, since no provincial governor was likely to spend his tax collections anywhere but locally, Yuan Shih-k'ai, in order to run the government and pay his troops, had to seek loans from foreign groups whose governments regarded him with favor. He was fortunate in that the Western powers not only thought he was the strong man China needed to prevent another Boxer revolt, should the revolutionary republicans take over, but also regarded him as the leader who would guarantee the continuation of foreign rights and privileges. The fact was, however, that financial solvency rather than leadership was the key to the stability and ability of the Chinese government.

All during 1912 and the early part of 1913, Yuan had been negotiating with a six-power syndicate for a reorganization loan, and in April, 1913, in the headquarters of the Hong Kong and Shanghai Banking Corporation, he signed a contract for a loan of 25,000,000 pounds. He signed despite the facts that (1) the National Assembly had previously rejected its onerous conditions and (2) in March President Wilson had forced the American participants to withdraw, stating that:

> The conditions of the loan seem to touch very nearly the administrative independence of China itself, and this Administration does not feel that it ought, even by implication, to be a party to those conditions. . . . The conditions include not only

the pledging of particular taxes, some of them antiquated and burdensome, to secure the loan, but also the administration of those taxes by foreign agents. The responsibility on the part of our Government implied in the encouragement of a loan thus secured and administered is plain enough, and is obnoxious to the principles upon which the government of our people rests.[3]

Yuan, however, was convinced that his action, though illegal, was best for China: "I, who have been entrusted with the safety of four hundred million people and their property, cannot tolerate the actions of these trouble-makers." [4]

Although the loan had neither constitutional nor legislative approval, the governments behind the banks involved rejected all protests and accepted Yuan's note in hand, at the same time refusing to recognize his government. They regarded Yuan Shih-k'ai himself as *the* government of China and the loans as a means of restoring order to a shattered land. For the bankers, the 1,750,000 pounds in fees and commissions was sufficient stimulus. The republicans were baffled by this attitude of the powers, having zealously believed that they would welcome rather than attempt to destroy another parliamentary state. What they did not realize was that the powers wanted not a strong China but a strong man in China.

On May 5, 1913, the Parliament, led by the Kuomintang, voted against the loan. Sun, returned from Japan, now urged military action against Yuan Shih-k'ai, but when, on July 15, 1913, he called upon China to revolt against its President, there was no response, and the uprising attempted in Kiangsi was easily put down. Sun's second revolution had found no support. The Chinese people and their leaders were for Yuan Shih-k'ai or, at least, for peace.

In October, 1913, Yuan was elected President of China for a five-year term. In November, with the concurrence of the military governors of the provinces, Yuan Shih-k'ai dissolved the Kuomintang (on the grounds of sedition), and its members were expelled from the Parliament. This left Parliament without a quorum, but Yuan, who liked the color of legality, replaced the members with his own people. Then a political conference was convened that prepared a new organic document, the Constitutional Compact, for promulgation in May, 1914. In effect, Yuan Shih-k'ai became dictator of China, and, sensitive to the past and the present, he decided to create a new dynasty. Through agents and friends, he prepared the ground for the restoration of a monarchy, while a public study committee began to consider whether a monarchy or a republic was best for China. Despite Yuan's modest protests, a national convention met in Peking in November, 1915, and, by unanimous ballot, all of the 1,834 members urged Yuan to take the throne. In December, 1915, Yuan accepted the mandate and moved to create a new organic law, a new peerage, and a name for his reign, and to prepare an enthronement ceremony.

This was his greatest mistake, for it brought against him a coalition of all of his enemies, who, for once, were more powerful than any forces he could muster. The Progressive Party, led by Liang Ch'i-ch'ao, which had once given him support now deserted him; his own military leaders began to distrust his ambition; and the radical wing of the Kuomintang, based in Japan, embarked on a campaign of terror against him. Meanwhile the foreign powers, led by Japan, sensing that the monarchial move was unpopular and might plunge China into serious internal difficulties, advised Yuan Shih-k'ai not to restore the monarchy.

Between the *coup d'état* of 1911 and the winter of 1915, the struggles for the Republic had been carried on by a relative handful of people, with the weight of foreign influence on the side of Yuan Shih-k'ai. But somehow the concept of a republic had taken root among the Chinese people. Certainly the monarchy was thoroughly discredited. Yuan's enemies increased their actions, and his supporters continued to fall away from him. He had already become the target of popular anger in early 1915, when he had yielded extraordinary privileges to Japan. Armed revolt broke out in Canton and Shanghai and, more importantly, in Yunnan, where Ts'ai Ao, the military governor, declared his independence. Kweichow and Kwangsi Provinces followed suit. By March, 1916, South and Central China were solidly against Yuan. In order to prevent South China from breaking into open revolt against him, on March 22 Yuan openly abandoned his monarchial scheme. This did not stem the opposition against him, and when he died of natural causes on June 6, 1916, he was an angry and disappointed man.

The Great Anarchy

> *China will never improve her situation until she gets rid*
> *of all her militarists, including me.*   —Chang Tso-lin

The judgment of his contemporaries on Yuan Shih-k'ai was a severe one, based as much on the anarchy that followed his death as on his actions in life. However, in order to judge him fairly, the following considerations must be taken into account. For one thing, faced as he was with the problem of governing a poor and divided country, he badly needed the financial support of foreign powers, and this support, which any Chinese government would have needed in some degree, was available only at a price. Then, not only had a significant number of China's leaders between 1911 and 1915 backed his programs, but his foreign advisers had assured him, in unfeigned belief, that constitutional monarchy was the best solution to China's problems. Yuan himself did have serious intentions of reintegrating the Chinese political system, and if he had almost no principles he had almost no prejudices—he simply looked upon power as a business that should be made to pay. Had he curbed his overweening ambition to be Emperor and accepted a permanent tenure as President of China, only death could have prevented him from ruling the Republic like a monarch.

On the other hand, the republican leaders of 1911-13 have been criticized by contemporaries for having attempted to establish a true Western-style republic, though it is difficult to see how, in 1911-13, republicans could have supported any other system of government. Critics also charged that the Western powers neglected to live up to their professed ideals by refusing to support the First Republic and thus were partly responsible for the failure of the experiment and the consequent tragic decades of anarchy. As in the case of the judgments against Yuan Shih-k'ai and the Kuomintang leaders, this view ignores the context of the age. The Western powers could not be expected to welcome a strong, independent republican China. In those times of empire, their thoughts were for a government strong only in the sense that it would guarantee the stability and peace of the country for the foreigners. Finally, with the second revolution of 1913, any hopes for liberal republicanism were smashed. Once they were dissolved, the republican forces again became a secret organization, guiding events through charisma and force, and loyal, not to principles, but only to a leader.

THE WARLORDS AND THE NORTH

The political history of China in the decade following the death of Yuan Shih-k'ai is best understood as the military history of the provinces and regions of China, while the history of the government at Peking is the story of the intrigues of the military leaders involved. After 1916, the central government at Peking lost any effective function in internal administration and, in a sense, had no prerequisite of national sovereignty. That is, it not only had no geographical area over which to function, for the provinces of China were practically independent, but its sovereignty over the remaining buffer areas of Tibet and Outer Mongolia was largely a fiction. It could keep operating only by giving exorbitant pledges for loans from foreigners.

The government of China in 1922 has been aptly described by two British bankers:

> The authority of the Central Government has shrunk to that of a mere municipality, its credit is exhausted and borrowing even at the most exorbitant rates of interest has become impossible. The provinces contribute no revenue, the salt surplus is pledged several times over, the outstanding debts of the railways to firms and manufacturers alone are estimated at over $40,000,000 and the total unsecured debt of the Government, internal and external, at approximately $500,000,000. It is clearly beyond the power of the Peking Government, cut off from all resources and dragging out an existence of political isolation, to cope with the burden of debt, which must continue to grow by the mere increment of unpaid interest, so long as these conditions continue.[5]

Between June, 1916, and May, 1926, China had six Presidents, one of whom (Tuan Ch'i-jui—November, 1924–April, 1926) was called a Provisional Chief Executive, and after May, 1926, China had no President, but only a cabinet. These six chief executives had a total of nineteen Prime Ministers, none with a tenure of more than a year. With Yuan's death the last political binding force was gone. For decades the centripetal forces—the dynasty, the official class, Confucian values—had been decaying and vanishing. China had nothing on which to fall back—no functioning government, no viable economy, no order, no armed protection, and in a sense, no roots. There seemed to be only a continuum of villages and a rising, angry pride.

Control of power was disputed among Yuan Shih-k'ai's former military subordinates, who had been trained in the command of the Northern Army. This clique split after Yuan's death into three contending groups: the Chihli group under T'sao K'un and Wu P'ei-fu, the Feng-tien (Mukden) group under Chang Tso-lin, and the Anfu (Anhui-Fukien) group under Tuan Ch'i-jui. Sometimes the three groups cooperated; more often they fought each other with their private armies.

The events of 1924-25 give a reasonable indication of the situation in China. Feng Yu-hsiang, the "Christian General" (Kansu, Shensi, and Inner Mongolia) was entrenched at Kalgan, fortified with Soviet arms and advocating Buddhism, war on England, and death for Chang Tso-lin. Chang Tso-lin (Manchuria, North Chihli, and Shantung), backed by Japanese money, had his headquarters at Mukden, and with a well-trained and well-armed force staffed with Russian *émigré* officers and men, controlled China from the Amur to the Yangtze. Wu P'ei-fu (North Hunan, Hupeh, Honan, and South Chihli), based at Loyang, was in control of the Yangtze provinces and those parts of North China not under Chang Tso-lin. Yen Hsi-shan ran Shansi and ran it well. Sun Ch'uan-fang controlled Kiangsi, Fukien, Chekiang, Anhui, and Kiangsu.

Wu P'ei-fu supported the central legal government at Peking, partly because it was run by his friends and partly because he dreamed of uniting all China under it by force of arms. Chang Tso-lin, who was Wu's mortal enemy, also dreamed of becoming dictator of a united China. Wu had beaten Chang in 1922 near

Peking, and Chang thirsted for revenge. In late 1924 war broke out between them. Later that same year Feng Yu-hsiang, who was an ally of Wu P'ei-fu's, betrayed him by seizing the city of Peking and the government. Wu, caught between the forces of Chang and of Feng, evacuated by sea from Tientsin. Chang and Feng agreed to put in their own man as President of the provisional government, but, while Wu P'ei-fu was re-organizing his forces in the Yangtze Valley, they quarreled. So Chang returned to Mukden and, announcing that he and Wu were now friends, began preparations to seize Peking from Feng. Thus ended the year.

These men, while moved by avarice and ambition, were nationalists in the sense of being patriots, and a few were re-formers endeavoring to establish modern education, industry, and government in their provinces. Indeed, these reformers were, at least in their own eyes, revolutionists. By tradition and inclination, all were regionalists, although most of them would have welcomed and supported a federal China, provided it legitimized their provincial or regional autonomy. None were prepared to yield their power, nor did they call themselves "war-lords." This was a term of opprobrium made popular in the 1920's by the resurgent Kuomintang, and once a "warlord" had come over to the rising nationalist revolutionary forces, the Kuomintang dropped the old term and called him a "revolu-tionary general."

SUN YAT-SEN AND SOUTH CHINA

Following the 1913 failure, the Kuomintang seemed doomed as an influential organization. Small and ridden by factions that disputed methods of organization and the use of power, for the next ten years it was again a party in exile, first in Japan and then in Shanghai. Sun, who had fled to Japan in 1913, could conceive of no better approach to reorganization than having each party member take an oath of personal loyalty to him. This directive of "follow and obey" was a throwback to the old revolu-tionary days, and anticipated the overcentralization of the Kuomintang later blamed on Communist influence. Sun got his new party organization in 1914 (as the Komintang or Revolutionary Party), although in 1916 he had to abandon the personal oath. The party was to remain small and to be kept in existence by a dedicated man who was more a catalyst for a leadership group than a leader himself.

When, in 1917, the Parliament at Peking was dissolved, the southern provinces protested. Taking this as a sign of hope, Sun came to Canton in July, 1917, to make that city the seat of a revolutionary government for China. In August he convened a parliament of sorts from a number of South China leaders and some of the members of the dissolved National Parliament. This group established the Military Government of the Republic of China, with Sun as Commander-in-Chief. In January, 1918, the Canton Parliament or, as it was called, the National Assembly, repudiated Peking and proclaimed itself the government of China.

The military governor of Kwangtung, increasingly concerned by the erosion of his own financial base as Sun's rump government seized the salt monopoly income of Kwangtung (and of Kwangsi) to support itself, in December, 1919, drove Sun out of Canton. In October, 1920, Sun's ally, the military commander Ch'en Ch'iung-ming, seized Kwangtung, and Sun was asked to return from Shanghai. He was elected President of the Republic of China (at Canton), but his efforts to establish a national regime at Canton were unsuccessful. He could not command the loyalty of the Kwangtung troops but only refugee troops from other provinces; he became embroiled with Ch'en over his demand that Ch'en's troops be removed from his command and placed under civil control; and he alienated the businessmen and merchants of Canton with his heavy taxation. In June, 1922, Sun was driven out of Canton again. But a multiple civil war between Kwangtung, Kwangsi, and Yunnan then drove Ch'en out of Canton, and in 1923 Yunnanese and Kwangsi troops asked Sun to return.

Sun now abandoned the title of President for that of Commander-in-Chief, and with the aid of Yunnanese troops took control of Canton. Yet he was not rooted in the hearts and minds of the Kwangtung populace. He was a poor administrator, and his control of Canton rested in the hands of his loyal and able police chief, General Wu. His failure to establish a popular base in Kwangtung—ever the most revolutionary area of China— and his definite ideological unpopularity in Canton induced him to build up his own military force, refurbish his ideas, and reorganize his party.

THE FIGHT FOR A CULTURE:
THE DEATH OF CONFUCIUS

The end of a dynasty and the subsequent tyrannies and disruptions were no new experiences for the Chinese people. Their ancestors had undergone massive anarchies and had not only survived but flourished. But in the first decades of the twentieth century the ancient groups that had made China an enduring and self-governing society—the family, the gentry, the guild, the village—were irreparably weakening. The struggle to emancipate women, the growth of cities with their factories, the development of business enterprise, and a new system of education were not remaking but destroying Chinese society. While the political revolution lay stagnant the cultural revolution was rising. Ironically the iconoclasms that contributed to the cultural change arose from one of the last efforts of "self-strengthening," the new education. Conservative reform had used the last of its strength only to overthrow itself.

The New Education

For almost fifty years now a steadily increasing number of foreign works had been translated into Chinese. The government itself had set up its own translation bureau and press in 1860, and by 1900 there were some forty publishers in China (government, private, Chinese, European) engaged in the same enterprise. The publications of these publishers were predominantly concerned with modern Western social and scientific thinking. As long as they remained outside the curriculum they constituted a separate and neglected fount of education of a kind vitally needed to help strengthen China and to assist the progress of evolutionary reforms under a monarchy. The traditional skepticism of the Confucians concerning metaphysical matters had made popular the translations of Descartes, Hume, Spencer, Darwin, James, Russell, Dewey, and Huxley. The translation and publication in 1898 of Thomas Huxley's *Evolution and Ethics* had proven enormously popular, for it fitted in with the evolutionary concepts of the dominant Confucian reformers, and especially of Liang Ch'i-ch'ao, who said of Darwin's work:

> Since Darwin produced his *Origin of Species* a new heaven and earth has been opened to the world of thought. Not only was natural science changed, but also history, political science, economics, sociology, theology, and ethics all have been deeply affected. Spencer arose and took everything together and threw it into the melting pot. He took the most diverse and inexplicable phenomena and linked them together on one principle, building up a great system with its trunk and branches. . . . Science—in the narrow sense of what in Chinese is called k'e chih—has advanced, and religion cannot hold its dying breath. By evolution the roots of age-old tenets have been thrown away. Every intelligent man recognises that the success of evolution is of the order of the universe.[6]

They therefore sought to incorporate this learning into the examination system. The trouble was that the classical examination system was beyond improvement, and as long as it provided the entrance to office, position, and honors, Western subjects would be neglected. The examination system itself had to go.

After the Boxer disaster the aged Viceroy Chang Chih-tung saw a critical need for a system of graded schools.

> . . . unless men of ability are trained it is impossible to strive for [national] survival; unless schools are opened it is impossible to train men of ability; unless the civil and military examinations are reformed it is impossible to open schools, and unless students study abroad, it is impossible to remove our deficiencies in opening schools.[7]

In 1901, the Dowager Empress abolished the ancient formal literary essay as the content of the examination and substituted essays on politics, history, and classical subjects. The results can be seen in a contemporary description of the new examination:

> In October 1906 fifty-three candidates took the new examinations for the highest degree. Forty-two of them had studied

abroad and of the twelve who passed first all had studied abroad in either United States or English universities. The examination took the better part of two days. Below is a description of the questions.

Three questions were given for the first day's examination: First, Define philosophy and distinguish it from science and ethics. Explain the following systems of philosophical thought: Dualism, Theism, Idealism, Materialism, Pantheism, Agnosticism. How would you classify, according to Western methods, the following named Chinese philosophers: Chang Tzu, Chang Tsai, Chu Tzu, Lu Tzu and Wang Yang-ming? Second, Explain why philosophy developed earliest in Greece. What are the leading thoughts in the teaching of Heraclitis? Why will his system, at one time almost obsolete, again become popular?

Third, Expound fully Mills' four methods of induction and mention some of the scientific discoveries and inventions which may be directly traced to them. On the second day of the examination the theme for the required essay was: Will it be expedient for China to adopt the system of compulsory education? [8]

However, the examinations were still regarded as primarily literary in nature, the form of an answer on politics as important as its content. And a degree from one of the new schools was considered inferior until 1904, when Peking declared it equivalent to a degree gained through the old examination system. For the first time since the late T'ang dynasty the school and not the examination became the means to honor, position, and power. Nevertheless, the chief aim of education was still deemed to be preparation for government service, a concept that did not change until after 1950.

In 1913 Yuan Shih-k'ai established a Ministry of Education and projected a four-step national school system, to consist of a lower primary school (four years), a higher primary school (three years), a middle school (four years)—included in this level were industrial and teacher training—and higher schools for successful middle school graduates, who could specialize in technical, legal, or university training. By 1921 there were 189 provincial normal schools, 41 provincial collegiate schools, and 18 collegiate institutions of higher learning, under the Ministry of Education, of which nine were in Peking. There were also 16 Protestant missionary colleges, 60 Roman Catholic missionary colleges, and 27 private collegiate schools. The total number sounds impressive, but many of the schools were quite small and varied greatly in quality, often affected by the turbulence of a given province.

The three best universities in China by the end of World War I were Peking National University (the most powerful and influential, although it had only two thousand students, and the Chancellor of which, Tsai Yuan-pei, was a master of both Chinese and Western learning); Southeastern University at Nanking; and Tsing Hua University in Peking (administered by the Ministry of Foreign Affairs with the United States Boxer indemnity money). In 1916 the Rockefeller Foundation took over the Peking Union Medical College, and in the same year the Chinese Geological Survey was founded. Between 1907 and 1919, it has been estimated, about ten million Chinese received some form of the new education. While only a fraction over 2 per cent of the population, it was a vital fraction, and its leaders, centered in Peking, were young and initiators of movements for a new language, literature, thought, and society.

The New Youth

The New Youth was the name of an enormously influential magazine founded in 1915 by Ch'en Tu-hsiu, and it spoke, literally, for a new youth. It called on all Chinese youth to be everything their fathers were not—to be progressive, scientific, independent. It addressed itself to the young men and women educated in the new schools and in the new thought. Many of them had studied in Japan, in Europe, in the United States. They had been exposed to the free exchange of ideas, Eastern and Western, old and new. They knew that 1911 had rid China only symbolically of the old officialdom and authority, that China was still an easy mark for foreigners. They believed they had come upon a working, acceptable substitute for the enfeebled and enfeebling orthodoxy. They felt that, as stated simply by Ch'en Tu-hsiu, the salvation of China lay in a new culture based on Science and Democracy: "Republican government in politics and science in the domain of ideas, these seem to me to be the treasures of modern civilisation." [9]

The proposed transformation of culture was to take place through several approaches. In part it was a literary revolution, launched in 1917 by Hu Shih, who called for an end to the bondage of Chinese literature to mere form and mechanical ability and for the displacement of the difficult classical language with the vernacular. The unintended result of this was to drive out the old literature and to create a new literature with revolutionary content. The first short story published in the vernacular and in the new style was the "Diary of a Madman" (1918) by the great Lu Hsun. The protagonist, driven mad by persecution, challenges the Confucianists and their values, calling them cannibals. Lu followed this with the most famous of modern Chinese stories, "The Story of Ah Q," a witty and punishing satire on the old ways.

The political transformation was to take place through a revolutionary program based on Western ideas, although in this period Western ideas stood for a heady brew of anarchism, socialism, idealism, pragmatism, materialism, democracy, and constitutionalism. There was also to be a social transformation in that the family system was to be dispensed with, the tyranny of filial piety ended, and women emancipated.

The movement had all the virtues of self-expression with all the vices of permissiveness. It was a tremendously exciting thing, as the historian Ku Chieh-kang indicated in writing of his youth in those days:

Those years in the Middle School coincided with the period when the Manchu court was turning a deaf ear to the popular demand for constitutional government. The result was that public opinion leaned more and more toward revolution, and I, too, was one of the multitude to be swept away by this tendency. The calm and willing self-sacrifice of men like Hsu Hsi-lin, Hsiung Ch'eng-chi, and Wen Sheng-t'sai, who lost their lives in the revolution, impressed me as something worth lamenting with tears or extolling in song. After the revolution of 1911 my zeal for the cause mounted yet higher. I fancied that there is nothing under the sun too difficult for men to accomplish; that the good, the true and the beautiful need only to be advocated, and they will become actualities. A race-revolution was only an insignificant part of our program. We would not consider our revolutionary task accomplished until we had abolished government, had discarded the family system, and had made currency unnecessary.[10]

But while the movement marched under many banners, it had definite goals. It was against the perpetuation of feudal political and military power; it was flatly against Confucianism as a social system, against the failure of China to face reality, against the enforced servility and ignorance of the Chinese people. The old guard, of course, fought back. Led by K'ang Yu-wei, it argued that such desperate times called for the binding force of a morality. (In 1913 K'ang had wanted to make Confucianism a state religion in order to preserve the "national essence" of China.) The Confucianists pointed out that since 1911 the revolution had gotten rid of everything but Confucius and Mencius and still China was not strong. Even anti-Confucianists like Yen Fu argued for the retention of Confucianism as an ethic that would soften the raw edges of the Chinese revolution. Why, then, get rid of the masters?

But both sides were fighting a straw man. By 1919 Confucianism was dead as an orthodoxy. What China lacked was not ideas but operational facilities to put ideas into effect—and, as some saw, the iron will to get these facilities.

As for the Western people, they are by nature warlike and aggressive so that such behaviour has become customary with these countries. From ancient times right down to the present day, there was religious war, political war, commercial war; not one word in the whole history of European civilization has not been written in blood. England acquired the most powerful position in the world by blood. Germany achieved her present glory by blood. Belgium and Serbia, being small countries, are fighting the great powers with freshly shed blood to protect their freedom. I believe these countries will not be crushed in the long run. The Eastern people might consider that such a spirit of endurance in overcoming hardships is madness; but if they could but slightly imitate this spirit, how could it happen that the peace-loving, reposeful, magnanimous and elegant inferior Eastern people could be forced down to the position of conquered peoples? The national character of the Western people [made them] rather fight and die than bear insults; the national character of the Eastern people [made them] rather bear insults than fight and die. A people possessing such mean and shameful characteristics—how can they boast about propriety, ritualism, and civilization without feeling ashamed! [11]

THE FIGHT FOR A NATION

The Rise of Nationalism

There has never been any clear evidence that Yuan Shih-k'ai sold out to Japanese demands in 1915 in return for Japan's support of his imperial adventure. If there was a bargain it was one-sided, for Japan received her rights and yet warned Yuan not to take the throne. But it is clear that after 1896 Japan's aim had been to dominate the fate of Northeast Asia and China. As expressed by Japan's leaders at the turn of the century, this objective was not selfish. It was an obligation wherein a modernized Japan could discharge her ancient cultural debt to China. Japan would help deliver China from her inertia to a point where she could resist imperialism. There was little China could do about this oppressive friendship. Considering her state of disrepair, any refusal to cooperate would only accelerate the demands for special privileges and the end of the remaining Empire.

When Japan defeated Russia in 1905 she gained the Russian rights and privileges in South Manchuria and became firmly ensconced in Chinese territory. From then on, as a complicated process of international politics worked to strip China of control of Manchuria, Mongolia, and Tibet, Peking was a bystander. Japan and Russia were each in control of a part of Manchuria. England and the United States were attempting to "neutralize" Manchuria by putting together an international group to buy out and internationalize its railroad system. Since both Russia and Japan had paid in blood for their positions in Manchuria, and since neither was able to afford any counterbalance to the railway proposals (which a hapless China was urging as a means of preserving her sovereignty), the two former enemies came together, in 1911, in a series of secret agreements. Manchuria was divided into two spheres of interest: Japanese South Manchuria and Russian North Manchuria; Japan recognized Russia's special interests in Outer Mongolia, and Russia recognized Japan's special interests in Inner Mongolia. Each agreed to join a common front against interlopers, including China.

The loss of Korea (which in 1910 became a Japanese colony) and of Manchuria, the spread of British trade and financial influence in the Yangtze Valley and of French influence in South China, and the continuing efforts of all the powers to obtain more privileges slowly bred a feeling of Chinese nationalism that, among some, quite early reached passionate levels.

Japan in China

Up to 1915 this surging antiforeignism was kept under control (save for occasional boycotts) not only by lack of leadership but by the commitment of so many students and revolutionary leaders to the ideals of Western institutions, and by the "Pan Asian" feeling between Japan and China. But by 1915 a tremendous feeling had built up against Japan, since she had led in the demolition of China's remaining empire.

Between 1911 and 1914 China lost control of both Mongolia and Tibet, and in neither case could it be blamed on Yuan Shih-k'ai. For generations there had been bitter feelings between the Steppe Mongols, who were breeders and stockmen, and the Chinese settlers who broke the land, fenced off the range, and through their money-lending activities owned the Mongol sheep economy. In July, 1911, the Mongol nobility requested their Russian friends to protect them from the influx of Chinese, and in December Outer Mongolia declared its independence of China and, under Russian protection, set up its own government at Urga under their Hutukhtu or Living Buddha. In April, 1912, Yuan Shih-k'ai ordered that Tibet become an integral part of China, but the British would not countenance this and demanded the "autonomy" of Tibet. In the fighting that ensued between China and Tibet, the Chinese lost. Two years later England, at the Simla Conference, recognized the independence of Tibet, and Peking was forced to accede against its will. In both of these cases ancient grievances had come home to plague China, yet this loss of power was not of great concern to the Chinese people. It was the ruthless demands and actions of Japan within China herself in 1915 that roused their bitter hatred.

With the outbreak of World War I in August, 1914, the entire balance of power in Eastern Asia changed at once. With the West engaged in Europe, there was little restraint on Japan's ambitions in China. When she declared war on Germany in accord with her treaty with England, despite the almost frantic efforts of the British Foreign Office to dissuade her, the British were under no illusion as to her intentions. In October, 1914, Japan occupied Tientsin, and by right of war took over Germany's possessions, leases, and privileges in Shantung. Peking protested.

The Japanese government, unmoved, publicly announced it had no other motive in occupying Shantung than to take it from the Germans and restore peace in China, but privately stated that "those who are superior will govern those who are inferior." When Peking refused to recognize Shantung as a war area, on January 18, 1915, Japanese Ambassador Hioki secretly delivered to Yuan Shih-k'ai a series of twenty-one Japanese demands. Their total effect, had they been agreed to, would have been to make China a protectorate of Japan. Yuan Shih-k'ai, caught between his need for Japanese support and the awful implications of the demands, leaked them to United States Ambassador Reinsch and to the Chinese newspapers. With the exception of the United States, none of the powers seemed to think these demands unreasonable, agreeing, perhaps, with Ambassador Hioki that: "When there is a fire in a jeweler's shop the neighbors cannot be expected to refrain from helping themselves." [12] The foreign reaction may have been based on the Japanese publication of a false list of demands, the infamous Group V being omitted.

Yuan Shih-k'ai might have utilized the intense popular reaction that the list evoked in China, but he did nothing. On May 7, 1915, Japan gave China forty-eight hours to sign. Peking accepted, and thereafter May 9 was known as National Humiliation Day. In addition, on May 25 a Sino-Japanese treaty was signed whereby Japan was assured dominant rights in Manchuria and in Fukien and Shantung Provinces, and fiscal and administrative control of the Hanyehping Iron and Coal Company. Group V was held in abeyance, but China did agree that the disposition of Shantung would depend on arrangements made after the war between Germany and Japan. In 1917, because of the desperate need of the Allied Powers for Japanese naval help in the Mediterranean, England, France, Italy, and Russia agreed to recognize Japan's claims to Shantung. These agreements were kept secret from both the United States and the Chinese governments.

In the midst of her imbroglio with Japan, China was called upon to decide whether she was at war with Germany. Insofar as they understood the European War, the Chinese were pro-German and certainly reluctant to support a cause that concerned them so little, a position the Japanese endorsed, hardly desiring to have China raise a modern national army. But by 1917 the Allies, in need of Chinese labor troops, prevailed upon Japan to bring China into the war. Japan assented—by this time she was heavily subsidizing Peking—and in March, 1917, Peking severed diplomatic relations with Germany, precipitating a factional fight within China during the next several months. The Peking militarists wanted to declare war in order to obtain loans from the Allies. The revolutionary forces in the South opposed a declaration of war, seeing it could only strengthen the military government. In April the warlords assembled in Peking, disbanded the Parliament, took over the government and proceeded to argue the question of war. The declaration, made August 14, 1917, was that of an illegal, unconstitutional regime, even by Chinese standards.

The United States, opposed to China's involvement in the war and appalled by the internal struggle over the decision, became increasingly convinced that China would fall even further under Japanese domination. In June the United States had sent Peking a note holding that the main problem before China was the creation of a "central, united, and responsible" government and that the matter of war against Germany was quite secondary. This statement of a policy toward China that every other power had now renounced, if only secretly, gave Japan pause. The United States was the only remaining power able to block Japan's ambitions in Eastern Asia, and the only power with which Japan had no agreement concerning China. Therefore, in August Viscount Ishii began talks with Secretary of State Robert Lansing, and from these talks came, in November, a Japanese-American agreement, which, although it firmly restated all the best wishes for the Open Door and the "integrity of China," nevertheless contained the following two-edged clause:

> The governments of the United States and Japan recognise that territorial propinquity creates special relationships between countries, and, consequently, the government of the United States recognises that Japan has special interests in China, particularly in that part to which her possessions are contiguous.[14]

Japan was jubilant, the people of the United States were shocked, and China felt betrayed. There were many shades of meaning to "special interests." On the strength of it Japan established its own civil administration in both Shantung and Manchuria.

THE MAY FOURTH MOVEMENT

The Versailles Conference and the May Fourth Incident

When the war ended China had a place at the peace conference, earned by her status as an ally and by the almost 200,000 labor troops she had sent to France. The Chinese delegation at the Versailles Conference was able and idealistic. When it became apparent that these men, led by C. T. Wang and V. K. W. Koo, had come not just to make peace with Germany but to get the Japanese and the Powers out of China, the other delegations became worried. The Japanese arrived with three main objectives: (1) to confirm possession of the former German Pacific islands north of the equator; (2) to confirm possession of the former German rights and privileges in Shantung; (3) to have the proposed League of Nations guarantee that

> The equality of nations being a basic principle of the League of Nations, the HCP [High Contracting Parties] agree to accord as soon as possible to all alien nationals of states members of the League, equal and just treatment in every respect, making no distinction, whether in law or in fact, on account of their race and nationality.[15]

Despite the opposition of England (backed by Canada, Australia, and New Zealand) the League Commission agreed 17-11 on equal treatment, but the chairman, Woodrow Wilson, ruled it out of order, since the vote was not unanimous. Wilson had earnestly backed the clause as a lever to get Japan out of Siberia and Shantung but, in the last analysis, could not bring himself to fight publicly for such a controversial issue in his own country.

Japan did receive the German islands but only as a mandate. Increasingly angry over the rejection of her claims, which had been assured by the secret agreements with her allies, Japan would not accept a reversal on the Shantung issue and threatened to withdraw from the peace conference. This was no bluff. Therefore the delegates, while reserving residual sovereignty for China, confirmed Japan's succession to Germany's economic privileges in Shantung. The news stunned China. Not only had Japan, by force, replaced Germany in China, and with the corrupt connivance of a rump government, but the ideals of the Western war had been betrayed. Thus the indiscriminate enthusiasm of Chinese intellectuals for Western culture received a fatal shock. Inasmuch as World War I had been understood by them, it was in terms of Wilsonian aims and ideals. They had believed the war was against war, for democracy and the self-determination of all peoples.

On May 4, 1919, students of Peking University began a solemn march to protest the Versailles decision. Intensified by anti-Japanese feeling built up over the years, the march erupted into violent action against the government. The students sacked the homes of certain officials believed to have sold out to Japan, and in a clash with the police one student was killed and thirty-two arrested. When the government sentenced the thirty-two to death, a virtual state of war followed between the government and the university students. Great pressures were placed on Peking University by the government, and the university administration, very much in sympathy with the students, resisted. Again the students struck, and this time a thousand were arrested. Protests began in other cities, not only among students but among merchant groups, and for a month there were large-scale strikes and demonstrations. With a massive general strike in Shanghai in June, the government yielded. The imprisoned students were released and the Chinese delegation at Versailles was ordered not to sign the treaty.

The "New Doubt"

The May Fourth march became the May Fourth Movement, for out of shame and anger came the motivation and potential for revolution. In North China, the movement was a catalyst that united large-scale organizations—students, labor, merchants, and guilds. It brought the New Culture to all Chinese intellectuals, and it also promoted revulsion for the West. World War I and its aftermath had made it clear that China no longer had to feel culturally inferior. If a war fought loudly for moral principles was to have an immoral resolution, then the West could explain its own sickness—when it could spare time from diagnosing China's ills.

Science and democracy were now challenged by Chinese intellectuals who had doubts as to how far a people could go on purely deterministic principles and by those who began to think it simple-minded to exclude moral idealism from life. But fundamentally the challenge was based on the failure of science and democracy in China. Here, as in the move to accept the West twenty years before, the most widely read author was Liang Ch'i-ch'ao. In 1920 he published his reflections on the spiritual and intellectual confusion of the West and found that it represented the absolute triumph of science, wherein the stability of life had vanished because history, religion, philosophy and their standards had been put away. Without these moorings how could men know what was good and what evil? In the face of what Europe had become, said Liang, it was ridiculous to say that China had nothing of her past to contribute to her future.

But there were more immediate reasons for turning from the West. By a coincidence of history the resurgent Chinese revolution was to come into contact with the new Russian revolution. Although Western officials in China had been sympathetic to the May Fourth Movement, Western businessmen in China regarded it as an offshoot of the new radical Bolshevism, and in 1919 the authorities of the International Settlement, against the advice of United States officials in China, expelled the movement from its haven in the settlement. This action by those who preached democracy and brotherhood while retaining their imperialistic rights played into the hands of the new Soviet state. In March, 1919, the Soviets had renounced (because they could not help but do so) Russian rights and privileges in China. When the news of this became public in 1920 (the telegram was withheld for eight months) such a favorable general reaction was created that, in September of that year, Peking was forced to break relations with the Russian legation. Chinese intellectuals were not interested in Bolshevik theory, which was regarded as rather crackpot, but they believed that in communism the Russians had come upon a weapon whereby to combat militarism and imperialism.

The failure of democracy for many intellectuals left them with science, and from there it was an easy step to Marxism. From France came not only returning students aglow with the Utopian romantic revolution and the rights of man, but also the tens of thousands of labor volunteers who had served in the war. These had not been coolies but students from poor families. The racial discrimination, language difficulties, harsh treatment, and poor pay they had experienced in France had taught them the value of uniting and organizing. The New Culture Movement itself fell apart. Ch'en Tu-hsiu and Li Ta-chao and their magazine, *The New Youth,* became Marxist and turned to political revolution, while Hu Shih espoused Western reforms and cultural evolution. All still claimed to be "scientific," Marxist on the one hand and pragmatic on the other. Still other groups, desiring to be neither Marxist nor Western, had ideas of their own. If there was a common denominator it was one of despair, disillusion, and of profound doubt about all values. Some years later Hu Shih summed up the thinking that was characteristic after 1919:

All these transvaluations of values in the Western civilization have had their reverberations in all the non-European countries. In China the effect of these criticisms is particularly noticeable because here these ideas have the strongest appeal to those who have been apologizing for the so-called spiritual values of the East, and to those who have found it difficult and uncomfortable to be in the age of the machine civilization which seems so radically different from the ideas and habits of the agricultural society. A nation which is only on the threshold of political democracy and capitalistic industrialism, therefore, begins to congratulate itself on not having gone very far in imitating blindly a civilization of which the fundamental blunders are being so loudly exposed by a unison of the voices of the Marxian Communists, sentimental social workers, pious religious leaders, anti-religionists, imperialistic junkers, and anti-imperialist reformers. Mr. Liang Ch'i-Ch'ao, who twenty years ago had been the most eloquent champion of Westernization, came out in 1919 as the standard-bearer to sound the warning of "the imminent bankruptcy of the scientific civilization." The young men of the country, who have never seen what a capitalistic civilization is like, are coming out with hundreds of pamphlets condemning the imperialistic and capitalistic systems of economics and government, and advocating Marxism, revolution, and dictatorship of the laborer and the farmer. Even the one-time liberals are wavering from their faith in democracy and are being attracted by the newer tendencies of fascism and other forms of dictatorship.

Thus has come the period of the "new doubt." All the values have been turned upside down, and the nation is standing at the parting of the ways, wondering which road to take, which prophets to follow. Will these new doubts retard the processes of China's modernization? Or, will these criticisms and challenges help China better to understand the real nature and meaning of the Western civilization which has probably been oversimpli-

fied by the earlier enthusiasts who, in their excessive zeal, saw
only one side of the shield? [16]

THE ORGANIZING OF THE CHINESE
COMMUNIST PARTY

In the summer of 1918 there were circulated throughout China
thousands of copies of a manifesto signed by Leo Karakan,
Deputy Commissar of Foreign Affairs of the U.S.S.R. It read, in
part:

> The Russia of the Soviets and her Red Armies . . . are march-
> ing toward the East. . . . We are marching to free the people
> from the yoke of the military force of foreign money which is
> crushing the life of the people of the East and principally
> China.[17]

In the same year the official Soviet newspaper, *Izvestia,* had
declared that:

> The Communist international should give serious attention to
> the East where the fate of the Revolution may be decided. For
> whoever shall know how to go to the enslaved peoples of the
> East and make comrades of them will, in union with them, come
> victorious out of this last war of labour and capital.[18]

In 1920 the Comintern had convened, at Baku, a Congress of
the Nations of the Orient, where it was agreed that there could
be no real world revolution until the peoples of Asia joined.
The majority of the delegates at the Congress were not Communists, the chairman noted, but the conference did represent a
chance to organize the common grievances of the Orient into
a revolutionary struggle against the imperialist powers, especially Great Britain, and show that backward Oriental countries
could, like Russia, have a successful revolution.

There were no Red Armies marching eastward in 1918 or in
1920, and Russia was exhausted from revolution and civil war,
but certainly events in China had given substance to the heady
dreams of the Communist International. The war industry had
created a depressed proletariat of nearly two million workmen
concentrated in a few cities, and there was a mercantile class,

small but powerful and articulate, whose ties were with the new
industry, rather than with the landlords or the political bureaucrats. Warlordism and regional particularism had made a
mockery out of government. There were widespread strikes and
protests, the national revolutionary party was dormant, and
agriculture had almost collapsed.

It is estimated that by 1920 almost half of the Chinese peasantry was landless and that wars and famine had displaced about
56,000,000 people, many of whom were now vagrants seeking
food or bandits seeking plunder or soldiers for the warlords.
The normal food requirements were greater than the total
domestic production plus all imports, and 1920 and 1921 were,
in North China, years of famines and drought. The Famine
Relief Commission despaired. Often the only means of trans-
porting food was by human back. Yet a man who could carry
a load of 133 pounds seventeen miles a day to a famine area,
an average distance of seventy-five miles, would arrive with
no food. For, accompanied by an average family of four, he
would have eaten his load in order to live.

The discontent, bitterness, and unrest evident among the intellectuals was spreading through all sections of Chinese society.
The Republic of China, ten years after the revolution, was a
series of fiefs. The recognized government at Peking was at the
beck and call of the northern military leaders. To many young
students Russia and therefore Communism seemed the only
ally in a hostile world.

Organized Communism in China began in 1920 with a small
study group called Socialist Youth in Shanghai, led by Ch'en Tu-
hsiu (1880-1942), who, in the magazine *The New Youth*, had set
forth Mr. Science and Mr. Democracy as the only possible successors to Confucius and Sons. Ch'en, a member of a well-to-do
family and a fine classical scholar who had also studied in
Japan and in France, had been exiled from China by Yuan
Shih-k'ai for calling for a really democratic revolution. He had
returned in 1915 to found *The New Youth* and in 1917 had become Dean of Letters at Peking University. He was a dedicated
student of the West, which he understood in terms of the
eighteenth-century Enlightenment and democratic revolutions,

who turned to Communism as the most efficient method for modernizing China. On the other hand, his co-founder of the Socialist Youth Party, Li Ta-chao, a fanatic nationalist, saw in Communism the weapon for destroying imperialism.

A year after the founding of the Socialist Youth Party, Ch'en and Li, with ten other Chinese and the Comintern agent for China, Voitinsky, organized the Chinese Communist Party, adopted the radical policies of class warfare and dictatorship of the proletariat, and joined the Third International. By 1924 the Party had only 600 members, but it was this handful who were to play a disproportionate part in the reorganization of the entire Chinese revolutionary movement.

THE KUOMINTANG-COMMUNIST ALLIANCE

We no longer look to the Western Powers. Our faces are turned toward Russia. —Sun Yat-sen, 1923

By 1922, Sun Yat-sen was disillusioned with the West, with many of his former followers, and with many of his former tactics. Few of the members of his organization seemed either to understand or to believe in his principles. Thus, there was little unity of purpose in the Kuomintang. Sun had stressed revolutionary action to the detriment of political propaganda and education and had but little contact with the mass of the Chinese people or students, although after the May Fourth Movement, he began, for the first time, to work with student groups and to work toward a well-organized and disciplined party with as broad a base as possible. The Russian Revolution provided the opportunity to revive his moribund revolution.

The Soviet-Comintern-Chinese Talks

It had not been possible until 1920 (after the defeat of the Kolchak government in Russia and the end of civil war in Siberia) for an emissary of the Soviet government to come to China to discuss the future of Sino-Soviet relations. And there was much to discuss: both Peking and Moscow opposed Japan's presence in China, and the status of Outer Mongolia and Turkestan was unclear—Russia and China each claimed the historic role of protector in those areas. Yurin, the first Soviet emissary (officially he came from the puppet Far Eastern Republic) was received only as a commercial agent, for at that time Peking still maintained an official relationship with the Legation of the Provisional Russian Government of Kerensky. It was the Yurin mission that resulted in the breaking of the relationship with the provisional government, but while it was followed by a Chinese mission to Moscow in September, 1920, no formal Sino-Soviet treaty resulted. The visit of Yurin's successor, Paikes, in 1921, was equally unproductive. But the 1922 mission of Adolph Joffe represented a Soviet Union on the way to recovery from the disasters of civil war and therefore able to make certain demands. Joffe presented three conditions for a treaty: Soviet forces would remain in Urga as long as anti-Soviet Japanese and White Russian forces were in Manchuria; the Soviets were to be given an interest in the Chinese Eastern Railway, which was being mismanaged; and, finally, if China continued to ignore all legitimate Soviet interests, the renunciations of 1920 might be invalidated.

The delay in reaching agreement, together with the fear of Japanese control of China, led the Soviet government to pursue parallel negotiations with the Chinese Revolutionary Party, through the agency of the Comintern. Meanwhile the negotiations for an agreement with the legal government was carried on through the Commissariat for Foreign Affairs.[19]

In 1922 Sun and Joffe had conversations in Shanghai and in Canton. Joffe promised a general policy of good will and hands off China. He stated publicly that Russia's intentions lay in helping to further a united, strong, and democratic China through Sun's movement and in helping those intellectuals who were "the real representatives of true national interests of China" to fight militarism and imperialism in China. A joint statement of Joffe and Sun added that this help was to be in the form of organizational aid; however, both men agreed, Communism was not to be propagated, for it did not suit China's need. Following this declaration, Sun sent a small party to Moscow, headed by his aide, Chiang K'ai-shek, to gain first-hand information on military organization, in order to form the Kuomintang's own dedicated and drilled revolutionary army.

The New Kuomintang

In 1923 a small group of Comintern advisers, led by Michael Borodin and Vassily Blucher (General Galen), arrived in Canton to put themselves "at the disposal of the Chinese National Revolution. . . ."[20] Earlier a handful of Sun's supporters had met in Canton to clarify the principles and practices of the reorganized party (now renamed Kuomintang), and in a statement to the party in January, 1923, Sun left no doubt that the days of divisive opinion and self-seeking were over.

> We recall when the Government was founded at Nanking (1911) how prosperous was the party and how bright its prospects. Why does the party, so prosperous then, present such a sorry condition at present when we are in Canton? The reason is found in the fact that the party is composed of too many divergent elements. There is such a heterogeneous group of men that the party begins to lose the respect of outsiders, so that they do not wish to join and help us in the struggle. For instance, many members of the party wish to get high positions in the Government. Those who had their wishes fulfilled and got high positions are satisfied. The psychology of these members of the party is that revolutionary work should stop once the object of high positions is reached. Those who are disappointed and failed to get the high positions turned to the enemy to oppose the party. While there are many who are devoted to party work and struggle really for its principles, the great majority of the members of the party look upon joining the party as a short cut to reach high positions in the Government. Because their aim in joining the party is to reach the high positions, so their character is despicable, and their presence in the party has produced such incongruity in its composition.[21]

This manifesto of 1923 called for an end to imperialism and militarism, the formation of a unitary national state without racial or class distinctions, the withholding of citizenship from those who opposed the triumphant revolutionary state, the equitable distribution of land through the instrument of taxation, the control of monopoly, and the creation of a united front with the Chinese peasant and worker. Above all, it called for the well-organized and disciplined party as the supreme authority. The principles of this manifesto were adopted by the First Congress of the Kuomintang in 1924, and with this the centralized Lenin-style party became Borodin and Sun's objective.

Borodin faced a heroic task. He had to rid the Kuomintang of adventurers, favor-seekers, and bureaucrats, and he had to, somehow, base the party firmly on the Chinese people. Meanwhile, in order to take advantage of the Communist methods of revolutionary organization, Sun decided to admit the members of the Chinese Communist Party into the Kuomintang. Drawing on Joffe's assurances, Sun told the Congress:

> The Communists are joining our party in order to work for the National Revolution. We are, therefore, bound to admit them. If our members are only active in their propagation of the principles of the party, and build up a strong organization and submit unquestioningly to Party discipline, we need have nothing to fear from Communist machinations. In any case, if the Communists betray the Kuomintang, I will be the first to propose their expulsion.[22]

For their part, the Chinese Communists, through their leader Li Ta-chao, pledged obedience to the Kuomintang but refused to give up their membership in the Communist Party. Actually, it appears that each group intended to use the other while both worked together for the revolution. Without doubt the Chinese Communists joined the Kuomintang as a party and not as individuals.

Despite the smallness of their numbers, the Chinese Communists could take heart from the thesis of Zinoviev at the Comintern Congress of 1924 that a Communist Party need not have numerical control, but just a decisive majority at a decisive place at a decisive time. And it was obvious the Chinese Communists had been provided with a decisive place and time for agitation. There was governmental chaos and political anarchy. Foreign control of Chinese industry and native feudalism had resulted in the most shocking of working and living conditions, and foreign attitudes in general had aroused deep resentment and hatred among Chinese of all classes.

Using these factors, Borodin was to reorganize the Kuomintang, propagandize among the masses, and get rid of the dead wood in the party—but primarily he was to swing Sun away from dependence upon individuals to dependence upon classes.

Indeed, it is impossible to overestimate the influence of Borodin and his aides upon young Chinese revolutionaries. They were tough and able professional revolutionaries, and they brought to China all of the techniques of organization, agitation, and propaganda of the Bolshevik Revolution and the civil wars. They provided the first real school of revolution in China's history, and their pupils were to go far.

The Three Principles of the People

To assuage the old-line members of the Kuomintang, who were irritated at the prominence of the new Communist members, and to quell the doubts of very conservative members, who saw everyone save themselves as Communists and were horrified at the appeal to the peasants, Sun gave a series of public speeches in 1924 in which he summarized his political, economic, and social philosophy, under the rubric: "The Three Principles of the People." These Principles had long been his guiding star, but to assure the members of his party that he did indeed have a set of principles and had by no means surrendered to Communist doctrine, he chose to make his ideas public.

Sun's Principles incorporate elements of both Chinese and Western political philosophy and were not new to his followers, for he had spoken about them for many years. But even in their summary restatement of 1923 they are neither clear nor precise, for Sun's mind was a reflecting mirror, throwing off images of all ideas with which he came into contact. While they are inadequate as a philosophy of state and society, they must be taken seriously as a guide to what the Kuomintang claimed to be able to do for China.

Principle of Nationalism: The old loyalty to culture, family, and clan was to be superseded by a conscious loyalty to a unified Chinese state, lest China be swallowed up by the colonial powers. Without national loyalty there could be no genuine political revolution. Corollary to this was the idea of a unified

Chinese people without discrimination, but a racial bias is implied, of yellow against white.

Principle of Democracy: Parliamentarianism as practiced since 1912 was seen as totally unfit for China, for China needed not liberty but discipline. In lieu of it a constitutional government of popular suffrage was to be reached, in stages, under the "tutelage" of a single benevolent party. A government of Five Powers was to be administered by an elite (those who directed), responsible to the popular will. Enemies of the Chinese Republic were to be excluded from participation in government. (The most significant part of the restatement on democracy is Sun's omission of his previous conviction that the period preceding constitutionalism should last only six years, under a bill of rights—thus the invitation to an endless period of "tutelage.")

Principle of the People's Livelihood: This was the most important, confused, and incomplete of the Principles (simply because it dealt with the land problem and the peasant). The state was to regulate capital by managing and controlling large-scale enterprise, the ownership of land was to be widespread through the state use of taxation, and workers and peasants were to be protected.

In 1924 the single burning principle was nationalism, for where the Communists had been unable to make a nationalist out of Sun Yat-sen, the British succeeded. That year the merchants and landlords of Canton, in joint action with the Kuomintang, had armed themselves against the corrupt administration of the city of Canton and the province of Kwangtung. But when the Kuomintang also invited the peasants and workers of the province to arm against the military rule of the area, their merchant allies became alarmed and organized themselves against the Kuomintang, inviting local militarists to take over the city and expel Sun. To forestall this, Sun confiscated the arms that were being imported from Hong Kong for the use of the Merchants Volunteer Association, whose leader was the Chinese head of the Hong Kong and Shanghai Banking Corporation. Driven back by force of arms into the Saikuan section of Canton, the dissident merchants appealed to the British. On August 26, 1924, the British Consul at Canton notified Sun that the senior naval officer in the city was instructed to take energetic action if the Kuomintang tried to wrest the Saikuan section from the merchants. Astounded at this interference in a purely Chinese affair, Sun wired the Labour government of Ramsay MacDonald and the League of Nations. Both remained silent. Sun then issued a manifesto saying that henceforth the battle cry of the Chinese revolution would be the overthrow of foreign imperialism in China.

In early 1925, there was a strike against Japanese-owned cotton mills in the Shanghai International Settlement, during which a Chinese striker was killed. The Japanese were protected by extraterritoriality from arrest. On May 30 students entered the International Settlement to distribute leaflets protesting the incident. A number were arrested, and were followed by the remainder to the police station. Here they were fired on by police under British command, and seven students were killed. Shanghai went wild. On June 23 a sympathy march was held in the foreign settlement at Canton. It, too, was fired on by British police, and 150 people were killed. The Chinese reacted with a fifteen months' strike and boycott at Hong Kong, and membership in the Chinese Communist Party, which had been about 1,000, mushroomed, reaching almost 60,000 by 1927. In addition, 1925 and 1926 saw a great surge of labor and peasant unions.

Not all the new Communists were ideologues. Many saw the Party simply as a way to express their nationalism, inasmuch as they understood that term.

> I know that really there were many very earnest men among them who, seeing China's increasing weakness, always sought to use the best means to make her strong and prosperous. To their minds the best means was what is called "nationalism." . . . Their nationalism was just a sort of emotion, a sort of sound wave; or, to speak more concretely, it was just the two slogans, "Eradicate the traitors within, resist aggression from without." Who the traitors within were, what the aggression from without was, how to eradicate it, how to resist it, they had not fully pondered so as to analyze it and reason it out.[23]

One extremely interesting aspect of nationalism after 1925 was that Christian schools in China were forced to place reli-

gious instruction on a voluntary basis. In effect, foreign evan-
gelism was at an end. If the missions wished to stay, they could
engage only in education.

In January, 1925, Sun entered Peking Medical Union Hospital
suffering from cancer of the liver. The news of his mortal illness
raised a storm in the Kuomintang, and as he lay dying, the party
started to split three ways. One group joined the pro-Japanese
militarists because of their opposition to the Russian orientation
of the party; a second group held to the party principles but
called for a revocation of the reorganization of 1924; and the
third and largest group, under Wang, Chiang, and Borodin, held
fast. In February, 1925, Sun died, leaving the party embroiled in
a fight for leadership.

THE POLITICS OF REVOLUTION

Sun had consistently lacked a capable and loyal army. At Canton
he had had to rely on the benevolence of the Governor of
Yunnan-Kweichow and the warlord of Kwangtung-Kwangsi for
military support. He had tried to remedy his situation by having
Wang Ching-wei build a party army under Ch'en Ch'iung-ming,
but when Sun and Ch'en had split in 1922, the army had gone
with Ch'en. Judging by the nature of Chiang K'ai-shek's mission
to Moscow in 1923—he was to talk to government and military
experts—it is entirely possible that Sun's chief motivation for
establishing a liaison with the Soviets was his need for arms and
military advice.

Whampoa

In May 1924, 499 cadets assembled at Whampoa Island, just
below Canton, to form the nucleus of the Kuomintang's elite
military force. The commander was Chiang K'ai-shek; the civil
administrator or political commandant was Liao Chung-k'ai. The
staff were Soviet experts and Chinese who had trained abroad
in foreign military academies, but the real military expert was
General Galen. Whampoa was supplied with its arms and ammunition by the Soviet Union, acting secretly through the

Comintern, since it would have been illegal to arm the revolutionary opponents of a friendly government.

By October, 1924, the first class at Whampoa had completed its six months' course and become the officers of two regiments (3,000 men), and in May, 1925, Chiang K'ai-shek was named Commander-in-Chief of the Kuomintang Army. By the end of the year the Whampoa group was established as a tough, efficient, disciplined cadre in control of the party's army, led by Hsu Ch'ung-chih.

When Liao Chung-k'ai was murdered by an unknown assassin in August, 1925, the chief moderating force in the party army was removed, and the army became the prize in a contest between the Russian advisers and Chiang K'ai-shek. Whoever came to control it would control the Kuomintang.

The Split in the Revolutionary Forces

A brief exposition of this complex situation is necessary in order to tie together the threads of intrigue leading to the coups of 1926, 1927, and 1928. By the beginning of 1926 there existed in Kwangtung Province in South China a well-organized and well-armed Chinese revolutionary movement with the avowed aims of liberating China from native militarism and foreign imperialism. The advisers and organizers of this group were Soviet emissaries. The Soviet state, acting through both the Soviet Military Attaché to the nominal Chinese government at Peking and the Communist International, was actively assisting this revolutionary movement with money, arms, and advice. The Kuomintang owed its organization and its resurgent success to the Soviets. However, prior to its reorganization, the party had largely consisted of Chinese merchants, landlords, and intellectuals, intent on ridding China of crippling internecine strife and placing the country under a single party government that would develop economic potentialities. The admission of Communists to their party vexed them, and the successful attempt of Communist organizers to tie the Chinese proletariat to the revolution with promises of land and tax reform filled them with the fear that the left wing was turning the revolutionary movement not only against native militarism and foreign imperialism but also against the native bourgeoisie. Furthermore, they were angered by their loss of prominence in the party organization and the consequent loss of prestige and emoluments.

In September, 1925, this conservative wing left the Kuomintang and proceeded to organize against Communism. Their efforts met with little success until they began a campaign of vilification against the two leaders of the Kuomintang, Wang Ching-wei and Chiang K'ai-shek, taking advantage of a Communist attack against Wang, who was openly anti-Communist and who fought the Communists on their own ground. However, since Chiang had little use for the old conservative clique, it was he upon whom they concentrated their propaganda. By elaborately devious measures, they succeeded in keeping Chiang ignorant of the Communist attack against Wang and even intimated that Wang was in alliance with the Communists. Chiang took these rumors seriously, for, if true, it would have meant his finish as a leader of the party. Meanwhile Chiang's old Shanghai financial associates planted the seed of ambition in him, saying that, with Wang and the Communists relegated to minor importance, Chiang would become the sole leader of the Chinese revolution. At Whampoa the Communists were already helping matters by trying to discredit Chiang as a commander so that they could take over the Academy. Most of their criticism was petty and unreasonable, but it was incessant and keyed Chiang to the pitch of retaliation.

On the morning of March 20, 1926, with Borodin absent in the North, and without consulting with his civil superior, Wang, Chiang suddenly declared a state of martial law in Canton. All Soviet advisers in the city were placed under house arrest, and political delegates in the army were placed under detention. Chiang was in control of Canton and of the party. Wang, who believed that the military should be subordinate to the civil organ of the party, resigned. The conservative factions sent telegrams of congratulations and it looked, in general, as though the Chinese revolution was now in safer hands. To the surprise of everyone, Chiang, on April 3, issued a manifesto stating that the Russian alliance was as strong as ever and should any reactionary or counterrevolutionist set foot in Canton he would be court-martialed. Borodin returned and became as cordial with Chiang as before.

Despite the surface appearance of solidarity, however, this episode marked the ascendancy of Chiang K'ai-shek to military control of the party. A plenary session of the Kuomintang in April, 1926, forced the Communists to hand over the lists of their members, and they were banned from serving as the heads of any party or government department. Moreover, all future instructions of the Chinese Communist Party to its members would have to pass the review of a Kuomintang committee. While this compromise and accord merely postponed the time when the serious ideological differences and aspirations for power within the Chinese revolutionary movement would break out into true interparty warfare, it provided the military leadership of the party (the civil leadership, a nominal position, was given to Chang Ching-chiang) with the opportunity to plan and launch an armed expedition to destroy the northern warlords.

The Northern Expeditions

In June, 1926, eight armies, comprising the three Army Corps of the People's National Revolutionary Army, began the march north from Kwangtung to Peking under the command of Chiang K'ai-shek. They were armies whose regimental strength varied widely from six to sixteen; their total force was less than 100,000. Russian military advisers had counseled against the campaign, and they expected formidable opposition from the combined armies of the five great North Chinese warlords. But the survival of the Chinese revolution now depended on its breaking from the confines of a single province. Against the odds they matched enthusiasm and good leadership. In Honan and Shensi they made an alliance with Feng Yu-hsiang, and they were preceded by activities of their propaganda bureau:

> In the large towns the workmen and artisans were given spe-
> cial attention; and in the country districts very patient and
> painstaking work was put into the campaign for the farm
> labourers, tenants, and small landholders. They were hard to
> move; but as the peasants' union began to grow it was able to

exert an increasing pressure in the good cause. Their "wrongs
and oppressions" were tirelessly urged on their attention, bigger
and bigger meetings were organized under high official patronage, enthusiastic speeches made, resolutions carried and levies
made for expenses.[24]

And the same careful and fervent organization went on within
the armies.

Two of the corps (with the Hunanese army now added as a
third corps) moved directly north to the Wuhan (Wuchang-
Hankow) area. They reached the Yangtze in August and took
Wuchang in October, 1926. The remaining corps, under Chiang
K'ai-shek, was to move up the rougher terrain of the coastal
provinces to take Shanghai and then turn upriver to seize Nanking. Here the way was difficult, for Sun Ch'uan-fang fought
stubbornly for his domain of the lower Yangtze, and not until
March, 1927, did Chiang's army stand outside Shanghai. But
Shanghai was an easy prize, the Communists having organized
the working population to seize the city and capitulate as the
army arrived.

On March 24, 1927, Nanking was taken. There was popular
violence against foreigners and foreign concessions, and a real
blood bath was prevented only when British and American warships laid down a barrage between the Nationalist forces and the
British concession. There had been sporadic violence against
foreigners throughout Central China and the Yangtze Valley, and
bloodletting at Wuchang and Hankow. The appearance of this
"red tide" rolling along the great river valley alarmed the
Powers, and preparations were made to reinforce military and
naval forces in China.

The Break-up of the Revolution

In January, 1927, the revolutionary government at Canton moved
to Hankow. Its Foreign Minister, who spoke no Chinese, was the
brilliant and patriotic Eugene Chen, born in Trinidad; its chief
domestic spokesmen were the pro-Russian Sun Fo and the intense supporter of the Chinese revolution, Soong Ch'ing-ling
(Madame Sun); and the other chief leaders, ranging from
moderate to Communist, included T. V. Soong, H. H. Kung, and

Hsu Ch'ien. The directing power, however, lay in the hands of Michael Borodin. During the spring of 1927 the actions of this government (which consulted in English, since Chen had no Chinese and the remainder had been educated in American or English schools) were pushing the Chinese national revolution to the verge of an explosive social revolution. Peasant unions and peasant rebellions in Central China, land confiscations in Hunan and Hupeh, and labor organization and property seizures in the Wuhan area presaged the complete rupture of the left and the conservative wings of the Kuomintang.

In March Chiang K'ai-shek refused to attend a meeting of the Central Committee at Hankow and was therefore removed from his chairmanship of the Study Committee. On April 7 he was demoted from Commander-in-Chief to Commander, First Army Group, and with Feng Yu-hsiang as Commander, Second Army Group, was ordered to proceed to Peking. Chiang K'ai-shek's reply on April 12 was to launch a merciless extermination of Communists, radicals, leftists, and their friends in Shanghai and to issue a call for a purged party convention at Nanking. Now both wings of the party expelled each other. The Central Executive Committee announced:

> Whereas Chiang K'ai-shek is found guilty of the massacre of the people and oppression of the Party. . . . The mandate is hereby issued that the Central Executive Committee has adopted a resolution that Chiang shall be expelled from the party and dismissed from all his posts and that the commanders and soldiers shall effect his arrest and send him to the Central Government for punishment in accordance with the law against counter-revolutionaries.[25]

Chiang, in a manifesto issued in Shanghai, stated "We started the revolution for the people as a whole not for the creation of the dictatorship of the proletariat," and "The Kuomintang is a responsible party and we cannot allow the Communists to wreck it." He accused the Chinese Communist Party of six main offenses:

1. They have created a reign of terror in the Kuomintang.
2. They have excluded the Kuomintang from workers' and peasants' organization.

3. They have forced the imperialistic powers into a united front against the Kuomintang.
4. They have dominated the party organization.
5. They have alienated the Army and interrupted troop movements, lest a rapid conquest leave them no time for propaganda.
6. They foment mob violence.[26]

Now joined in an uneasy alliance with Wu P'ei-fu, Chiang set up a rival Nationalist government in Nanking and isolated Wuhan. But the government at Wuhan had two good armies, the Fourth (Iron) and the Eighth, the great Hangyang Arsenal, and its own unreliable ally, Feng Yu-hsiang. In the summer of 1927 the two warring factions were being held in balance by Feng Yu-hsiang (due to his very unreliability, since both his allies and enemies waited to see which way he would jump) when the entire direction of the revolution was altered. In late May, Joseph Stalin, who had never really understood what was going on in China, ordered the Chinese Communist Party to take over the Kuomintang Party and government at Wuhan, to proceed with land confiscations, and to form an independent workers' and peasants' army. An indiscreet Comintern agent leaked the instructions to the non-Communist left, led by Wang Ching-wei, who at once expelled the Communists and began a purge of them in the Wuhan area. The Communists and their allies, revolutionary troops and peasant movements, were now dispersed and fighting for their lives, while Borodin and his party fled to Russia.

In September, the remaining factions of the Kuomintang (the Wuhan group, the Chiang K'ai-shek group, and the resurgent reactionary group that had left the party in 1924) joined in a temporary Nationalist government at Nanking. Between September and December, 1927, the three factions fought for power. By January Chiang had emerged as the leader with the greatest financial, military, and political support. His chief rival, Wang Ching-wei, was discredited by the continuing Communist insurrections, and thus the right wing went to Chiang. Chiang was reinstated as Commander-in-Chief of the Nationalist Army and

Chairman of the Central Executive Committee of the Kuomintang.

The final task of the renewed government was to take Peking from Chang Tso-lin, who led the northern coalition, in control of the area from Shanhaikuan to Peking-Tientsin. As Kuomintang armies drove on Peking, Chang abandoned it to take the last train out. Enroute to his headquarters at Mukden, he was killed when his train was blown up by a land mine, thus bringing the Peking government to an end. But when the combined Nationalist forces moved into Shantung Province the Japanese took Tsingtao and Tsinan from them to bar them from advancing into Manchuria. The Japanese had arranged for the assassination of Chang Tso-lin and desired no other power in Manchuria save theirs.

By the end of 1928 that "irresistible union of scholar and peasant, the key to success in China" [27] had been hammered apart by factional and personal power fights and by foreign interference and intrigues. The revolution it sought had aborted. The strength of the nation and the making of a new Chinese society lay in the hands of a factious combination welded strongly to tradition, intent upon self-preservation, often opposed to the very principles by which it had come to power, and destined to govern under the shadow of Japanese arms, peasant rebellions, and Communist resistance.

NOTES

1. Jerome Ch'en, *Yuan Shi-k'ai 1859-1916* (Stanford: Stanford Univ. Press, 1966), p. 129.
2. O. E. Clubb, *Twentieth Century China* (New York: Columbia Univ. Press, 1964), p. 43.
3. Tang Leang-li, *China in Revolt* (London: Routledge and Sons, 1930), p. 87.
4. Ch'en, *op. cit.*, p. 292.
5. H. Fox and A. George, *Report on the Commercial, Industrial and Economic Situation of China in July 1922* (London: Dept. of Overseas Trade, H.M.S.O., 1922), pp. 8-9.
6. E. R. Hughes, *The Invasion of China by the Western World* (New York: Macmillan, 1938), pp. 210-11, citing Liang Ch'i-ch'ao in 1902.

7. W. Franke, *The Reform and Abolition of the Traditional Chinese Examination System* (Cambridge, Mass.: Harvard Univ. Press, 1960), p. 52.

8. J. K. Goodrich, *The Coming China* (Chicago: McClurg, 1911), p. 195.

9. As cited in O. Briere, S.J., *Fifty Years of Chinese Philosophy* (London: Allen and Unwin, 1956), p. 23.

10. Ku Chieh-kang, *Autobiography of a Chinese Historian*, trans. A. W. Hummel (Leiden: E. J. Brill, 1931), p. 28.

11. Dr. Huang Sung-k'ang, *Lu Hsun and the New Culture Movement of Modern China* (Amsterdam: Djambatan, 1957), p. 11.

12. P. Reinsch, *An American Diplomat in China* (Garden City, N.Y.: Doubleday, Page, 1922), p. 137.

13. W. King, V. K. *Wellington Koo's Foreign Policies* (Shanghai: Kelly and Walsh, 1931), pp. 89-90.

14. Lansing to Ishii, November 2, 1917, from *Foreign Relations of the United States 1917* (Washington, D.C.: Govt. Printing Office, 1922), p. 264.

15. H. B. Morse and H. F. MacNair, *Far Eastern International Relations* (Boston: Houghton Mifflin, 1931), p. 604.

16. Hu Shih, *The Chinese Renaissance* (Chicago: Univ. of Chicago Press, 1934), pp. 41-42.

17. R. T. Pollard, *China's Foreign Relations, 1917-1931* (New York: Macmillan, 1933), p. 125.

18. *Izvestia*, March 8, 1918.

19. The double operation being carried on in China in 1920-28, at various levels, by the legal Russian government and the illegal Comintern with the legal Chinese government, the illegal Kuomintang, *and* the warlords is much too complex to narrate in a general history.

20. Tang, *op. cit.*, p. 159.

21. T. C. Woo, *The Kuomintang and the Future of the Chinese Revolution* (London: Allen and Unwin, 1928), p. 162.

22. Tang Leang-li, *The Inner History of the Chinese Revolution* (London: Routledge and Sons, 1930), p. 178.

23. "Kuo Mo'jo, Poet with the Northern Expedition," trans. J. W. Bennett, *FEQ*, III, 2 (February, 1944), p. 168.

24. H. Owen Chapman, *The Chinese Revolution 1926-27* (London: Constable, 1928), pp. 23-24.

25. Clubb, *op. cit.*, p. 137, citing *The China Yearbook 1928* (Tientsin, 1929), p. 1370.

26. Chiang K'ai-shek, *Manifesto to the People* (Shanghai, 1927), pp. 6-7.

27. C. P. Fitzgerald, *Revolution in China* (New York: Praeger, 1952), p. 56.

Four

The Chinese Revolution —
The Tragic Era
(1928-49)

THE NATIONALIST ASCENDANCY

The Struggle to Govern

The Nationalist government at Nanking, created by a single party modeled on the excessively centralized Bolshevik Party of the Soviet Union, was a pyramidal structure with all power at the top. Its cumbersome and premature five-branched system of government was based on Sun Yat-sen's concept of co-equal legislative, executive, judicial, examination, and supervisory functions of government. The overelaborate structure climaxed in the Council of State and the President, both chosen by the party. The office of the President of China was of itself a government, for it directed three suboffices: budget, civil affairs, and military affairs, which controlled matters of foreign and domestic policy, finances, and war and peace. The divisions of this government were manned by party men, and the executive power had no check upon it save as might arise through intra-party feuds.

Sun had been opposed to interference of one branch of government with another or to any outside check on the operation and conduct of government during the time when China would undergo the transition to constitutional government, under tutelage of the party. Tutelage was envisioned as a means of assisting the people to become self-governing, district by district. As soon as any *hsien* (equivalent to a county) became able to govern itself, it could then participate, through representation, in the central government. When every hsien in a province became self-governing, that province could elect its own government. When a majority of the provinces had become self-governing, then a national constitutional government would be established, and the party would relinquish its tutelage.[1]

At the local level there was an attempt to revive a system of local government, but it did not work any more than the national government worked, for, despite the desire to create local independence, power was still retained by landlords and by government officials. At no level of government did the Nationalists ever create an efficient administrative machine.

Meanwhile the Chinese Communists were learning the value of and tactics for mass organization of villages.

THE PARTY

After 1929 the best that the riven Kuomintang could seem to do was maintain an equilibrium between its various factions, while the ideals of Sun Yat-sen and all reform principles fell by the wayside. The party, based on a self-perpetuating membership, at first had drawn quite heavily on students, but it now failed to attract new members or new ideas. Also, being no longer a revolutionary party, it excluded peasants and city workers from membership. It had become transformed into a party representing three main groups—the urban bankers, merchants, and manufacturers, who were for order, peace, economic reconstruction and against taxes; the gentry, living on their land rents, who were for the status quo and against taxes; and the army, which needed taxes and the support of both other groups.

The Kuomintang, whose estimated membership ranged from 3,000,000 to 4,000,000, was organized in small local units, culminating in the Central Executive Committee. This, in turn, was run by its standing committee, until 1938, when the post of Party Leader was created (the title of President had been permanently and posthumously conferred on Sun Yat-sen in 1926). Both party and government candidates were nominated by the Central Executive Committee. In actuality the party was the government, and the government was the party. Both, with their internal factions, were held together by the party leader, whose ultimate source of power was the army.

THE MILITARY DIVISIONS OF CHINA

At the onset of its regime the purged Kuomintang and its Nationalist government controlled only the provinces of the Lower Yangtze area; the remainder of China was still in the hands of various allied warlords, and within a short distance of the new national capital bandits levied tribute. Outside China proper, too-hasty efforts were made by Nanking to bring the great border areas under central control before China itself was united. Six new provinces were created along the Mongol-Tibetan frontiers (Sinkiang, Ninghsia, Tsinghai, Suiyuan, Chahar, Jehol), but they were run by Moslem or Mongol officials who paid scant heed to Nanking, and rather than helping to prevent local independence or foreign penetration, their support and defense was a constant drain. Efforts to reassert Chinese power in Central Asia (Sinkiang) were equally fruitless. A Moslem rebellion against Chinese officials, garrisons, and taxes raged there from 1931 until 1934, when it was subdued by the Soviet Union, which subsequently dominated the area.

Within China proper, the success of the Nationalist government hinged on securing the demobilization and unification of those loosely allied armies that had fought together for North China. In theory, they were all army groups under the National Revolutionary Army, but in fact, they represented at least six different armies, of which Chiang K'ai-shek could count only on his own Whampoa-led Central Army. All Manchuria was under Chang Hsueh-liang, the most loyal and dedicated of Kuomintang allies but still a man who cherished his independence. General Yen Hsi-shan, "the model general," ran Shensi Province; Hunan Province was under Ho Chien; Kwangtung

Province, the "government of the South," was under Ch'en Ch'i-t'ang; Kwangsi Province was under Li Tsung-jen, China's ablest commander; in Hopei and Shantung a large and powerful force was under Feng Yu-hsiang, the "Christian general." In addition there existed separate forces and governments in Yunnan, Kwei-chow, and Szechuan Provinces.

In January, 1929, Nanking brought the commanders together in an attempt to disband these swollen forces and to form a core of the best into a standing army that could be supported by the central government. The effort was rejected by all because the proposed plan placed both the new army and the new government under one man, Chiang K'ai-shek. Most of the generals resigned their posts in the government and went home. The continued need for the government to coalesce or conquer their armies led to a number of field campaigns, 1929-30, particularly in the North, against Yen Hsi-shan and Feng Yu-hsiang, and in Central China, against Li Tsung-jen. Despite government victories in these campaigns, the defeated generals remained essentially independent within their home areas, and in various alliances they formed regional and provincial military cliques, as well as coalitions within the Nationalist government. It is, in part, this crazy quilt of private and semiprivate armies and of regional loyalties, now proffered and now withdrawn, that makes the history of the Nationalist period that of groups of local areas drawn to the central government by the attractions of money and power, as well as by personal loyalties. But whenever these centripetal forces were overcome by local self-interest and ideological disagreement, Nanking suffered the consequences.

The attitude of intelligent Chinese who stood aside from all self-seeking factions was marvelously expressed in an obituary, written by Lin Yu-tang in 1931:

THE DEATH OF THE DOG-MEAT GENERAL

So General Chang Tsung-Chang, the "Dog-Meat General," has been assassinated, according to this morning's report. I am sorry for him, and I am sorry for his mother, and I am sorry for the sixteen concubines he has left behind him and the four times sixteen concubines that had left him before he died. As I intend to specialize in writing "in memoriams" for the bewildering generals of this bewildering generation, I am going to begin with the Dog-Meat General first.

So our Dog-Meat General is dead! What an event! It is full of mystic significance for me and for China and us poor folk who do not wear boots and carry bayonets! Such a thing could not happen every day, and if it could, there would be an end to all China's sorrows. If it only would, you could abolish all the five Yuan, tear up the will of Dr. Sun Yat-sen, dismiss the hundred-odd members of the Central Executive Committee of the Kuomintang, close up all the schools and universities of China, and you wouldn't have to bother your head about Communism, Fascism, and Democracy, the universal suffrage, and emancipation of women, and we poor folk would still be able to live in peace and prosperity.

So one more of the colorful, legendary figures of medieval China has passed into eternity. And yet Dog-Meat General's death has a special significance for me, because he was the most colorful, legendary, medieval, and unashamed ruler of modern China. He was a born ruler such as modern China wants. He was six feet tall, a towering giant, with a pair of squint eyes and a pair of abnormally massive hands. He was direct, forceful, terribly efficient at times; obstinate and gifted with moderate intelligence. He was patriotic according to his lights, and he was anti-Communist, which made up for his being anti-Kuomintang. All his critics must allow that he wasn't anti-Kuomintang by conviction but by accident. He didn't want to fight the Kuomintang; it was the Kuomintang that wanted to fight him and grab his territory, and being an honest man, he fought rather than turn tail. Given the chance, and if the Kuomintang would give him back his province of Shantung to rule over, he would join the Kuomintang.

He could drink, and he was awfully fond of dog meat, and he could swear all he wanted to and as much as he wanted to, irrespective of his official superiors and inferiors. He made no pretense to being a gentleman, and didn't affect to send nice-sounding circular telegrams, like the rest of them. He was ruthlessly honest, and this honesty made him much loved by all his close associates. If he loved women, he said so, and he could see foreign consuls while he had a Russian girl sitting on his knee. If he made orgies, he didn't try to conceal them from his friends and foes. If he coveted his subordinate's wife, he told him openly, and wrote no psalm of repentance about it, like King David. And he always played square. If he took his subordinate's wife, he made her husband the chief of police of Tsinan. And he took good care of other people's morals. He forbade girl students from entering parks in Tsinan, and protected them from the men-gorillas who stood at every corner and nook to devour them. And he was pious, and he kept a harem. He believed in polyandry as well as polygamy, and he openly allowed his concubines to make love with other men, provided he didn't want them at the time. He respected Confucius. And he was patriotic. He was reported to be overjoyed to find a bedbug in a Japanese bed in Beppu, and he never tired of telling people of the consequent superi-ority of Chinese civilization. He was very fond of his executioner, and he was thoroughly devoted to his mother.

Many legends have been told about Dog-Meat's ruthless honesty. He loved a Russian prostitute and his Russian prostitute loved a poodle, and he made a whole regiment pass in review before the poodle to show that he loved the prostitute that loved the poodle. Once he appointed a man magistrate in a certain district in Shantung, and another day he appointed another man to the same office and started a quarrel. Both claimed that they had been personally appointed by General Dog-Meat. It was agreed, therefore, that they should go and see the General to clear up the difficulty. When they arrived, it was evening, and General Chang was in bed in the midst of his orgies. "Come in," he said, with his usual candor.

The two magistrates then explained that they had both been appointed by him to the same district.

"You fools!" he said. "Can't you settle such a little thing be-tween yourselves, but must come to bother me about it?"

Like the heroes of the great Chinese novel Shui Hu, and like all Chinese robbers, he was an honest man. He never forgot a kindness, and he was obstinately loyal to those who had helped him. His trousers pockets were always stuffed with money, and when people came to him for help, he would pull out a bank roll and give a handful to those that asked. He distributed hun-dred-dollar notes as Rockefeller distributed dimes.

Because of his honesty and his generosity, he was beyond the hatred of his fellow men.

This morning as I entered my office and informed my colleagues of the great news, everyone smiled, which shows that everyone was friendly toward him. No one hated him, and no one could hate him.

China is still being ruled by men like him, who haven't got his honesty, generosity, and loyalty. He was a born ruler, such as modern China wants, and he was the best of them all.[2]

But the intelligentsia were restricted to a role on the sidelines. Men without arms had no influence on the course of events. Nanking in fact was plagued with divisions, defections, and insurrections from 1929 to 1937. It never really ruled the North at any time, and it only held the South after 1937. During these same years it faced Communist rebellions in Kiangsi and Hunan and a Japanese invasion of North China. It is little wonder that Nanking saw the unification and the governing of China almost exclusively as a military problem, wherein it had to reduce the territorial bases of both the independent generals and the Communists in order to extend the national authority beyond its narrow confines. Social and economic problems were also treated as military matters, subordinate to the creation and care of the army.

It was tragic that a revolution against regionalism and militarism resulted in a regional government founded on military power; it was ironic, despite the government's endorsement of military power in the pursuit of modernization, that the commander of the army neglected to modernize his military thinking or organization, seeming instead to live in a twilight world of old-time warlord and bandit armies, with whom one could make a deal or whom one could defeat by ancient military academy tactics.

Beginning in 1927, Chiang K'ai-shek replaced his Soviet advisers with German Reichswehr officers. They were charged with reorganizing and training a national army designed to be independent of government but responsible to the President of China. This plan in itself gave rise to much of the party friction during the next four years and led to Chiang's temporary resignation in 1931. Many within the party pressed for an end to one-man rule of the military, and when Chiang returned to government in 1932, a military committee was established, of which he became chairman.

Able German officers, under Generals Von Seekt and Von Falkenhausen, worked between 1934 and 1938 to build an efficient, tough, and smartly commanded army. Despite their efforts and their warnings, however, the entire new structure (from the General Staff School to regimental commands) was dominated by the graduates of the Whampoa Academy, who were inadequately trained in modern military methods—and who did not care. Their military upbringing had been the day-to-day field expedients of revolutionary warfare and bandit campaigns, and they had a fatal contempt for such desk work as planning, logistics, and administration. While at times the task of the Reichswehr officers seemed hopeless, nevertheless, by 1939 Nanking could count on an army of some 80,000 first-class, trained troops, armed with German weapons.

POLITICAL FACTIONS IN CHINA

Political factionalism within the Nationalist Party was as grave a problem as military factionalism without. While Chiang K'ai-shek controlled the financial and military strength of the party, Hu Han-min and Wang Ching-wei commanded the larger political following, including members of Chiang's own family. Both Hu and Wang claimed the mantle of Sun Yat-sen, and each claimed that the new Kuomintang had betrayed the founder, thus following the lead of Sun's widow, who had, in July, 1927, excoriated Chiang K'ai-shek and his faction:

> Dr. Sun came from the people. He has told me a great deal about his early days. He came from the peasantry. His father was a farmer and the people of his district were farmers.
>
> Dr. Sun was poor. Not until he was fifteen years old did he have shoes for his feet, and he lived in a hilly region where it is not easy to be a barefoot boy. His family, until he and his brother were grown, lived almost from hand to mouth, in a hut. As a child he ate the cheapest food—not rice, for rice was too dear; his main nourishment was sweet potatoes.
>
> Many times Dr. Sun has told me that it was in those days, as a poor son of a poor peasant family, that he became a revolu-

tionary. He was determined that the lot of the Chinese peasant should not continue to be so wretched, that little boys in China should have shoes to wear and rice to eat. For this ideal he gave forty years of his life.

Yet today the lot of the Chinese peasant is even more wretched than in those days when Dr. Sun was driven by his great sense of human wrongs into a life of revolution. And today men, who profess to follow his banner, talk of classes and think in terms of a "revolution" that would virtually disregard the sufferings of those millions of poverty-stricken peasants of China. . . .

Dr. Sun's policies are clear. If leaders of the party do not carry them out consistently then they are no longer Dr. Sun's true followers, and the party is no longer a revolutionary party, but merely a tool in the hands of this or that militarist. It will have ceased to be a living force working for the future welfare of the Chinese people, and will have become a machine, the agent of oppression, a parasite fattening on the present enslaving system! [3]

The political and ideological disunion within the Nationalist Party was complex and tragic. Between 1929 and 1932 three separate Nationalist governments were in some sort of operation. At the Third Conference of the Kuomintang several of Wang Ching-wei's men were expelled, and he was accused of political deviation. The result was that with Feng Yu-hsiang and Yen Hsi-shan he tried to set up a Nationalist government in Peking. In 1931 Hu Han-min's followers attempted to establish their own National government at Canton. However, the Japanese seizure of Manchuria, in late 1931, moved the rivals toward unity, the more so as it was obvious that any central government, if it were to function, would have to include Chiang K'ai-shek.

Chiang returned to a reorganized coalition government in early 1932 and to a party whose standing committee now included three of his enemies, Hu Han-min, Wang Ching-wei, and Sun Fo, the son of Sun Yat-sen. Chiang became Chairman of the Military Committee, Wang Ching-wei Chairman of the Civil Executive, and Eugene Chen Foreign Minister, thus repeating the uneasy and explosive balance of authority that had existed in the party in 1924-27. This balance was destroyed within the year over the policy of resistance to Japan. Chiang wanted to temporize with Japan, while his opponents wanted immediate armed resistance. This time Eugene Chen, Sun Fo, and Wang Ching-wei resigned.

In this same year civil war erupted in Kweichow, Shantung, and Szechuan Provinces; the Communists were in rebellion in Kiangsi and Hunan Provinces; and meanwhile Japan was probing North China. In 1933, when Japan seized the major pass through the Great Wall and took Peking[4] and Tientsin, Wang Ching-wei reentered the government. But the increasing danger from Japan failed to bring about political harmony. Because of a truce between Nanking and Tokyo in 1933, Feng Yu-hsiang announced that he was unilaterally taking command of the defense of Chahar Province, and Hu Han-min accused Nanking of treason. This was followed by the establishment of a separatist government in Fukien Province with Eugene Chen as Foreign Minister, which threatened Nanking's tenuous hold on the South. To prevent the chance that the Communist forces in Kiangsi might join with non-Communist separatists in Fukien and that together they might link up with the powerful and independent Kwangsi and Kwangtung governments and with the dissident Southwest Political Council, Nanking, in January, 1934, took the cities of Amoy and Foochow.

TUTELAGE GOVERNMENT

To abate separatism and political division, Chiang resorted not only to military pacification and intraparty compromise but also to the creation of a loyal government-party machine. Through the Central Political Institute, a training center he had established at Nanking, he groomed his personal cadres for the party, which brought him, in time, the same dominion over party he had held, through the Whampoa graduates, over the army. It was perhaps inevitable, given an ambitious, pragmatic, and old-fashioned Confucian like Chiang K'ai-shek, that he would be turned by the politics of war and revolution and the continuing divisions of China to personal government. Personal government would demand that the apparatus of control be a kind of dictatorship exercised through a party, an army, and a government whose command was interlocking.

Chiang K'ai-shek, the Last Confucian

THE NEW LIFE

If unity could not be achieved by political or military means then it was natural for Chiang K'ai-shek to assume that it might be accomplished through morality and a return to sterner values. He was, in the old-fashioned sense, a moral and upright man. As early as 1927, he had established within his army the Officer's Moral Endeavor Corps whose members pledged themselves to a frugal habit of life and to abstain from drinking and smoking. The New Life Movement Promotion Association, under the sponsorship of the Kuomintang and Chiang K'ai-shek, was founded in March, 1934, to "achieve a new life" for a distraught people that would at the same time unite them and teach them political discipline. It is important to see this movement not in cynical terms—as the personal action of a Christian convert or the desperate retreat to morality of a besieged government—but as an earnest attempt to revive Confucianism.

The Nationalist government had reached the stage where it was seeking to base its power on legitimacy more so than on conquest. It was no longer a revolutionary party and having abandoned new principles, it was only reasonable to seek old ones, under a leader whose own principles were held up as exemplary, the more so as by now the identity between leader and party was complete. Prior to 1931 Chiang's ambivalence toward revolution was well known, but in that year he hardened in his feeling to where he was ". . . against all rebellions in Chinese history, going back to the Red Eyebrows and the Yellow Turbans." [5] This attitude typifying the Kuomintang's emphasis on Confucian principles and its evasion of fundamental agricultural and industrial problems was also true of the New Life Movement, whose patron was Madame Chiang K'ai-shek. The purpose of the Movement was to restore the classic virtues of *li* (right attitudes), *yi* (right conduct), *lien* (a sense of integrity), and *ch'ieh* (a sense of shame), the latter two signifying the ability and willingness to distinguish right from wrong. Thus, by ancient means the Chinese hoped to accomplish such immediate practical goals as the eradication of opium smoking. Members of the association were required to examine their own life, in terms of ninety-six specific rules of conduct and action, before acting as missionaries of the New Life among their friends. A sizeable organization developed, although oddly enough it was directed not to the great rural population but to the urban minority. Its members worked to improve public sanitation and personal hygiene, consoled the hungry and ill, and conducted military training and air raid drills for citizens. Unfortunately they also occupied themselves with general snooping, the public correction of the private habits of others, and the banning of smoking, drinking, and dancing among students. This blend of paternal salvation, Confucian ethics, and fundamentalist morality met a mixed reception among the Chinese populace, although it was supported by the Protestant missions, who saw in it a simulacrum of the Christian ideal.

The movement was dissipated by the beginning of the Japanese war in 1937, and an attempt to revive it in 1941 was unsuccessful. Yet Chiang K'ai-shek was never to lose his belief in the efficacy of what he believed Confucianism to be—that necessary social discipline achieved through the correct observation of tradition. This is why the Kuomintang supported not good government but a good gentry, why it tried to revive the old collective-responsibility household system in the villages, why it printed the classics primarily for spiritual indoctrination, and why it seemed to put the renewal of a culture ahead of the struggle for a sound government and economy.

The movement was aided by the persistence of bookishness in Chinese schools from primary grades through the universities. Learning was dispensed by overworked and underpaid staffs who taught their students too much about the past and too little about contemporary China. The intellectual stimulation of the scientific and literary movements had not really penetrated the school system, and in the 1930's students were being burdened with memorization of texts rather than trained in vocational agriculture, mechanics, and crafts. This produced, at the upper levels, an unfortunate number of half-educated talkers, and also produced a good many students who became increasingly dissatisfied with the disparity between their textbooks and Chinese society as they knew it. There existed in China a sizeable body of able men who were anti-Japanese and anti-Communist but who also differed with Chiang K'ai-shek and who had been, with their various political groups, outlawed as early as 1937. While they possessed no armed force, that open sesame to the world of Chinese politics, they had great personal influence. Their primary aims were to win the war against Japan, rid the country of tutelage, establish a multiparty government, and get about the business of building China on the Three Principles. It was pressure from this group that forced the Kuomintang to draft a new organic law in 1936. Unfortunately, the new constitution strengthened executive power but evaded the matter of tutelage, and it shook the confidence of many Kuomintang wellwishers.

By 1938, the leaders of China's government had become fatally inbred. Chungking was not only cut off from material support but also from the moderate and leavening influence of the large urban middle class. The students and professional men who had retreated upriver with the government to set up schools and universities for Free China were increasingly alienated by the censorship forced on them, and after 1939 their criticism began to center on Chiang K'ai-shek, for indeed it seemed there was no one else to blame. He was the leader of the party, army and government, and the worse the war became, the more power he took to himself, as if in his will alone lay China's salvation. Chiang neither understood nor sympathized with the non-Confucian generation, and he viewed their demands for the end of tutelage and their criticisms of his government as a perilous annoyance to the conduct of the war. Therefore they were repressed.

CHINA'S DESTINY

Chiang K'ai-shek was not and never pretended to be a democrat in the Western or the American sense of the word. He was brought up to be a traditional Chinese gentleman and had been given a military education, and he was a profound patriot. He was prepared to use every means to maintain those values he believed to be vital for China's security. His philosophy is best expressed in two books, *China's Destiny* and *Chinese Economic Theory*, published in 1943. Both of these works glorify China's cultural past, and both are intensely anti-Western, indicting not merely Western imperialism but also Western individualism and egoism. In *China's Destiny* Chiang blames the plight of his country on China's having scorned and abandoned her own cultural heritage and proposes a solution to economic problems. The state must control natural resources and business enterprise to prevent misery and exploitation among the people and to place China in permanent readiness for mobilization for defense. Significant among his ideas is that it is more important for a country that its leader understand human nature and correctly regulate human conduct than it is that he understand material wants and move to satisfy them.

Quite aside from the frank and honest content of the books, their timing was troubling to China's wartime allies, who were puzzled and dismayed at the depth and passion of Chiang K'ai-shek's nationalism. The Communists used these books to propagandize him as a reactionary militarist. The loyal intellectuals read them as open rejections of "The Three Principles of the People." Yet, as a modern scholar has noted, there was nothing unusual in what he said, for he was in the mainstream of modern Chinese intellectual and emotional tensions.

> It is nearly meaningless to say of a twentieth-century Chinese thinker or politician that he is striving to select from the Chinese past the principles of enduring value and to adapt them to meet the problems of the modern world, for in various ways that is what they all have done with the exception of the leadership of the Communist party. For all the others, the hold of the traditional has been too powerful for the most ardent modernizer to escape, and the demands of the modern too compelling for the most confirmed traditionalist to ignore. The core of all intellectual and political controversy in China's turbulent twentieth century has been the restatement of Chang Chih-tung's formula: *Chung-hsüeh wei-t'i; hsi-hsüeh wei-yung* (Chinese studies as the basis; Western studies for practical use).[6]

The true impossibility of his course of thought and action lay in attempting to revive a Confucian system without the checks and balances and safeguards of the old system, and most particularly without that overriding concern that the old order had for the peasant, the land, and the crops.

Economic Reconstruction

FISCAL REFORMS

The great and real successes of the Nationalist government were in the monetary, fiscal, and credit reforms undertaken by T. V. Soong and H. H. Kung. Between 1931 and 1937, despite the wars and depression, they ended likin, paid China's foreign debts, gained tariff autonomy for China, set up a national budget, and created a sound currency, the latter done, miraculously enough, without inflation and despite the fact that almost alone in the world China was on a silver standard. China's being on a silver standard placed her money at the hazards of the fluctuation in the supply and the value of silver, and thus the basic value of her money was really out of her control. After 1935 China was forced to abandon the silver standard, largely because the United States overpriced silver and thus drained Chinese reserves, pushing the cost of replenishment beyond her capacity. So China was forced into a managed money economy just as the Japanese invasion became a full-fledged war and was moving the costs of government beyond calculation.

However meritorious and brilliant the early fiscal reforms, they were diminished by the failure to reform the land tax system or to make the largest spender of government, the army, account for its funds. While a budget was created, it was determined by needed expenditures and not anticipated revenues. Some 80 per cent of the total revenue went to military costs, and since these military costs were unquestioned, unaudited, and increasing, and since the interest and principal on the foreign loans had to be paid if China were to preserve her credit, there was never any money left for reconstruction. The government was even hard put to meet its meager nonmilitary running expenses because its sources of income were limited. In 1928 it had had, to a large extent, to abandon the land tax to the provincial rulers. It drew revenues from the customs, the salt monopoly, a transactions tax on manufactured goods, and loans from Chinese banks, in which the government itself was a heavy stockholder.

THE INDUSTRIAL SITUATION

In Chinese industry the Kuomintang inherited a heavy and onerous burden of foreign rights and privileges. As it had done in economic fields Nanking drafted and passed model legislation that was unenforced and unenforceable, and it did not touch the underlying ills. Since 1900 all major Chinese cities had become industrial centers. The heaviest concentrations were cotton, silk, and flour mills (in Canton, Shanghai, Tientsin, Tsingtao, and Wuhan) and coal and iron works (in Tangshan and Wuhan). Foreign and domestic investors in these enterprises demanded, expected, and often received 100 per cent returns. Therefore, high-yield, short-term speculative investment was favored over low-yield, long-term constructive investment. The primitiveness of Chinese industry with its lack of the corporation and of modern business techniques, and with its speculative price structure and cutthroat competition, made the lowest possible labor costs essential to assure high returns. The description by Fong of the conditions in the mines and mills at the beginning of the 1930's is not atypical:

> Match factories are particularly bad: large sheds seething with women and children who shiver with cold in the winter and suffocate with heat in the summer, so dark that artificial light is necessary even at high noon. In the old filiatures of Shantung the ceilings are barely man-high, and the workshops are so narrow that there is scarcely room for two rows abreast of the primitive looms, separated only by a narrow passage with an earthen floor full of accumulated rubbish. The atmosphere is steaming hot summer and winter, so that the men have to work stripped to the waist; and if they have to go outside, they do not take the trouble to cover themselves, even in the bitter cold common in northern China during several months of the year. The prevalence of tuberculosis is hardly surprising in these circumstances.[7]

Every morning at about six o'clock, a group of coolies are seen waiting in front of the mill's gateway. In a few minutes a staff member comes forward with a bundle of numbered sticks and throws them toward the coolies. A struggle immediately ensues, and those coolies are employed for the day who are in possession of the sticks.[8]

As the overwhelming majority of Chinese mines use contract labor, it should always be borne in mind that the amount paid out for wages by the mine administration is never that which is actually received by the miners. According to the authoritative estimate of the China Geological Survey, there is a difference of about *twenty per cent*, on the average, which still is—we regret to state it plainly—an entirely legitimate, extremely heavy toll on the miner's earnings for a hardly justified benefit of the contractors, who are nothing but entirely superfluous middlemen.[9]

Industrial unionism, which began to emerge in the early 1920's, was brought under control by the Trade Union Act of 1928, which forbade any union to enter into a labor agreement without government approval. Since the bulk of the domestic investors and operators was composed of absentee landlords, returned overseas Chinese, and many civil and military officials, conflicts of interest between government and owner prevented beneficial unionism from starting and also negated the Factory Act of 1929, which had prohibited child labor, set a work day of ten hours, and called for health and safety measures in the factories. If Nanking could not control or ameliorate the actions of Chinese owners, it was even less effective in dealing with factories or mines that were foreign owned, which constituted about half of China's total industry. One result was a wage scale called the lowest in the world and conditions of near slavery in the mines. Another was that production seriously lagged behind population growth and the needs of China.

THE AGRICULTURAL TRAGEDY

For the hundreds of millions of farmers the ascendancy of the Kuomintang represented little if any change from their experience of war and natural disaster. Between 1911 and 1949 there were 400 distinct civil wars in China, in addition to the war with Japan that broke out in 1931. In 1920-21 and again in 1928 there were widespread famines in Northwest China, and in 1929 a drought, while in 1931 and again in 1935, there were great

Yangtze floods. In 1938 the Yangtze dikes were breached against the invading Japanese, and that river was not controlled again for ten years. Whole villages along its banks migrated, their women and children were sold, and banditry was rampant. Politics was the least concern of a population so stricken.

The gravest default of the Nationalist reconstruction was its abandonment of farm and agricultural problems. Against natural disasters, of course, no government could prevail, and against social institutions such as the fragmentation of the land through equal inheritance no government could have prevailed by less harsh methods than collectivization. It was, however, largely the failure of the Kuomintang to help in the grave problems of exorbitant rents and interest rates that alienated it from the countryside, a condition abetted by that large section of the membership of the Kuomintang who were absentee landlords and obviously against Sun Yat-sen's principle of equalization of the land. Since 1911 the old paternal rural relationship between landlord and tenant had broken down, and the stabilizing force of the gentry had vanished. By the 1930's farms were increasingly in the hands of absentee owners. It has been calculated that in the period 1930-40 10 per cent of the population owned 53 per cent of the cultivated land; 40 per cent of the farmers had to borrow food to live; and 30 per cent of the farmers were in the hands of usurers.

Amidst this impoverishment came the army of tax collectors from the warlords and the provincial authorities to squeeze money from 70 per cent of the cultivated land (some 30 per cent of the cultivated land, belonging to officials and warlords, was unregistered and exempted from taxes). In many instances the tax collectors extorted undue payments of crops and, depending upon the need and rapacity of the local officials, collected the taxes for years in advance.

The attitude of government has been succinctly stated by Ping-ti Ho:

[During the 1930's] we . . . did not attempt to put a special check on great landlords. A more truthful way of putting it is that fundamentally we did not pay any attention to this problem.

This was because we believed that in the Chinese ethical society the landlord and his tenants lived together like members of the same family. Moreover, our social institution was based on the custom of equal inheritance by all sons. However large a landlord might be, after two generations his estate was bound to be divided into a number of small households.[10]

The Communist Insurrections

> *The people are the sea, we are the fish, so long as we can swim in that sea, we will survive.*
> —Mao Tse-tung

The neglect of fundamental reforms would not have been sufficient to bring about the fall of the Nationalist government without the burden of three wars, each against a different enemy. These were, first, the intermittent civil war with other provinces and regions of China; second, the Japanese invasion; and third, the continuing Communist insurrection. Moreover, the Nationalists were intrinsically incapable of defeating either the Japanese or the Communists. And of these opponents the most difficult were to be the Communists, for they demonstrated a quite uncharacteristically Chinese ability to organize peasants and scholars who had fallen by the wayside in the Nationalist triumph. China had no more training in the organization of mass political parties than she had in the organization of mass industry or business. Therefore the ability of the Communists to organize was always to be greater than the ability of the Nationalists to exterminate.

Yet in 1927 the Chinese Communist Party had been almost decimated at the hands of either Chiang K'ai-shek or Wang Ching-wei, and those alive were in flight to places of safety. The Fourth Nationalist Army, stationed at Nanchang, had mutinied in the debacle of 1927, and parts of it had dispersed to Kwangtung, Hopei, and Honan Provinces. One column, led by Chu Teh, in obedience to standard Communist Party doctrine, had tried to seize the cities of Changsha, Amoy, and Canton, had failed badly, and had retreated and holed up in the mountains of Kiangsi Province. Here Chu Teh met another refugee, Mao Tse-tung. It was here in the Kiangsi fastness that Mao and Chu began the debates on Communist strategy and tactics whose outcome was to be momentous for China.

The Chinese Communist Party, as orthodox Marxist-Leninists, had believed that the peasants were necessary and desirable allies but that a revolution must be led by the industrial workers. Added to this was the traditional contempt that the Chinese Communist leaders, who were all of the educated class, had for the poor landworker. But when the Northern March began, the peasants in the path of that march rose in such enormous and enthusiastic masses to assist the cause, because of the dedicated labor among them of a handful of Communist organizers, that some of the younger Communists, especially those with experience in the countryside, concluded that a revolution in China could be led by the peasants. Had the Communists paid more attention to their Chinese heritage, this would have come as no surprise, for every mass movement in China's past derived its force from the peasantry. But entrapped in the Western orientation of Marxism-Leninism, they had been able to see revolution only in European terms and doctrines. Mao Tse-tung had intimate experience with peasant organization and saw them as the very base of the revolution. In 1927 he reported to the Communist Party on his work among the peasants of Hunan:

> The poor peasants (especially the very poor) secured the leadership of the Peasant Associations because they were the most revolutionary . . . *this leadership by the poor peasants is very essential. Without the poor peasants there will be no revolution.* To reject them is to reject the revolution: a blow at them is a blow at the revolution.[11]

Needing both a territorial base and mass support, the Communists in Kiangsi saw close at hand the peasants who fed them, gave them information, and furnished recruits for the Red Army they were building. Between 1927 and 1929 Mao Tse-tung urged a change from the orthodox theory and tactics advocated by the leaders of the Communist Party who were in sanctuary in Shanghai. He wanted to translate Marx and Lenin to the Chinese situation, in effect to Sinicize them. He did not want to subordinate the Chinese revolution to the international interests of the Soviet Union and he proposed that the Party build itself with the peasantry before extending its efforts to the cities. One could sense the slow rise of revolt in the country-side against hunger, exactions, extortions, and military rule, he argued, and one should build with the good materials at hand. The Kiangsi group agreed with the 1927 report on the lack of Communist success, which stated:

> This defeat tells us very clearly, a purely military adventure without calling upon the broad peasant [masses] to arise was bound to fail. Yet after having gone through this experience some people are basically doubtful about the peasants, considering them to have no strength. We should sternly oppose this errone-ous concept.[12]

The founder of the Chinese Communist Party, Ch'en Tu-hsiu, city-bred, insisted that this was impractical.

> "It seems to me too romantic," Ch'en Tu-hsiu replied, "for you to insist upon a Communist movement in the rural districts, because the main force of the Communist movement must necessarily consist of industrial workers. In such a country of small farmers as China, over half the farmers are petit-bourgeois landed farmers who adhere firmly to private-property conscious-ness. How can they accept Communism? How can the Com-munist movement extend itself successfully in the mass of rural China where there are many landed farmers?"[13]

Mao was insistent on the principles he had expounded in his 1927 report, and the Communists in the Kiangsi fastness went along with him, while the Central Committee of the Chinese Communist Party, led by the orthodox Li Li-san and the op-portunistic Chou En-lai, continued, with Moscow's blessings, the task of basing the revolution on the nonexistent industrial proletariat of the cities. It is probable, because of his heresy, that Mao Tse-tung was for a while officially expelled from the Party; for certain, he and his followers were in disgrace. But they mustered and commanded the only real armed force the Party had, and from 1931 (when the Chinese Soviet Republic was declared) to 1934, the perfection of the force's guerrilla tactics proved sufficient to hold off the attacks of Nanking's armies, who launched one "bandit suppression campaign" after another against the Kiangsi Communists. By 1932 Mao, having in 1930 seized and executed the supporters of Li Li-san's line within the Kiangsi area, was powerful enough to force the Shanghai headquarters to move to Kiangsi, and in 1935 he became chairman of the Chinese Communist Party.

As the internal Communist struggles went on, Chiang K'ai-shek directed all of the financial and military resources of his government toward a single objective, extermination of the Communists. The Kiangsi state within a state, far more dangerous, because of its economic and social ideas and its unremitting hostility, than any mere warlord-dominated area, was beginning to spread into parts of Hunan and Kiangsu Provinces. Despite the brutality of some of its methods, such as the execution of landlord gentry, it gained power among villages through the distribution of land and through its image as a beneficent force, opposed to warlords, tax collectors, usurers, foreign powers, and the government. The peasants, although nonpolitical, fought with the Communists for one elemental reason. Since the Kuomintang was publicly against any rural reforms save such as could be comprehended within its vision of Confucianism, their return meant the return of the landlords. It was this fear that enabled the Communists to beat back four major Kuomintang attacks. In the process they so equipped themselves with arms yielded by Kuomintang deserters or taken from defeated Kuomintang armies that they were able to put in the field a partisan force of almost a quarter of a million men.

In 1934 the Kuomintang forces, under General Von Seekt, were organized in a close blockade of the Communist area, a noose that was drawn tighter and tighter. Faced with starvation and slow annihilation, the Red forces, almost 90,000 men, women and children, broke out of Kiangsi and set off for Western China. This was the famous Long March, whose route went along the edges of the snowy peaks of Tibet and through Central Asia to Shensi province in the poor and arid Northwest. Here, among the hill caves of Yenan, 20,000 survivors set up camp and proceeded to build another Chinese Soviet area.

CHINA UNDER SIEGE

Japan Moves on China

With the end of the Kiangsi and adjacent "soviets," the internal armed threat to Nanking so diminished that the Kuomintang planned to take economic and political measures toward genuine strength and unification. This brief interlude, with the promise of a more stable China working in concert with Western powers, threw the Japanese military command into a panic and doomed the prospects of improvement for China. This military clique, which by now dominated Japanese life and government, was resolved to extend Japan's occupation from Manchuria to North China, and to use North China as the base from which to dominate China and expel Western influence.

Japan had taken the position in 1928 that the Nanking government was at best the government of only a part of China. Behind this lay Japan's fear that a true Chinese central government aligned with the West was an enduring menace to Japan's ordained prospects on the continent of Asia. Having murdered Chang Tso-lin, the Kwantung Army found his son and successor, Chang Hsueh-liang, military boss of Manchuria, even less amenable to Japanese control; indeed, he was a true patriot who put the Manchurian provinces under the Nationalist flag. Therefore, in September, 1931, the autonomous Kwantung Army, without the knowledge of the civil government of Japan, and upon a pretext of "banditry," which it had itself staged, seized and occupied Manchuria. In February, 1932, this prize became the puppet empire of Manchukuo under an emperor, Henry Pu-yi, whose last throne had been, briefly, that of the Manchu Empire in 1912. From Manchuria, the Kwantung Army began to seep into North China under the continuing excuse of "bandit suppression," beginning a process that was to wreck irretrievably whatever stability existed, not only in China but in all of Asia.

Diplomatic pressures exerted by other countries and by the League of Nations failed to dispossess Japan from Manchuria. Unable to face the Japanese in the field, Chiang K'ai-shek decided on a policy of slow attrition and diplomacy; of negotiating with Japan without yielding anything; and of hoarding his forces until the Japanese tired of trying to digest China. However, a great wave of popular anger swept China, and a general boycott was begun of Japanese goods. This proved so effective that the Japanese, on the excuse of protecting their nationals in Shanghai (two of whom had been murdered by Chinese mobs), assaulted that open city by air and sea bombardment and then landed troops, in February, 1933, using the International Settlement as their operating headquarters. For thirty-four days the Nineteenth Route Army, against orders from Nanking and without support, held the Japanese at Shanghai. Under heavy international pressure and because Nanking promised to "demilitarize" Shanghai, but most probably because of the gallant and unexpected Chinese resistance, the Japanese withdrew.

Almost immediately, however, they again began a penetration of North China. In 1933 they added the province of Jehol (the eastern part of Inner Mongolia) to their Manchukuoan empire, and they moved into Chahar Province, which they set up as an "independent" Mongol state. By virtue of their rights under the Boxer treaties, they held the Peking-Tientsin railway line, which gave them an interior position in North China and a constant excuse to protect themselves. Now, in addition to Chahar and Jehol, they began to nibble at Suiyuan and Hopei Provinces, and it was not until May, 1933, that this advance was stopped. In that month Nanking and the Japanese Army signed the Tangku Truce, which created a demilitarized buffer zone between Jehol and Hopei Provinces that the Chinese were pledged to police against anti-Japanese elements, while the Japanese were to withdraw their forces into Manchuria.

The Japanese Army in North China, as ambitious as its parent Kwantung Army, did not abandon its plans to create a separate state in North China. They gave aid to pro-Japanese Chinese officials, drew the tax revenues from the areas they dominated, and made these areas into Japanese monopoly markets. They engaged in propaganda and large-scale smuggling and became the largest handlers of narcotics in the world, for by the widespread and cheap sale of opium, morphine, and heroin they hoped to demoralize and enfeeble the population. By 1935 they had succeeded in "neutralizing" Hopei Province, although North China was not so easily gained as Manchuria, for the population, both urban and rural, was hostile. But Nanking was forced to remove loyal troops and commanders from Hopei, whereupon the Japanese began to edge into Kiangsu and Hunan Provinces. Wherever it was possible local Chinese forces fought bravely, but formal large-scale actions were limited, partly by the confusing political divisions in North China and partly by the overwhelming strength of the Japanese force. Nevertheless, the German military advisers now advised Chiang K'ai-shek to strike at the flanks of the advancing Japanese. This he refused to do. He was sensible of the limited force at his disposal, which, should it have been wiped out, would have left Nanking without any army whatsoever, and he was opposed to creating a people in arms and throwing North China into a widespread guerrilla war. Above all, he was fixed in his belief that the Communists regrouping in Shensi were a worse menace to him than the Japanese and that internal pacification must precede resistance to Japan.

Actually what was taking place was not a war. The Japanese formally proclaimed their movements police actions to protect the rights of their nationals and to prevent "communization" of China. Nor did the foreign powers call it war, for no one wanted to treat China as a belligerent power, who would, under the rules of war, be denied any assistance whatever. All in all, because of their command of the air, sea, and land, the lack of effective large-scale Chinese resistance, and the treason of a substantial number of Chinese officials, the only opposition the Japanese encountered was local guerrilla action. Therefore, from the Japanese point of view, the "no-war" was both easy and profitable.

However, had the Japanese any foresight, they might well have been concerned over their failure to develop a political base, for they controlled only the areas they could garrison. They might also have done well to worry about the increasing demand in China for resistance at any costs, the rise within the Kuomintang of a powerful resistance group, and the appearance in Northwest China of a skillful Chinese guerrilla force.

The Second Kuomintang-Communist Alliance

The Shensi area, where the Long March had ended in 1934, was barren, impoverished, and small in population, and the problems of survival seemed insuperable for the Communists, cut off as they were from material Soviet help, barely able to live off the land, forced to manufacture their own small arms and ammunition, and blocked by Nationalist armies. Yet, surprisingly, they replenished themselves and took control of the local government. They received reinforcements from other Communist groups in China, which migrated from Central China between 1934 and 1936 to join forces in Shensi. Above all, the Communists revived themselves by taking the public lead against Japanese aggression. In effect, they appropriated nationalism from the Nationalists and made it a powerful Communist weapon.

THE COMMUNIST-KUOMINTANG CONFLICT AND
ANTI-JAPANESE NATIONALISM

The Kiangsi Soviet had declared war on Japan in February, 1932. At the same time it had called on all Chinese to join the Communists against the Kuomintang. Both the Communists and the Kuomintang operated from the same premise—that the other had to be exterminated before there could be an effective struggle against Japan. As an earnest of his intentions, Chiang K'ai-shek placed the Northeastern Defense Army of Chang Hsueh-liang, headquartered at Sian, on the line in the Northwest to blockade the Communists. Meanwhile, the Communists, from their headquarters at Paoan, carried on a vitriolic propaganda campaign against the Kuomintang and conducted such guerrilla operations as they could in the bordering areas.

In 1935 the Chinese Communist Party imposed the death sentence *in absentia* on Chiang K'ai-shek. In return, the Kuomintang put a price of $100,000 on the head of Mao Tse-tung, who during this time had been the leader at Shensi. This mutual hostility seemed destined to end in a successful Kuomintang campaign against Shensi, directed by Chang Hsueh-liang, but, unknown to Chiang K'ai-shek, his careful planning for the disposal of his internal enemies was being subverted. Chiang calculated not only that Chang's army would crush the Communists, but that the army would suffer sufficient casualties itself to remove Chang as a force in China. But by 1935 the Communists had changed their line. In that year, the same year that Mao became Chairman of the Chinese Communist Party, the Soviet Union, threatened by Hitler on its western frontier and Japan (in Mongolia) on its eastern frontier, and seeing the wreckage of Communist parties around the world, initiated a policy of the United Front. The Chinese Communists responded by urging a union of all Chinese against Japan, and even appealed to Chang Hsueh-liang at Sian, for it was well known that he and his men hated the Japanese far worse than they hated Chinese Communists.

At the same time, public opinion had turned against Nanking for its failure to do anything more about Japan than make patriotic speeches and engage in empty attempts to negotiate. Chiang's intolerance of criticism and his impatience with any opposition embittered the students especially. They wanted China to fight Japan, and it seemed unreasonable to them that China's army should be fighting other Chinese. In massive, indiscriminate protest, they attacked Kuomintang headquarters, the Foreign Ministry, and the Foreign Ministers, and in 1936 they formed the National Salvation League. Within the Kuomintang itself there was a growing demand to take a stand on Japan. But Chiang K'ai-shek firmly disregarded all evidence of a nationalist fervor boiling up in China that could not be controlled, diverted, or ignored but only led.

THE UNITED FRONT

The same unrest pervaded the Northeastern Army, which preferred to quit fighting the Communists and start fighting the Japanese, who had taken over their homeland of Manchuria. In 1936 there were military revolts in Kwangsi, Kwangtung, and Shantung Provinces. While the Nationalist First Army in Kansu was cracking under Communist attack, Chang Hsueh-liang was warning Chiang K'ai-shek from Sian that his men had no heart for what they were doing. Suddenly, in August, 1936, the Communists offered to fight in a united front with Chiang against

Japan. Chiang could ignore the Communist offer but not the impending defection of the Northeastern Army, which threatened to upset the entire Nationalist strategy. In December, 1936, Chiang went to Sian to order Chang Hsueh-liang to mount a full attack against the Communist bases in Shansi. Chang refused, his troops mutinied, and Chiang K'ai-shek was kidnapped and held as a prisoner while Chang Hsueh-liang and his senior commanders issued a manifesto to the nation:

> At this juncture, our Central Leader ought to encourage both military and civilians to organize the whole people in a united war of national defense. But while those soldiers at the front endure death and bloodshed in the defense of our national territories, the diplomatic authorities are still seeking compromises.
>
> Ever since the unjust imprisonment of the patriotic leaders in Shanghai, the whole world has been startled; the whole of our people has been filled with anger and distress. To love one's country is an offence! This is a terrifying prospect.
>
> Generalissimo Chiang K'ai-shek, surrounded by a group of unworthy advisers, has forfeited the support of the masses of our people. He is deeply guilty for the harm his policies have done the country. We, Chang Hsueh-liang and the others undersigned, advised him with tears to take another way; but we were repeatedly rejected and rebuked.
>
> Not long ago, the students in Sian were demonstrating in their National Salvation movement, and General Chiang set the police to killing these patriotic children. How could anyone with a human conscience bear to do this? We his colleagues of many years' standing, could not bear to sit still and witness it.
>
> Therefore we have tendered our last advice to Marshal Chiang, while guaranteeing his safety, in order to stimulate his awakening.[14]

The manifesto went on to request an end to civil war, a restoration of political freedom, and a united front against Japan. There was panic in both Nanking and Sian. Nanking was prepared to launch a full-scale air and land attack against its own mutinous troops at Sian, and in Sian a number of the mutineers wanted to execute Chiang K'ai-shek. No one knows the details of what happened at Sian between December 12 and December 24, but one thing seems clear. The Chinese Communist Party certainly influenced the Sian kidnapping, and Moscow was instrumental in obtaining Chiang's release. The Soviet Union warned the Chinese Communist Party that the kidnapping and possible execution of Chiang was a danger since an ensuing Chinese civil war would open the gates of China and Asia to Japan. It ordered the Chinese Communist Party to put all possible pressure on Chiang's captors to free him. Edgar Snow says that "Mao Tse-tung flew into a rage when the order came from Moscow to release Chiang." [15]

Chou En-lai arrived in Sian on December 17. After seven days of conference, Chiang, yielding none of his basic principles, agreed to fight Japan and end the anti-Communist war. He was freed on December 24, and his only public statement, made at the Nanking airport, was, "I want no more civil wars." Chang Hsueh-liang voluntarily returned to Nanking as a captive "for punishment," and the Northeastern Army was withdrawn from the Shensi front and sent to Central China.

In February, 1937, the Chinese Communist Party made an open offer to the government:

(1) to stop our program of conducting armed uprising throughout the country for the overthrow of the National Government in Nanking; (2) to change the Soviet Government into the Government of the Special Region of the Republic of China and the Red Army into the National Revolutionary Army under the direct leadership of the Central Government and the Military Affairs Commission in Nanking; (3) to enforce the thorough democratic system of universal suffrage within the special regions under the regime of the Government of the Special Region; and (4) to put an end to the policy of expropriating the land of landlords and to execute persistently the common program of the anti-Japanese united front.[16]

In return, they asked for an end to civil wars, political freedom, and a coalition government to carry on the Japanese war.

In September, 1937, after the Japanese had captured Hopei, Chiang responded by congratulating the Communists on joining

the common struggle and on foregoing their Communist principles to carry on the Three Principles of the People. He urged
that there be no arguments over the past and that all Chinese
should loyally serve the Republic, for he would welcome any
organization that would join him under the banner of the National Revolution.

From 1937 on the Soviet Union chose to back the Kuomintang and not the Chinese Communists. In 1937 a Sino-
Russian nonaggression pact was signed although neither signa-
tory had "any illusions with respect to the other." [17] As an
earnest indication of their feeling, the Russians agreed to put
up $50,000,000 in aid, including fighter planes and pilots. For
the first time in many years China was united, reluctantly, it
is true, but presenting a common front to Japan. But for Kuomintang and Communists it was merely an expedient union.
If Japan were to be defeated, the two would again dispute for
control of China.

Greater East Asia

FROM "INCIDENT" TO "UNDECLARED WAR"

The oral agreements at Sian and the Communists' open offer of
February, 1937, were treated by Japan as mortal challenges to
their China policy, which was the creation of a Japanese economic and political protectorate over that country. The Kwantung Army and the new nonparty Japanese government announced that they would now take whatever means they deemed
were needed to preserve the peace throughout East Asia. On
the night of July 7, 1937, Japanese forces on maneuvers outside
of Peking fired on Chinese troops. The fire was returned, and
what Japan had long planned as a relatively easy piecemeal
seizure of North China opened into a general war. Neither
country could back down. The whole course of modern Japanese history had pushed her past this point of no return, while
the Chinese were united in their resolve to yield no further.
The Japanese poured troops into Suiyuan and Hopei Provinces,
attempting to cut off Northeast China by a double envelopment
of Shansi Province. Tientsin and Peking were taken in August

and Suiyuan occupied in October. From Tientsin a Japanese army moved into Shantung Province, but it met very stiff resistance and did not secure that area until the following year. In the northern Shansi mountain passes the Japanese also met ferocious opposition from Yen Hsi-shan's troops, and at T'uancheng Pass and Hsin'kou Pass the Japanese North China Army suffered more than 60,000 casualties. Although they took the provincial capital, Taiyuan, in November, they were held out of southern Shansi for another two years.

Meanwhile, on August 13, the Japanese Yangtze Expeditionary Force landed at Shanghai. The Chinese Nineteenth Route Army bravely held that city until November, when they were outflanked and forced to withdraw up the river. The Japanese, following swiftly, took Nanking, which was ill defended, on December 13. With the capital of China, the coast of China, and most of its major cities and rail lines in their hands, the Japanese command, believing the campaign was over and that the Nationalist government had no option but to surrender, turned loose their troops for celebration in Nanking. What followed in this undefended city was an orgy of destruction, murder, looting, and rape such as has seldom occurred in modern warfare.

At the beginning of 1938 the Japanese moved to link their North China and Central China forces by taking the important rail junction of Hsuchow. Outside Hsuchow they were trapped and badly beaten by Li Tsung-jen, who held them long enough for the main Chinese forces to withdraw to Szechuan, but Japanese reinforcements encircling him forced him to break out to the west. The Japanese now drove westward along the rail line from Hsuchow toward Chengchow to complete their hold on China north of the Yangtze, but the Nationalist Army, without warning the Chinese population, broke the Yangtze dikes, killing an uncounted number of Chinese but stalling the Japanese advance. The Japanese attack then shifted back to the Yangtze River line, through Ankang and Kukiang, to the seizure of the provisional capital of Hankow, which was taken in October, 1938. The Nationalist government now retreated to Chungking in Szechuan Province.

THE "CO-PROSPERITY SPHERE"

By the end of 1938, Japan, convinced that China was isolated and that the government and remaining forces had to seek peace, went about setting up what she termed a "Greater East Asia Co-prosperity Sphere." By this Japan meant that her only aims were the stability and prosperity of East Asia and that she had no territorial ambitions. A corollary slogan was "Asia for the Asiatics," which could more properly be read "Asia for the Japanese." Japan had established a provisional government of China at Peking in December, 1937, and when Nanking was captured, she had established a second government there, the Reformed Government of China. Japan was quite willing, if Chiang K'ai-shek sued for peace, to keep him at the head of a pro-Japanese government, providing Japan could garrison China at China's expense. Since Chiang would not yield, the Japanese looked for the support of those Chinese who hated the Communists worse than the Japanese and Chiang K'ai-shek worse than either, those who were opportunists, those with no future, and those who honestly believed that Japan meant well for China. In 1938 the various provincial puppet governments merged into the United Council of China, which two years later formed the Central Government of China at Nanking, under Wang Ching-wei.

While the Japanese Army ran the government, it milked the economy through "development companies." It owned a piece of every business and racket in Occupied China and controlled the cities, ports, railways, and major resources and industries, as well as the salt and customs revenues. The Japanese needed this income, for the vast army in China was an intolerable strain on Japan's already weak domestic economy. Indeed, after 1940 there was a question as to which would give first—the Japanese economy or Chungking.

THE THREE-CORNERED WAR

What was the fan jet power which thrust the Communist party from its 1935-1936 position as a marginal force in Chinese politics to its 1945 position as the control center of an administrative system governing ninety million people?

—Howard L. Boorman[18]

Looking back at the passionate clash of men and ideas in wartime China, together with the generally ill-informed reactions in the United States, it is too easy to forget that the real revolutionary force in China was neither the Communists nor the Nationalists. It was the Japanese invasion, which loosed war on North China for fifteen years, and in so doing subjected the Chinese to such suffering that they could no longer comprehend who was friend or enemy. They became equally weary of war and politics.

At the beginning of the war the combined major forces under Nationalist command had numbered between 200,000 and 300,-000 good troops. The majority of these were lost by the end of 1937, and by the end of the next year, China was exhausted of trained troops and officers. The Nationalist government was also now starving for money and military supplies. It could not both buy arms and support its currency without totally exhausting its assets. It had lost all revenues from the areas occupied by Japan and had become dependent on the poor, rural interior. Despite the United States' unlimited purchases of Chinese silver in 1937, the government was forced into an inflationary position from which it never recovered. In July, 1937, it began printing money.

The same year, the French, under Japanese economic pressure, stopped shipping arms to China via the Haiphong-Kunming railway, and in October, 1938, the Japanese took Canton, thus ending trade through Hong Kong. Now China's only connections to the outside world were the old Silk Road to Russian Turkestan, the Kunming-Lashio Road (Burma Road), literally built by hand in 1938, and the flights of China National Airlines from Chungking, over enemy territory, to Hong Kong. The only substantial foreign help came from the Soviet Union, which sent in regular Red Air Force squadrons. By the end of 1939 there were 1,000 Soviet planes, 2,000 Soviet pilots, and 100 Soviet military advisers in China. The Soviets were also pinning down Japanese troops in Mongolia and Manchuria, and in

1937-38 had taught the Japanese a bitter lesson in three border battles.

For several years the Kwantung Army had been probing the Soviet borders in Inner Asia, seeking to find a weak spot, and three times it was repulsed, first in July, 1937, in a river war fought on the Amur in front of the main Soviet town of Blagoveshchensk. The following summer a "border incident" on the Korean-Siberian frontier escalated to a battle of divisional strength, in which the Japanese were beaten back and heavy losses sustained by both sides. In August, 1939, a full-scale tank battle was waged at Nomonhon on the steppe of Outer Mongolia near the Khalka River, and the Japanese were badly defeated.

In April, 1941, the Soviet Union, anticipating the German attack in June and desiring to protect her eastern frontier from attack, signed a five-year nonaggression treaty with Japan. The previous September Japan had invaded French Indochina and brought sufficient pressure to bear on England to force her, in July, 1941, to close the Burma Road. Although in November the government of India gave permission for flights from China to Assam, the supplies that could be carried over that hazardous route were a mere token. By the middle of 1941 China was truly under siege.

In August, 1939, the civil and military organs of the Nationalist state were superseded by the Supreme National Defense Council, whose chairman held emergency powers. Its high command was an unwieldy, overstaffed structure spotted with incompetence, for often posts were allotted to friends or to factional leaders. The strategy planned by this command, from its position of isolation, was one of hoarding strength and waiting, keeping the army intact for one final smashing offensive. Meanwhile the official defense of China depended upon the Chinese civil population, *without* the army, to take the blows and act as the buffer between the enemy and the Nationalist forces. Thus, after 1939 the Kuomintang fought a siege warfare from South China and abandoned North China to the Communist forces, who were quite prepared to wage guerrilla warfare with the help of the Chinese civil population.

In order to understand Communist plans and operations in this period it is necessary to understand how the peasants viewed resistance, reform, the Communists, the Nationalists, and the Japanese, because it was not, certainly in the beginning, nationalism and resistance alone that attracted the peasants to the Communist cause. The peasants were disaffected, and the root cause lay in the disruption of the rural economy by the civil wars and then the destruction of that economy by the Japanese invasion. In North China the Japanese invasion and the subsequent guerrilla war in the countryside reduced the man-power available for production because men were either con-scripted or fled the area. Farm markets closed down, tools and livestock were destroyed, and handicraft industries were wiped out. Food was no longer on sale in the towns that were isolated from the countryside, and villages were shut off from neighbor-ing villages. How the Communists were able to capitalize on this is best seen in microcosm by what happened in Shansi Province between 1935 and 1939.

Shansi was a "model" province under a "model" governor, Yen Hsi-shan, who attempted to promote industry, to educate, and to institute reforms. He held the province tightly and literally eradicated the Communists. Yet he admitted in 1935 that, given their head, 70 per cent of his people would go over to the Communists. Yen Hsi-shan was unique in realizing quite early that neither he nor any other government in China would enjoy mass support until fundamental reforms were in-troduced. Yen's prophecy was proven in 1936 when, with the help of the peasants, a small, poorly armed Red Army invaded Shansi and took one-third of the province—this, despite Yen's large, well-equipped army and his having been the best pro-vincial governor in China, for years vigorously resisting Japa-nese penetration. Only when heavily reinforced from Nanking did Yen drive out the Communists, but in 1937 he invited them back to help fight the Japanese thrust at Shansi. Again, in the bitter two-year fight for southern Shansi (1937-39) Yen's troops and Nanking troops fought bravely without support from the Shansi peasants, for most peasants regarded the war with Japan as just another contest between rival warlords, but they flocked

to the Communist Eighth Route Army, which played a minimal
part in the Shansi fight, "the good army," as they saw it, that
did not "harm people or do evil things." [19]

As they had promised, the Communists gave up land redistribution and their autonomous government in the Northwest, but they proceeded to concentrate as much on territorial
expansion and political control as they did on fighting the
Japanese. Their vigorous call to arms was incommensurate with
their limited ability to fight. Their greatest asset lay in gaining
the maximum number of friends so as to fight the minimum
number of enemies. Mao was smart enough to move in the great
tradition of peasant rebellion, and he was not burdened, as was
Chungking, with conducting a government. His Eighth Route
Army was a disciplined force that did not plunder, unlike the
retreating Nationalist armies. It fought the Japanese as necessary, but its main activity was political. To Mao power rested
on the army, and in 1938 he stated:

> Every Communist must understand this truth: Political power
> grows out of the barrel of a gun. Our principle is that the Party
> commands the gun; the gun shall never be allowed to command
> the Party. But it is also true that with the gun at our disposal we
> can really build up the organization in North China. We can also
> rear cadres and create schools, culture and mass movements.
> Everything in Yenan has been built up by means of the gun.
> Anything can grow out of the barrel of the gun. Viewed from the
> Marxist theory of the state, the army is the chief component of
> the political power of a state. Whoever wants to seize and hold
> on to political power must have a strong army.[20]

In the areas that came under its control, it carried out a social
revolution. It reduced taxes, controlled usury, offered free education, and gave medical help. In all this, it was unwittingly
helped by the attitude of the gentry in North China, who refused to support the war against the Japanese with either money
or men. To be anti-Japanese and to be revolutionary meant one
and the same thing to the peasants, and they attacked wealthy
Chinese collaborators who wanted to preserve the status quo

under Japanese protection. Thus, Communist guerrilla forces, who stayed in North China after the Nationalist forces retreated or were destroyed, were able to make tremendous inroads into the loyalties of the population. This situation was apparent in Chungking, where a section of the government agitated to treat the Communists, rather than the Japanese, as the major enemy. A rupture between Yenan and Chungking was prevented by neutral Chinese leaders acting as go-betweens, but Chungking continued to be disturbed over the extension of military control in North China by the Eighth Route Army, and even more so by the extension of Communist ideas and political influence.

In 1940 the Communists created a new army, the New Fourth Army, to operate in Chekiang, which the Kuomintang considered their area of operations. Chungking ordered the New Fourth to cross north of the Yangtze, and because it did not move at once, accused it of insubordination. When it did move, it was surprised during the river crossing by Nationalist troops and badly mauled. Chungking then cut off the flow of medical supplies and arms and ammunition to the Communist forces and again blockaded the Shensi area. This was a basic miscalculation, for not only did the Communist forces survive but their successes led them to make extensive and excessive claims. As they became entrenched in the North, they began to exercise the powers of a government. They gained arms and recruits from the Nationalist armies sent against them, and their confidence increased. At the same time Mao Tse-tung made no bones about his eventual aims. In *The New Democracy* (1940) and in *On Coalition Government* (1944), he stated that although the Chinese Communist Party might have to reach its goals through an intervening period of bourgeois coalition government, it would eventually achieve a Communist China.

The New Fourth regrouped, and the Communists, now cut off from any help against the Japanese, fell back on swimming in the peasant tide. The brief united front was over, and from 1941 on a three-cornered war took place in China—Nationalist against Japan, Communist against Japan, and Communist against Nationalist.

The Decline of the Kuomintang

THE MILITARY DECLINE

The Japanese attacks on American bases in the Pacific in December, 1941, and the entry of the United States and England into the war marked a great change in Chungking's military strategy. The spread of the war was an enormous relief to the tortured Chinese government, which at last had allies. Its siege policy now seemed justified, for it could continue to hoard its forces in the rugged interior and depend upon the United States to carry the military brunt of the war. This was not an articulated decision, but it was implicit in the actions and pronouncements of Chungking. They expected, as their due, replenishment and help for the lone stand they had put up over the years until 1941, while reserving their major striking forces intact for use against their internal enemies once the war was won. For its part, the United States, which had never felt comfortable about its neutrality while China was being battered and which was afraid that Chungking might collapse and sign a separate peace, moved to provide economic aid and military aid. In 1941, under the Lend Lease Act and with the blessings of the United States government, the American Volunteer Group, under Col. Claire Chennault, began operating in China against the Japanese air force. The following year the United States gave Chungking a $500,000,000 credit, with no strings attached, although this was of little avail against the enormous flood of inflated paper money now circulating in China.

In the spring of 1942 the Allied Forces under General Joseph Stilwell were driven out of Burma by the Japanese, and in that campaign China lost one-third of her trained troop reserve and the Burma Road (which was not reopened until 1945). Now, save for the flights over the route called "the Hump" and the Central Asian caravan route, China was totally cut off from material help. The Hump was a brave man's flight but hardly a supply route, and Russia turned down requests in 1942 for materials to be sent in through Turkestan when she found out they would be used by the Kuomintang armies in the Northwest against the Communists.

In mid-1942 serious friction developed between China and the United States, although both governments kept it secret. At the highest levels a debate began over Chiang K'ai-shek's desire to be treated as an equal ally of Churchill's and Roosevelt's. As a symbol of this he wanted materials (which he could not have used even if they could have been gotten in to China) and representation on the Joint Staff and the Munitions Board. On lower echelons, United States military representatives in China, who wanted rapid military reforms and, above all, a significant change in Chinese military leadership, were consistently pessimistic and derogatory about China as well as about her chances. The civilian personnel of the United States State Department and Treasury Department, better acquainted with China and with the agony she had been going through, were much more optimistic in their reports, although they despaired about the controlled rate of exchange, which, under the increasing inflation, was costing United States forces in China prices such as $75 for a sparkplug.

The struggle between the governments was represented in China by two proud, stubborn men, each convinced that he was right. General Joseph Stilwell, Chief of Staff to Chiang K'ai-shek and field commander of the China-India-Burma Theater, had served years in China, knew the language, and had a vast appreciation for the Chinese soldier's qualities when he was decently fed, trained, and led. To achieve good troops, he pressed constantly and, at times, intemperately, for significant changes in the Chinese command structure. He also wanted to incorporate within the Chinese army all trained elements, including Communists, and to use this reorganized force for offensive action. Chiang K'ai-shek, now more than ever convinced that his proper course while the Japanese and Americans fought was to hold back his force for the domestic struggle with the Communists, was acting for the preservation of his army, his party, and his government. Certain in his own mind that China's long struggle against Japan deserved every possible support, he refused to heed Stilwell or any other American adviser.

It is difficult today, more than twenty years after the end of the war, to assess exactly the politics of the military situation in China in the years 1941-45, but one thing seems beyond doubt—the strategy, the command, and the organization of the forces of the Nationalist government were hopelessly archaic and inefficient. On this point, observers, Chinese and foreign, who agreed with each other on nothing else, were agreed.

F. F. Liu, who was a Nationalist officer, described the command situation:

> As late as the nationalist period, a Chinese commander was partly a combat leader and partly a medieval lord who commanded the allegiance of his followers as a sort of district governor and family head. Most had had some variety of narrow military training at such schools as Paoting, Whampoa, or Pei-yang, but few indeed had enjoyed the benefit of training at Chinese or foreign staff colleges. Hardly a handful had had the combination of administrative, teaching, and command assignments which go into the making of the average Occidental commander. The Chinese commander's school had been the battlefield and there he had learned his tactics. His chief qualifications were some talent for personal leadership, courage, and resourcefulness.[21]

Nevertheless, there was a persistent refusal by Chungking to reform army abuses, and this was complicated not only by widespread corruption but by an indifference to the incredible sufferings of the civil and military defenders of China. Even as late as 1943-45, students and professional men were exempted from military duty or were allowed to leave China. The ranks were kept filled with peasant conscription. Too, not all of the Nationalist Army was amenable to Chungking's orders. Many southern provincial troops were commanded by warlords of dubious allegiance, and even more secure sections of the army were commanded by generals whose loyalties were gained, shakily enough, by subsidies and persuasion. Of almost 14,000,-000 Chinese conscripted for officially listed duty, only a small percentage went into service. An astounding number of men died or deserted before they reached their units, others deserted later, many died in recruit training, while many more were carried off by disease and starvation. Food, drugs, doctors, and equipment were in critically short supply. Two sympathetic observers, one American and one Chinese, have left their impressions of conditions in the Nationalist Army.

The Chinese did not fear to fight for their country; there was no deficit in patriotism. But they knew what recruiting camps were like. Government regulations could be read with a mirror. Officers were forbidden to mix sand with the rice they fed the recruits; they were forbidden to seize any clothes, baggage, or personal possessions a conscript carried with him; they were forbidden to torture, tie up, or lock their recruits in barred rooms at night; they were forbidden to ask families of deserting recruits to pay for the uniforms and food the soldier got at the induction center. Conditions in combat units were horrible, but by comparison to conditions in induction centers they were idyllic. Recruits ate even less than the starving soldiers; sometimes they got no water. Many were whipped. Dead bodies were allowed to lie for days. In some areas less than 20 per cent lived to reach the front. The week that the Belsen and Buchenwald stories broke in Europe coincided with the height of the conscription drive in China; the doctors who dealt with the recruit camps about Chengtu refused to be excited about German horrors, for descriptions of the Nazi camps, they said, read almost exactly like the recruit centers in which they were working. Near Chengtu one camp had received some 40,000 men for induction. Many had already died on the way; only 8,000 were still alive at the camp at the end of the drive. One batch of 1,000 inductees was reported to have lost 800 recruits through the negligence of its officers.[22]

Draftees were chiefly from the lowest classes, and they were often treated as military coolies. Many conscripts had to walk hundreds of miles to join their units . . . and suffered from lack of food, shelter, warm clothing and medical attention. It is not surprising that thousands upon thousands were lost, through desertion or death, before they could reach their units. General Stilwell found that in 1943 only 56 per cent of all recruits reached their assigned units. The rest died or "went over the hill" on the way.[23]

Those Chinese who finally got to fight did so with great courage. Many units literally obeyed their orders to stand to the last man. The Chinese soldier in action proved the assessment foreigners had made of him for decades. Properly taken care of and commanded, he was brave, tough, resourceful, smart, and the equivalent of any fighting man in the world. But save for the divisions being trained under the Americans in Burma, there was no one to take care of him. As late as the end of the war, the commander of a Chinese army received lump sums to pay his troops and was allowed to determine the pay rates.

It was this situation, plus the growing antagonism between Nationalists and Communists, that led Stilwell to warn Washington that any time the Japanese chose they could mop up the expensive and painfully constructed American air bases in East China. In April, 1944, the Japanese did exactly that, sending a striking force to smash superior numbers of Chinese, and by September forced the Americans to abandon every one of its bases. It was during this campaign that Chungking received another shock from the internal political situation. As T'ang En-po's Nationalist Army retreated from Honan, ravishing their own people as they went, the Honanese population turned on them and destroyed them.

Yet despite this attack upon a Chinese army by the Chinese people, no reforms in command structure, discipline, or supply was undertaken. When President Roosevelt then urgently suggested that the reorganization of the Chinese army be undertaken, Chiang K'ai-shek demanded that the vinegar-tongued General Stilwell be recalled, citing as a main reason Stilwell's insistence upon arming and equipping Communist forces to fight the Japanese. Stilwell was recalled to preserve the alliance between the two countries. He was replaced by General Wedemeyer, who was to have little more success, if any, as Chief of Staff of the Nationalist Army. In addition, President Roosevelt sent a series of high-level personal representatives, for by 1944 reports of American representatives and observers already in China warned that, if unchecked, the conflict between Kuomintang and Communists would erupt into civil war, weakening China beyond repair; Japan would then easily gobble up the still unoccupied South and Southwest, and the war would be prolonged. American advisers were particularly sensitive to the growing political alienation of the Kuomintang from the rest of China. The Chinese Communists were now using nationalism and war weariness to gather tremendous support, and there was a good probability that when the war ended the Communists could win the ensuing civil war.

POLITICAL COMPLACENCY

In 1939 the government had created, in the People's Political Council, a representative body to advise the government on the conduct of the war, but it was a powerless group because the government politely ignored it. Thus, once again the Kuomintang leadership lost the loyalties of an important group of Chinese. The fact is that in the stalemated war of 1940-44, the Kuomintang, sensing that Japan could not win, became dangerously complacent. It identified its critics as Communists and justified suppression as a survival measure. In time every group cast out from the Kuomintang was to find its home with the Communists, who were now seeking the widest possible cooperation toward establishing their own eventual political goals in China.

However, in 1939 these middle groups had gained the support of Madame Chiang K'ai-shek and Sun Fo, the son of Sun Yat-sen, in asking for a system of domestic power that would end civil war. This time their demand for a constitution was resisted by Chiang on the grounds that war was no time to effect fundamental political changes. But the pressures continued, and in 1943 the government announced that it would call into being the National Assembly, *which had been elected in 1936-37.* While this convening of a body of delegates elected six years previously seemed a cynical service to many, it did lead to the meeting in 1946 of an effective National Assembly. This tumultuous assembly drafted the best of Chinese constitutions to end tutelage and paved the way for national elections in 1947. But by 1947 the future of China lay not in elections but in the open clash of arms.

Victory and Defeat

The disastrous military reverses on the mainland were not due to the overwhelming strength of the Communists

but due to the organizational collapse, loose discipline and
low spirits of Party members.

—Chiang K'ai Shek[24]

THE TRUCE

Despite their truly implacable animosities, between November,
1944, and June, 1945, the Communists and the Nationalists were
actually negotiating on China's future under the auspices of the
United States. The Communists had moved a long way toward
agreeing to participate in a postwar national government, providing it was a new one where all parties were represented,
when the United States destroyed Hiroshima and Nagasaki with
atomic bombs, ending the war with unexpected suddenness.
The Japanese surrender found the Kuomintang in control of
South and Southwest China and the Communists in control of
North and Northeast China. Each side could muster effective
armies of about 1,000,000, and where the Nationalists had an
absolute superiority in heavy weapons and air power, the Communists could call up some 2,000,000 peasant militia. General
Douglas MacArthur ordered the Japanese in China to surrender
to Nationalist forces. Since only Communist armies were facing
the Japanese in North China, the United States began to move
Nationalist troops there. Meanwhile the United States Fifth
Marine Amphibious Corps held Chinwangtao, Tientsin, Tsingtao,
Peking, and the connecting rail lines. The Communists, however, refused to await Chungking troops. They called on the
Japanese to surrender, and when they resisted, the Communists
attacked and drove them out of their positions. By October,
1945, the Communists held the rail lines and countryside of
North China, and Nationalist and American attacks on the lines
failed to dislodge them.

Negotiations had been resumed in August when Chiang K'ai-
shek's representatives went to Yenan to work out peace terms.
It was agreed that a political conference be set up among representatives of the various organized groups in China. The Communists were willing to permit the Nationalist Army to absorb
and command the Red Army if, in turn, the Nationalists cleaned
their house of corruption, recognized the "people's governments"

of the "liberated areas" and pursued fundamental reforms. Intolerable as these terms might seem to Chungking, a considerable breadth of agreement was reached at Chungking between Chiang K'ai-shek and Mao Tse-tung but, while both sides were talking, both were also racing to occupy Manchuria. Although General Wedemeyer warned the Nationalists not to move their best troops into Manchuria but to use them to consolidate their position south of the Great Wall, they were supremely confident.

On November 15, 1945, the battle for Manchuria began; it was this that caused the United States to send a mission to attempt a settlement by peaceful means. Officially, the United States was committed to assist the Nationalist government, but at the same time it was resolved to stay detached from the Chinese domestic struggle. Obviously there was a policy conflict. The United States had already involved itself. While, on the one hand, it was legally, materially, militarily, and emotionally committed to the Nationalists, it had, by the Yalta Treaty of 1945, placed the Soviet Union in an unwonted legal position in China. This treaty established a Sino-Soviet condominium over the great Chinese Eastern and South Manchurian Railway complexes. The treaty was incomprehensible to the Nationalists, who were not represented at Yalta, because the Soviets had renounced all such rights and privileges years before and had sold out its interests in the Chinese Eastern to Japan in 1935; furthermore, it had never had any interests in the South Manchurian. The eventual effect of this treaty, in which the United States took part to gain Russia's entrance into the Japanese war, was to give the Chinese Communists a powerful foothold in Manchuria.

The American dilemma was serious. It knew that the sudden Japanese surrender would give the Communists *de facto* control from the Great Wall to the Yellow River, with the Nationalists holding the remainder of the country. It feared that within a few years, given their proven organizational ability, the Communists would have all China. The United States could then choose between abstaining from intervention and risk seeing China go Communist, or it could intervene and risk a war it might lose. What the United States might have done is best left to the "ifs" of history. What it did do was to help the Nationalist government reestablish its power and at the same time seek a truce between Communists and Nationalists to work out a political settlement.

In January, 1946, a conference, the Political Consultative Conference, met with General George C. Marshall serving as mediator. The representatives included eight Kuomintang members, seven Communist members, fourteen members of middle groups, such as the Democratic League and the Youth Party, and nine men not affiliated with any party. By February the conference had agreed on a truce, to be supervised by American officers, with no relinquishment of territory. It further agreed to a State Council representative of all parties in China, a new National Assembly, and a new national army. The agenda of the conference was sensible, and there was an astonishing amount of agreement and compromise. From the point of view of a united China it seemed the Marshall mission would be a success. But suddenly the conference broke down over the issue of Manchuria. The Kuomintang had refused to permit the truce to be extended to Manchuria, and both sides were maneuvering for that still Soviet-occupied area.

When the Soviets finally withdrew in March, they punctiliously turned it over to the Nationalists. However, they first stripped the cities, mines, and industries of everything portable as "war compensation," save for Japanese stockpiles of infantry arms and ammunition, which were turned over to the Communist partisans. At the conference, the Nationalists accused the Communists of moving their forces into Manchuria. The Communists denied it, stating that the Communists in Manchuria were Manchurian and not Chinese. Actually both sides were guilty of breaching an agreement—by using force to occupy territory.

The Nationalists were sure that with United States aid they could hold Manchuria. The Communists were equally sure that they could take it. General Marshall, returning to China, after consultation in Washington, in April, 1946, pointed out the implications of the situation, on which the majority of the conference participants concurred, but neither of the two armed parties would listen. Then Marshall warned the Nationalists that although they were seemingly winning the battle (it had opened on March 18) for Manchuria, at best they were holding their own while draining away those forces needed to hold China proper. Marshall's mediations continued through the summer of 1946, but neither side would give. In his private view, Marshall believed that China's hope lay with the middle groups, but these were helpless, and he knew it. When he left China in July, both sides moved confidently into full civil war. (Whoever did win, the United States would somehow lose. A large number of Chinese were coming to regard the United States as the abettor in an internecine war that could bring death and misery to millions of innocent Chinese.)

Americans, who held some delusory ideas about both the Nationalists and the Communists, believed for the most part that the Kuomintang could win a civil war. American-trained Kuomintang divisions were well armed, well led, and had good morale, and the Nationalists, through the United States, had sole command of air and sea. In addition, in an early test in November, 1945, the Nationalists had decisively beaten the Communists at the supposedly impregnable Shanhaikwan Pass (the Pass had been thoughtfully turned over to the Communists by the retiring Russians). We now know, from Yugoslav Communist sources, that Stalin did not believe that the Chinese Communist insurgents had a chance, and he had advised them to retreat from the war and concentrate on political action.

But both American and Soviet prognoses rested on the belief that the Kuomintang would act wisely and swiftly. The Americans had envisioned a rational strategy and efficient command for the Nationalist forces. Neither materialized. Trapped in the vision of the total reconquest of China, the Kuomintang demonstrated that during all the years of war they had learned nothing of its methods. First, at the end of the Japanese war Nationalist troops, save for the American-trained divisions, were demobilized and an enormous number of men thrown out on the countryside, eventually to be recruited into Communist ranks.

Second, a substantial number of China's good field commanders were forced out and their places taken by Whampoa-trained staff and desk officers. Third, troop movements were controlled by party rather than government, which alienated many Chinese. Fourth, the best strategists, Generals Marshall, Wedemeyer, and Barr, advised the Nationalists against attempting to dislodge the Communists from Manchuria until they had consolidated their own hold on China south of the Wall, pointing out that the armies would only be wasted in a struggle for the looted Manchurian cities. Their advice was disregarded. The civil war got under way with competent Nationalist officers pigeonholed, with the High Command in confusion, and with good divisions placed in indefensible positions. Finally, the end of the war saw a ruined agriculture and an inflation in North China. Floods in 1946 brought famine in some areas, and the systematic destruction of roads and bridges by both sides in the civil war blocked the cities from getting supplies of fuel and food, while in the villages it was almost impossible to market what was grown. In the midst of this situation the Kuomintang persistently conscripted the peasants and taxed them.

ECONOMIC AND POLITICAL COLLAPSE

By 1947 the American advisers were reporting that the military situation was dangerous and that political and economic blunders were sapping Nationalist strength in their own strongholds. The use of Chinese puppet troops and surrendered Japanese troops to oust the Communist forces from North China positions; the clean bill of health given to puppet leaders and their governments "for keeping order"; the assignment of General Okamura, the former Commander-in-Chief of the Japanese Army in China, as military adviser to the Kuomintang: all of these were political blunders. When in 1947 the minor political parties were outlawed and the university campuses raided and the faculty dismissed, arrested, or executed, it seemed as if the Kuomintang were determined to maintain themselves even if it took a police state to do it. The United States, continuing its support, now became part and parcel, in the minds of those affected, of a despotic government.

Indeed, the United States increased its aid, thus, unwittingly, nursing the delusion of Nanking that, no matter what happened, the United States would intervene with its own troops to win the civil war. Up to 1945 American aid had totaled about $1,500,000,000 exclusive of the payments made to Chungking for the support of American forces and operations in China. After the Japanese surrender, a further $642,000,000 was granted, plus military supplies, and there was an additional hundreds of millions of supplies in UNRRA aid. Despite the continuing inflation, the Nationalists returned to North China in a relatively good financial position. North China had, like Manchuria, been built up by the Japanese and offered a sound industrial and commercial base. Instead of cherishing this base, the Nationalists treated North China as enemy territory. It was plundered by returning civil and military officials. A small number of people were aggrandizing the industry and commerce of Kuomintang China, and, in addition, inflation was destroying the economy—by late 1948 the rate of exchange was 12,000,000 to 1.

The terrible inflation was less the result of the scarcity of goods than of an undue reliance upon the printing press. The issue is complex, but it can be stated simply that there was an excessive creation of paper money with a consequent loss of confidence, hoarding, and price rise. This set in after 1945, for, until that time, the Nationalist government had cleverly managed the currency situation. The effect of inflation was serious upon the army, which was supplied only with rice and whose officers and men had to buy all other food from their pay, and upon the fixed income civil service and the faculties and students of the wartime universities. By late 1948 the average price level was 6,250,000 times the average price level at the beginning of the war.

In the countryside the Kuomintang returned the land titles of the landlords and permitted them to demand impossible back rents and interests for the years they had been absent. In addition, returning officials attempted to collect back taxes for the years of Japanese occupation. No actions could have been more calculated to enrage the peasants and throw them into the waiting arms of the Communists. Reoccupying their native land as if they were conquerors, the Kuomintang permitted extortion, carpetbagging, and profiteering, all of which brought about an identity of interests between city and country.

MILITARY DEFEAT

As the Nationalist armies moved north, the Communists, abandoning the cities, moved south and positioned themselves on the flanks and communications lines of the Nationalist forces. In March, 1947, the Communist armies (now the People's Liberation Army) who, it was assumed, would be unable to take the field in the bitter Manchurian winter, began to probe at the Nationalist positions. In the spring and summer, fortified with heavy American weapons gotten from deserting or defeated Nationalist forces, they began full-scale attacks, bottling up the Nationalists in the cities and cutting their supply lines. Through the unimaginative and overconfident strategy of their own command, by mid-1948 the best Nationalist divisions had been trapped in Manchuria. The People's Liberation Army trapped and cleaned up some 700,000 men in Kirin, Mukden, and Changchun. Then they paused to regroup prior to striking out for North China.

The Nationalist situation was desperate and confused. Chiang K'ai-shek had taken personal direction of operations and was frequently in conflict with his own headquarters. Thus the defense of North China was conducted by two Nationalist headquarters without particular reference to each other. Communist strategy, meanwhile, continued successfully in Northwest and Northeast China, where traps were closed on Nationalist armies placed in indefensible positions. By November, 1948, the battle for Central China began. Called the Battle of the Hwai-hai, it was the last great entrapment, and it caught the major concentration of Nationalist troops around Hsuchow: sixty-six divisions surrendered or were destroyed. In the same month, Peking and Tientsin were occupied by the Communists, who now controlled China from the Amur River to the Yangtze.

In July, 1949, Chiang K'ai-shek asked for peace and for the intervention of the Powers, promising the latter military bases in China and the restoration of the unequal treaties. Neither the Powers nor the Communists replied. Chiang then resigned again as President (he had resigned after the Manchurian defeats of 1948, but the army groups had overriden the civilian groups and reinstated him), and General Li Tsung-jen was given the responsibility of holding the Yangtze line. This was an insuperable task, since Chiang still retained actual military control and China's reserves in money and men were being moved to Formosa.

On April 20, 1949, the People's Liberation Army crossed the Yangtze. Now Chiang decided to abandon the old defensive positional strategy and to hold South and Southwest China by mobile warfare. But by October the remaining Nationalist armies had surrendered, while the Nationalist government fled to Formosa.

NOTES

1. Tutelage beginning in 1928 was formally terminated in June, 1948. By that date not a single hsien had become self-governing.

2. Lin Yu-tang and Hu Shih, *China's Own Critics* (Tientsin: Chihli Press, 1931).

3. T. C. Woo, *The Kuomintang and the Future of the Chinese Revolution* (London: Allen and Unwin, 1928), pp. 271-72.

4. In 1928 Peking was renamed "Peiping" by the Nationalists. In 1945, after World War II, the name reverted to "Peking."

5. Mary C. Wright, *The Last Stand of Chinese Conservatism: The T'ung Chih Restoration 1862-1874* (Stanford: Stanford Univ. Press, 1957), p. 519. In that same year, the birthday of Confucius was made an international holiday.

6. Mary C. Wright, "From Revolution to Restoration: The Transformation of Kuomintang Ideology," *FEQ*, XIV, No. 4 (August, 1955), 531-32.

7. H. D. Fong, "Industrial Organization in China, "*Nankai Economic and Social Quarterly*, IX, No. 4 (January, 1937), 953.

8. *Ibid.*, p. 960.

9. *Ibid.*, p. 958.

10. P. T. Ho, *Studies on the Population of China 1368-1953* (Cambridge, Mass.: Harvard Univ. Press, 1959), p. 223, quoting Ch'en Kuo-fu.

11. Conrad Brandt, Benjamin Schwartz, and John K. Fairbank, *A Documentary History of Chinese Communism* (Cambridge, Mass.: Harvard Univ. Press, 1952), p. 88.

12. C. Martin Wilbur, "The Ashes of Defeat," *The China Quarterly,* No. 18 (April-June, 1964), 37.

13. Shinkichi Eto, "Hai-lu-feng—the First Chinese Soviet Government," *The China Quarterly,* No. 8 (October-December, 1961), 177.

14. *United States Relations with China* (Washington, D.C.: Govt. Printing Office, 1949), p. 521.

15. Edgar Snow, *Random Notes on China 1936-1945* (Cambridge, Mass.: Harvard Univ. Press, 1957), p. 2.

16. *United States Relations with China,* p. 522.

17. *Ibid.,* p. 21.

18. "From Shanghai to Peking: The Politics of a Revolution," *Journal of Asian Studies,* XXIII, No. 1 (November, 1963), 115.

19. D. Gillen, " 'Peasant Nationalism' in the History of Chinese Communism," *ibid.,* XXIII, No. 2 (February, 1964), 281.

20. Mao Tse-tung, *Problems of War and Strategy* (Peking: Foreign Language Press, 1954), pp. 14-15.

21. F. F. Liu, *A Military History of Modern China* (Princeton, N.J.: Princeton Univ. Press, 1956), p. 150.

22. Theodore H. White and Annalee Jacoby, *Thunder Out of China* (New York: William Sloane, paperback ed., 1961), pp. 274-75.

23. P. T. Ho, *op. cit.,* p. 251.

24. "Reform of the Kuomintang" (speech delivered July 22, 1950), in *Selected Speeches and Messages of President Chiang K'ai-shek 1949-1952* (Taipeh: Office of the Govt. Spokesman, 1952), pp. 45-54.

Five

The People's Republic of China

Earth revolves. Time is short.
Ten thousand years is too long.
Seize the morning and the evening,
The four seas are in fury, the clouds and water rage,
The five continents erupt with gales and thunder.
Wipe out all harmful creatures
Until no enemy remains.

—Mao Tse-tung

A CAUTIONARY NOTE

The platitude "Changeless China," which for so long informed the pages of Western works on China, persists despite contrary evidence. Before the Communist regime the theme was stated in a kind of sorrow at the hopelessness of China's ever surmounting her traditions and entering the modern, progressive, and aggressive world. Since the Communist takeover the theme is stated in a kind of desperate hope that so much that was admirable about traditional China will temper modern, progressive, aggressive China. The world outside China cannot have the China they want or have back the China they remember. Only the Chinese can determine what China is to be, and observers will be able to understand this only by realizing that the most enormous, basic changes have taken place. The reader has seen

the origins and some of the development of these transformations in economics, politics, society, and intellectual comprehension of the world by Chinese.

Since 1949 these transformations have taken quantum jumps,
and this chapter will examine them. But China today is like the
Indian story of the blind men and the elephant. Each of the
blind men, having felt a single aspect of the beast, described it
in terms totally different from those of the other blind men.
China is the world's elephant, for detailed and accurate information is hard to come by. Ordinarily one acquires information by
living intimately within another culture or by absorbing reliable
information concerning it, but no American has freely reported
on China since 1951, much less lived freely within it. Other
Westerners and Asians who do visit China as reporters or guests
or members of visiting delegations, and those who live there as
members of missions are quite restricted in what they may see
and report. Another way of studying what is going on in a
country is by studying statistical reports. But the new regime in
China started business without a good national statistical service and did not create one until late 1952. The Chinese themselves regarded its product as only fair, and in 1959 the state
statistical service broke down. Since then the Chinese have not
openly published statistical data. What is left for the considera-
tion of the world is what Peking chooses to tell us in its newspapers and journals and on its radio.

Doctrine bends to experience, to the need for training new
Party members and educating young Chinese. Much can be
gleaned from the widely distributed texts and pamphlets by
which the Party instructs the people. A good deal can be inferred, but there is also a good deal that no one knows. With the
exception of a dozen men, hardly anything is well known of the
backgrounds, opinions, or morale of those who control, operate,
and administer that overarching tripod—Party, Government,
Army—that both supports and embraces the system. As for the
masses of the people—particularly the urban dwellers, the general run of the educated, the rank and file of the armed services,
or the cadres of the Party—we have no reliable information

about their conditions or their thinking. What we have are working hypotheses strung over a slender framework of facts.

THE PEOPLE'S GOVERNMENT

Throughout the stage of New Democracy there cannot be and
therefore should not be in China a system of one class dictatorship and one party government.
                    —Mao Tse-tung, *On Coalition Government,* 1945

In March, 1949, a plenary session of the Chinese Communist
Party stated that the center of Party work had now shifted from
the country to the city, and that the Party had to learn how to
build up and govern the cities. To do this it had to attract thousands upon thousands of cadres (deeply committed Party members) from the intellectuals and middle classes of the cities and
train them for work in the country, while the limited number of
experienced Party men worked in the cities. This task obliged
them at the outset of their regime to foster wide cooperation
among all groups in China, for without this cooperation enormous areas could not be brought into political and economic
order. It was in this spirit that, in September, 1949, a People's
Political Consultative Conference was opened whose 662 delegates represented some 45 different parties and groups within
China, and among whom the Communist delegation, while
large, was not a majority. This conference adopted the Organic
Law, established a common program, elected a Council of Government, and on October 1, 1949, proclaimed the People's Republic of China.

The Organic Law set the theory of state power and created a
structure of government. The People's Republic of China is "a
state of the people's democratic dictatorship, led by the working
class, based on an alliance of workers and peasants and allying
all the democratic classes and various nationalities within the
country." [1] The new state guaranteed liberty but reserved the
right to punish those who opposed "the cause of the people."
This new regime had been clearly defined by Mao Tse-tung in
July, 1949, as a people's democratic dictatorship in which only

the people could voice their opinion, while the reactionaries were to be deprived of this right. The new state designated two classes of people, People and Citizens. Citizens were those re- actionaries who could not enjoy the rights of the People but had to observe the obligations of citizenship. They might become People through re-education. The People as well had to be re- educated, but whereas the re-education of Citizens was com- pulsory, the re-education of People was persuasive. It is impor- tant to note that Mao Tse-tung regarded the Chinese as "blank" and had added, "This may seem like a bad thing, but it is really a good thing. Poor people want to change, want to do things, want revolution. A clean sheet of paper has no blotches and so the newest and most beautiful words can be written on it." [2]

The state and its program of re-education was to be guided by a National People's Congress elected through universal suffrage every four years and called into meeting every three years, later annually. Until such time as the First National Congress was elected and called, its work was to be done by a council of 180 members, which would elect, from among its own mem- bers, a Central People's Government Council of 75 members. This latter council, whose chairman was Mao Tse-tung, ad- ministered China through the State Administrative Council, which was somewhat akin to a cabinet. The State Administrative Council, in turn, spun off four major committees: Finance and Economics, Culture and Education, Political and Legal, People's Supervision. These, in their turn, supervised the work of an extraordinary number of ministries, whose proliferation showed the determination of the state to guide and dominate every as- pect of life. While a number of non-Communists were included in high, middle, and low positions, each ministry had Party mem- bers in consequential posts, and the whole net was tied together by a few men acting as an interlocking directorate—for example, Mao Tse-tung was named head of the Party, Chairman of the State Council, and Chairman of the Revolutionary Military Committee. The army was kept apart from the government and under absolute Party control, for it represented the largest single source of disciplined manpower. Therefore, not its commander,

Chu Teh, but the Party chief, Mao Tse-tung, chaired the Military Council. The Ministry of Defense simply executed Party policy.

As time passed certain names changed, some ministries were deleted and others added, and numbers changed. In September, 1954, a unanimous vote of the delegates to the First National People's Congress approved a constitution superseding the Organic Law. But all the new constitution did was increase the centralization of power. The structure of government as servant of the Party remained—and remains—the same. Power is supposed to flow from the village to the national level by a series of People's Congresses to the National People's Congress, a prestigious but powerless and largely ceremonial body. China is governed by the Party and administered by the Council of State (Premier, Vice Premier, and Ministers) who direct the work of the apparatus.

The Party

The People's Republic of China, born of the long, shuddering collapse of traditional China, was the child of the Chinese Communist Party. It had taken the Party over twenty years of civil war to come to power, and unlike any other Communist party, it had succeeded without the urban working class. Instead, it had come into an unusual alliance with peasants and scholars. Its goal was the total and radical reorganization of the institutions of Chinese life and society, but its triumph was not just the end result of mindless historical forces. With the help of—and sometimes despite—these forces, the Party triumphed through the work of totally dedicated men, among them such movers and shakers as P'eng Pai, who founded the first peasant unions; Chu Teh and P'eng Tei-huai, who devised the guerrilla strategy and tactics; Liu Shao-ch'i, theoretician and organizer; and, above all, the leader, Mao Tse-tung. For over forty years this highly realistic man has used and adapted the general theories of Communism as his guides to action. Comprehending perfectly the brutality into which Chinese life had plunged, he also understood the power latent in the vast peasantry. He rode the events of a

long revolution, the witness of whose times had been suffering
in a society where neither duty nor obligation obtained.

To understand the Chinese Communists as people one must try
to understand first this background that gave them the mixture
of disillusion, callousness, selflessness, courage and desperation.
When we look back at history we realize that, although it is easy
for us to locate the mistakes of the past, we would very likely
have acted in the same way as our ancestors did were we in
their place. To live close to the Chinese Communists who, like
other people, are products and victims of their environment,
often gives one the same feeling. It is hardly possible for them
not to be ruthless once they are in power. They are quite as hard
on themselves as on others. Hundreds of trained political workers were sent to work among the aborigines soon after the Communists entered Yunnan. The aborigines lived in a primitive
form of society based on slavery and they would not be inter-
fered with. Hundreds of the political workers were butchered,
but the Party ruled that there should be no reprisals and hundreds more were sent. Charges of hard-heartedness cannot touch
them, not so much because they envy as because they despise
those brought up "on velvet and milk" who wail at every pin-
prick. On 27 February 1957, Mao Tse-tung said that from the
beginning of the People's Republic till then the Communists
eliminated half a million people in China, "not twenty million
as Hong Kong newspapers claimed." Western readers would
certainly think half a million quite a lot of people to kill in a
change of government, but the Communists are most unlikely
to think so. The Sino-Japanese war killed some twenty million
Chinese, a flood in North China took away two or three million,
and in any case the population increases by at least twelve million
annually. Many foreign commentators on modern China tend
to forget that this has been a period of violent seeds and violent
fruits, when desperate conditions justify harsh measures, and
the turmoil has not yet subsided. Mao Tse-tung could talk of
half a million counter-revolutionaries eliminated as if reviewing
statistics of road accidents because his followers and friends
were also killed by the Kuomintang by the thousand. In 1949,
before the retreat to Chengtu, the last stop of the Nationalist
Government on the mainland, hundreds of Communists in the
prison at Chungking were put to death. The theory of class
struggle of course made it impossible for the chain of violence

to be broken by the Communists, but even if it were theoretically possible to attain to a united and stable China peacefully, as some people thought after the recent Sino-Japanese war, it was highly improbable, for psychological reasons, that that would have actually happened. Western observers must continue to judge the Communists with the moral standards of a peaceful democratic society, because they are by habit incapable of doing otherwise, but moral feelings should not stifle sound understanding by pushing the emotional background out of the picture. It requires imagination for those who have never seen China to understand that the country has been too poor for its common people to see any good in democratic ideals. In times of crisis it was not even a matter of choosing between different types of morality; it was simply a situation in which any morality, even the traditional Chinese type, lost meaning, and only practical measures, moral or immoral by peace-time criteria, to save life and provide food were relevant.[3]

Mao Tse-tung was born of a peasant family in Hunan province in 1893. At the age of fifteen he left the farm to attend school, and in 1913 he was admitted to the very good Changsha First Normal School. He was swept up in the New Youth movement, and in 1920, in Shanghai, he underwent the transition to Communism. From 1921 to 1927 he was a Party organizer among the peasants, mostly in Hunan. He was a profound nationalist, equally willing to support the Kuomintang as long as it was truly nationalist, and he backed the Northern Expedition. It was after the break with the Kuomintang that he started to mold his own kind of party. Working in Kiangsi, independently of the Chinese Communist Party in Shanghai, he became the most powerful Communist leader in China. In the obscure days of the Long March he had become Party Chairman, and by 1935 he had attained control of the Chinese Communist Party without owing anything to the U.S.S.R. For fourteen years at headquarters in Yenan he planned for, organized, and led an unusually disciplined and indoctrinated party, which, by 1945, was in control of 90,000,000 people. With the ultimate victory of March, 1949, he moved to Peking as the ruler of a one-party government whose titular head he became in October, 1949. His leading personal qualities were pragmatism, self-assurance, an acute sense of past and present, and an utter conviction of right. He despised his enemies, but he fought them—one by one— and by the succession of victories his and the Party's mission seemed confirmed. This sense of destiny is what now underlies China's policy toward the world.

Mao's greatest achievement was the Chinese Communist Party. It is a party whose most powerful cohesive factor is not so much ideology as an unlimited willingness to sacrifice for the common welfare, and one whose custom when in power is to demand of all other Chinese the same brute dedication. Fundamentally Mao is not a theoretician. His writings are quite dull, and despite the efforts of the Party propagandists to build him up as one of the great creative thinkers of Communism, his theoretical contributions as seen in his speeches and writings are pedestrian. But what he says commands attention, for his words lead to action.

In the years from 1929 to 1935, when he was building his own position and developing the peasant revolution, he was so engaged in organization and tactics that his written works were concerned only with practical problems. Not until after the Long March, when he became Chairman of the Central Committee, did he reveal his thinking on Marxism and Communism. In these writings he shows that knowledge begins and ends in practice. That is, situations change, and theory must accommodate the situations. In 1938 he wrote that Marxism is not an abstract but a living thing when put into a specific national form. The corollary to this was his belief that Chinese Marxists could not separate themselves from the Chinese past nor the Chinese milieu. The discrete kind of Chinese Marxism that he was developing through practice meant a rejection of the Soviet model and the Soviet experience for China and, at least as early as 1935, Mao stated that Chinese Marxism was a unique model better not only for China but for all colonial people. Behind what has come to be called Maoism lies Mao's enormous confidence that the people of China can do anything, and will do it, under his leadership.

In essence Mao's theory seems to be that one pushes until one comes either to failure or to success. Either way, one learns. This is the doctrine of a revolutionist, chauvinist, and supreme technician of organized power, and not the doctrine of an ideologue.

Mao's Party was more cohesive and flexible than any other Communist party in the world. It deliberately fostered a perpetual, internal self-criticism to bar the least glint of deviationism, and it continually took soundings of public opinion, lest it move too far apart from the people. But most importantly it tended to rule by reason as well as force, and in this it has attempted to reform the "thought" of the largest population on earth. The Party was from the onset an elite group organized for the exercise of total power, and its success lay not in any kind of degree of orthodoxy but in the fact that it prevailed empirically. From 1928 to 1948 the Party survived under extreme hardships, and during these years it maintained its purpose and vigor. It was a small party, which developed an iron nerve and concentrated on working at the bottom of Chinese society. It evolved without corruption, fear, or favors, and it began to accrete larger and larger masses of adherents as war loosed the inertia of China.

> The Communist forces were swelled by enormous additions, by whole armies of Kuomintang troops which switched allegiance in the field, ex-puppet forces originally created to police the country under Japanese control, and semi-independent partisan armies which had operated previously at great distances from effective Communist control. The Communist armies became an agglomeration of plebeian soldiery with roots in the land and in the peasantry but with no fixed social or economic orientation. They had nothing to lose and everything to gain from the success of their new allegiance. They were, by and large, declassed masses of men, held together by submission to the authority of the party and of the army and by acceptance of the party program and promises and orders as the quintessence of the higher wisdom. The party leadership itself consisted of a hard core of skilled and able men, practiced in balancing themselves above and between different class groupings, with a well-established system of monolithic party authority and of suppression of any significant dissent. It was able to draw, as its victory became inevitable, on the student youth, with all its passionate and uncritical devotion, as well as upon the inevitable horde of

latecoming adherents, band-wagon jumpers, deserters from the old regime, and middle-roaders leaping into the new orthodoxy. These were, in general, elements which could be counted on to be even more zealously uncritical, and far less high-minded, than the older party cadres. Thus the party and the army both had been converted into instruments quite capable of carrying out, without undue wrenching, any tasks of organization and reorientation that the situation required.[4]

The Chinese Communist Party, as the representative of the working class, leads the people. According to its Constitution, "All questions of a national character or questions that require a uniform decision for the whole country shall be handled by the central party organizations so as to contribute to the centralism and unity of the country." The Party is under the nominal control of its National Party Congress, which meets at irregular intervals (there were no meetings between 1945 and 1956) upon the call of the leadership. This Congress is governed by a Central Committee on which sit 192 members. The Standing Committee, which was selected by the Central Committee, is the core of the Congress and perpetuates itself. The Congress is simply an assemblage of the faithful come to receive the Party line and elect the Central Committee. While the highest organ of the Party is the Central Committee, this too meets only at the call of the leaders. While plenary meetings of the Central Committee were supposed to be held twice a year, it met only seven times between 1945 and 1956, and since 1956 has met only in 1962 and 1966. Between its meetings power is exercised by the Central Political Bureau of nineteen voting members, who vote on policy. Even this is not the apex, which lies in the Standing Committee of the Political Bureau, established in 1956 and consisting of seven members. This topmost leadership is not only small in number but is old in average age. The Political Bureau, like the Central Committee, has become a rubber stamp for the actions of such ad hoc groups as Mao Tse-tung chooses to work through. At the very top, of course, is Mao Tse-tung, who, holding no formal position now in the government, is the unique supreme authority in China. The Party is so organized that its major administrative divisions parallel those of govern-

ment, and in the sense that these components elucidate and enforce policy, it *is* the government.

The Law

At the beginning of the People's Republic, and despite the cry
for cooperation, there was resistance to the Communists, and
large sections of China were kept under military control. The
resistance came from Kuomintang remnants, secret societies,
and anti-Communist groups, and when the Korean war began
it seemed to intensify. Like all dictatorships, the People's Republic created a large secret police force, whose euphemism is
"Social Affairs Department of the Central Committee." With
all means at its command, the new regime was forced to undertake "bandit suppression" campaigns throughout all China.

It is extremely difficult to determine the degree and scope of
resistance and its component parts. But by reading the official
press the firm impression is gained that until 1956 there was
sufficient dissatisfaction with the aims or the pace of the new
regime for the government to launch campaigns against "bandits" or "brigands" each year from 1950 to 1956, and that, after
1951, the substantial resistance was apolitical and came from
hungry villages. After 1956 the specific objectives of government
campaigns are more difficult to determine, for they were undertaken against "counterrevolutionaries" and this is a term applied
to the slightest opposition to the social order. The only certainty
is that opposition exists, is probably unorganized, and abides
largely among farmers.

Yet for the enormous majority, campaigns are not needed.
Satisfaction with China's first peace and unification since 1911
and pride in China's achievements are great binding forces. The
operation of the law, the insistence of propaganda, and the
discipline of education are sufficient controls. The law, based on
the norms of Communist behavior, is a weapon in the hands of
the state for the defense of the proletariat against counterrevolution. China has courts, law, lawyers, and punishments. There is
no adversary system, for the purpose of the criminal law is not
adjudication but education, the reformation of the individual or
the group through public confession or mass trial. Settlement of

civil actions and prosecutions of criminal cases are undertaken in the interest of the Party. It is the Party that, through directives, states what the law is, and every individual case is treated not in accord with the interests of the party at law but with those of the state. Thus crimes are acts of counterrevolution and are set down in broad categories. That is, specific crimes are not defined, while punishment is in accord with the status of the accused and the will of the local Party leader. "There is no law to rely on. When the authorities say kill, we kill. When they say release, we release." [5] Law is the will of the state as understood by the cadres.

In sum, China is governed as a state on a war footing. The enemies are those whose actions or thoughts impinge upon the beliefs of the Party or upon any prospect of leadership that might complement or supplement that of the Party. The undoubted transformation and achievements have been obtained by the imposition of a system of total government of a type literally unknown in the world before, for not only is the familiar uniformity of action and expression sought, but also a uniformity of interior belief, indeed of emotion. The commanders of the war are the Party members (some 12,000,000 in 1964) who work in obedience to the directing leaders of the Party. Knowing this, one cannot assume that they will always act from rational self-interest for the simple reason that on occasion they act according to their "law of history," which states there will be times when they will, inevitably, be at a disadvantage. Those times are to be suffered because it is their duty to take the determined road, no matter how difficult, that leads to the future. In the total context of the People's Republic, it is futile to talk of Changeless China:

> For the substance of the respective orthodoxies must count for something, and Confucian harmony is not Marxist struggle, Confucian permanence is not Marxist process, Confucian moralism is not Marxist materialism. And the rationalizations of the intelligentsia's power count for something, and Mencius' cool account of the way of the world—that those who work with their hands always support those who work with their heads— is not the pious Maoist profession that the workers inspire the

intellectuals who, simply by chance of their having education in a society still largely illiterate, necessarily take the official posts at first in a complicated system. Nor is the educated man's prestige as an amateur in Confucian society the prestige of the technically specialized product which Chinese communist education is seeking. Marxist classics, communist bureaucracy, even Huai River water-control are not so suggestive of old China exclusively that all Chinese history since the Opium War, with its social upheavals and intellectual agonies, should be reckoned just sound and fury. The categories of Chinese communist thought are not traditional. This is the salient fact. And it is belied neither by some communist taste for traditional achievement (Tun-huang frescoes or the odd phrase from a Confucian classic), nor by some communist casting in traditional roles.[6]

The Transformation of Society

The aims of education were set forth by Mao Tse-tung when he stated that educational policy must enable everyone who gets an education to develop morally, intellectually, and physically and become a cultured, socialist-minded worker.

The same aims have been stated more succinctly as "Reds first, specialists second," for Mao believes that no one can become an expert on anything unless he first becomes a Communist. Therefore the objectives of the entire school system are to produce those who are both "Red and expert."

THE INTELLECTUALS

The Chinese Communist Party had to draw on a bank of intellectuals—that is, Chinese who had graduated from a school—whom it considered of uncertain loyalty to the new creed. Sick of war, corruption, and inflation, these intellectuals had fallen away almost totally from the Kuomintang. Yet they were not Communist; they simply hoped that, with the Communists, they could give China peace, stability, and strength. The Communists who had to use them did not trust them. Many of them, especially those in their thirties and older, had been trained abroad and were regarded as either too deeply rooted in Western values or in the Chinese past to be trustworthy. But they formed the only source of managerial, administrative, and technical abilities.

The Party began a dual program of re-educating the non-Party intellectuals and of ensuring the future by reorganizing and reorienting the entire educational system. The younger ones were already committed; the older intellectuals, however, were a problem. But, on the premise that thought determines action, the Party was certain that "re-education" would work. It knew it could use clichés on the masses but that the re-education of intelligent men demanded a certain finesse. The answer was found in the application of well-known psychological principles, combined with some positive controls. Under the supervision of leaders who reported on their groups to the next highest authority, study groups gathered together each day for several hours. These were mandatory meetings of small membership wherein the principles of the Party and the revolution were endlessly discussed in relation to the life and work and thought of each individual in the group. No one could remain silent, for through the criticism of others, even conformable positions were ruthlessly analyzed until one admitted that only a single way was right.[7] Whether repeated exposure led from pretense to the acceptance of "reality" can only be known in individual cases but, generally speaking, the endless routine of self confession did produce a conformity. The confessions themselves were meaningless to the authorities. It was enough that for a few the process created genuine conversion, and for the many, fear.

Ordinarily the confession process, creating both fear and humiliation, is sufficient; if a man persists in remaining intractable he will starve, since there is no hope of jobs outside government favor. Outright persecution is not needed, for unemployment and hunger are sufficient weapons. But if this informal method does not work, more positive controls come into operation. Beginning in 1951, for example, stubborn intellectuals were put into special reform centers. Other controls are the declassing of intellectuals by making them participate in the lives of workers and peasants; the forced participation in what can only be called "hate campaigns," such as "Resist America"; the consistent indoctrination of teachers, artists, writers, and professionals against "bourgeois ideology"; and placing able men under the direction of Party cadres (young, intolerant people who prefer the "Red" to the "expert" and who direct the work of the expert according to the current line in everything from biology to literature). From 1950 to 1956 there was an intense re-education campaign, followed, in that last year, by a relaxation that produced a torrent of criticism against Party incompetence, with the result that in 1958 the orthodoxy was tightened.

The conflict between intelligence and servitude, rooted in Marxism, is the dilemma of intellectuals under the Chinese Communist regime. They support the ends that are the strength and the pride of modern China, but they do not like the means. Nevertheless, they cannot escape. This is the kind of system where everyone must participate and no one can withdraw. By and large the situation is rationalized. Loyalty to the doctrine is equated with loyalty to China. A man declasses himself by accepting a lower standard of living as a glorified privation; and if he forfeits his conscience, he assumes, as a substitute, faith in a materialism from which, eventually, all things will flow.

THE SCHOOL SYSTEM

Between 1949 and 1953 education was totally reorganized. Private schools were abolished, although the government permitted communes, factories, and organizations to set up their own schools—that is, to pay for them while the government controlled them. Six years of elementary schooling were given. These were not free, for China is too poor to support the army of teachers called for by the enormous demand for literacy and education. Therefore, fees are demanded that vary according to the locality. Admission to schools above the elementary level is by examination. Education is political, designed to produce fighters in the class struggle. Youth are indoctrined in the general line of love for and obedience to the Party, which is taught as "Communist morality." The solidarity of the collective life is taught in groups, not only by work, play, and study, but by the downgrading of personal ambitions for excellence, which is defined as that which is at the service of the whole group and not the individual.

At the highest level of education a vast number of new universities were created rapidly. Many of them were short-term revolutionary universities for the training of cadres drawn from the workers and peasants. Students were given food and clothing, and there were no entrance examinations. Nor were there books. Instruction was by lecture and discussion, and the subject was the study of history as the development of class struggle. Students were graduated after four months and went to work for the state and Party where needed. The old universities and the new permanent universities were set up as a system of specialized institutes. There was a drop in the number of general universities and a great surge in the number of technical schools. Weak schools were eliminated and their staffs incorporated into the stronger schools. Enormous emphasis was given to highly specialized training wherein a student became not a civil engineer but a highway specialist or a specialist in bridge building; not a mechanical engineer but a specialist in boilers. Everything Western was purged, and Soviet methods, teachers, and texts were adopted wholesale. The ability to read Russian was held at a premium. Collegiate examinations were set by both the instructor and the class, and grades given were subject to review by class discussion. The theory behind this was that the old examination system was tyrannical and bourgeois. No matter what one's specialty, everyone spent three years in study of the Russian language and a substantial amount of time in political study and discussion.

The push toward narrow technical specialization was in answer to the great need for research, management, and literate workers. But the speedup in training sacrificed quality. The short course meant sketchy training. Doctors were being turned out with two years of medical school and no internship, and while on the one hand this gave medical help to people who never in their lives had had medical assistance, on the other it was a dead end, for such a system devours itself, providing no time or training for real research or for real teachers. And, while there had been exceptional advances in the pharmaceutical, petroleum, and chemical industries since 1949, the subordination of scientific to political training was impairing the long-range supply of scientists and technicians. The quality of scientific and technical graduates was low and there was not a sufficiently qualified supply to replace the aging Western-trained scientists. Also there existed no overall objective research policies for science.

The quantification of education and the emphasis on producing "Communist man" damaged the academic role of schools, for both teachers and students, at all levels, were at the constant beck and call of nonacademic needs, as can be seen in this description of a student caught between politics and education:

> Our mother country anxiously awaits institutions of higher learning to cultivate construction personnel, but I witnessed the following situation at Fu-tan University. A [woman] student in biology, who is a Communist Party member and a member of the Organization Committee of the local [Party] branch, flunked two of the seven examinations this time, scoring 51 in chemistry and 41 in physics. . . . Since the opening of school, she has participated in countless big meetings, small meetings, discussion meetings, and report meetings, etc. She attends meetings during the day, during the evening, and sometimes deep into the night, consuming all of her rest hours, and study and class time. Of the five chemistry assignments she fulfilled only one, and all three physics assignments were neglected. She is physically exhausted to sickness, taking medicine and shots regularly. She knows well how to learn, but the works ordered by the [Party] leader cannot be declined; she has no choice but to attend the meetings.[8]

The education of "Red experts" demanded that students be put on half-work and half-study programs, with the labor duty serving as a disciplinary measure. But by 1958 it was evident that education, if it were to be good and useful, was a full-time job in itself; and that same year there began an intensive concentration on short-term and highly specialized technical study and work, a sort of on-the-job training, in a series of new "universities." The results of this plan were poor, and in 1961 there came a major shift in education from doctrine to honest specialized study. It was admitted that waste and mediocrity occurred in science where dogma and politics had taken charge. The values of academically sound scientific education were now put at the fore, and those academicians in other subjects were reminded that their duty was to produce the New Man while their scientific colleagues produced the technicians and engineers. In 1963 an intensive propaganda campaign was started, urging all to achieve a socialist education by studying and emulating Mao Tse-tung, and in which China was told that:

> To study the thinking of Mao Tse-tung one must learn his firm proletarian stand and his consistent revolutionary spirit, learn his methods in tackling and solving problems with dialectical materialism and historical materialism, learn his elaborate and agile art in waging the revolutionary struggle and learn his work style of maintaining close contact with reality, of concerning himself with the life of the masses, of keeping close touch with the masses and of adhering to hard work and plain living.[9]

Education became China's greatest factory, with the state determining the number, size, and type of schools, the number and classification of students admitted, the various curricula and even the retention or dropping of students. Then, in mid-1966, coincidental with the Great Proletarian Revolution, the entire school system was shut down for an indefinite period. At least all admissions to school were deferred from June, 1966, to an indefinite date in 1967. The closure was based on Peking's finding that the educational system was, like much of Chinese society, politically unreliable and that the universities in particular had been spawning grounds for "revisionism." "Bourgeois-royalist" university presidents were removed and a new educational system was planned when the schools opened. Only students sufficiently indoctrinated in the principles of the revolution were to be admitted—meaning politically reliable workers, peasants, and soldiers who already comprised over 60 per cent of the student body of the Chinese university system—and to ensure this, entrance examinations were to give their greatest weight to political factors, while entrance to graduate work would demand membership either in the Chinese Communist Party or in its youth organizations. The content of education and its length were to be altered. Class prejudice was to be eliminated from education by dispensing with marks, and it was believed possible to dispense with textbooks and to teach entirely from the thoughts of Mao Tse-tung. University courses of study were to be, at a maximum, three years, with a part of each year devoted to work in the factory or on the farm.

The goal of Chinese education then, even of the best, is to serve the state and build for the people. To this end, despite the years of experimentation, teachers, students, materials, and curricula are controlled by the Party.

The Hundred Flowers

In the mid-1950's the conflict between ends and means seemed to affect a substantial number of intellectuals, professionals, and students. They had seen through the verbal placebos of the regime, and the Party decided to let them complain openly because in fact the Party seems to have believed that the complaints were trivial and that it had indeed achieved a reorientation of thought. In 1956, with the slogan "Let a hundred flowers blossom together; let a hundred schools of thought contend," the door was thrown open for public criticism. The intellectuals were invited by Chairman Mao himself to criticize constructively the regime as "gentle breezes or mild rain." This was the year of the Hungarian revolt, a lesson to all Communist parties in party-people relations. At first the response was most cautious; but goaded by the Party to really speak up, a torrent of criticism broke in early 1957. Hardly any restriction or authority were left untouched. A bitter, outspoken, and voluminous attack broke loose particularly from university students. The Party was stunned, for the prevailing tone was not anti-Marxist but anti-Party. All complained of the political domination of education and the arts; all spoke against the controlled press, against the corruption of justice, against the irrational worship of the Party. Particularly resented was the politicalization of education. African students, for example, left Peking resentful about being socially segregated and getting a bad education.

No narrative can do as much justice to the Hundred Flowers campaign as the following excerpts from a rare collection of letters of the students at Peking University:

At present, many people are responding by saying "yes" out loud but meaning "no" in their hearts.[10]

The problem is that the Party has taken the place of the government. The Communist Party is the party in power; its prestige is very great and it is the seat of all real power. The law is only a matter of formality.[11]

I protest against Chairman Mao's recent statement to the [Youth] League Central [Committee] that "the Party is the leadership core in all work, and any deviation from socialism is erroneous." This statement should be translated as follows: "It is necessary to accept Party dictatorship; anyone who opposes the words of the super-emperor is wrong and should be killed forthwith." They've prostituted the words "People" and "Social-ism." [12]

The Chinese people have been deceived. When they coura-geously drove out the imperialists and the Chiang K'ai-shek gang, they put their trust in the wrong man. We used a robber's knife to drive out another robber. When one robber had been killed, we gave the knife to the other one.[13]

Getting "poisonous weeds" instead of flowers, the Party struck back with a campaign against "Rightists." There was a severe repression of the critics, public confessions were extorted, enemies were forced out of office at all levels and in all walks of life. Student privileges were withdrawn and the universities placed under surveillance. Beginning in 1958, students were forced to devote less time to study and more time to mass meet-ings. A great busyness was designed to keep students in safe and unrevolutionary activities and to leave them little time for re-flection, much less criticism. Nevertheless, the Party's vision that whole classes could be educated into socialism was shattered. It realized it could never relax, for there were seemingly in-destructible bourgeois elements among the intellectuals. Indeed, since 1957 no open criticism of the Party has been invited.

Propaganda and Culture

Like all good mass propaganda, Peking's propaganda consists of simple statements repeated over and over again. People, the premise states, will believe something if they hear it often enough and if there is no basis for comparison. In the early years of the regime, the people were told that not the United States but Russia had defeated Japan. This was, originally, treated with ridicule, for masses of Chinese knew quite differently, but as time went on the statement began to be taken seriously, as people began to wonder whether perhaps under the Kuomintang the truth had been hidden from them. With such strokes of black and white the whole world is presented to the Chinese people. The state gained complete control of all means of communication. With the Communist conquest, Kuomintang newspapers and radio stations became Communist newspapers and radio stations, often with identical staffs. These media restricted their news to that which happened in Russia and Eastern Europe. There was nothing else to read and nothing else to hear. Whether this fully succeeded can only be answered generally. Among the older generation it did not succeed. Among the children it succeeded well. Those who attained their majority under the present regime have the normal cultural arrogance of the Chinese along with a vast and willful ignorance of the world.

> The young Chinese, in striking contrast to the young Russian nowadays, does not imagine that he can learn anything from the West. To judge by those I met, their ignorance of life beyond their own borders is stunning, although perhaps no greater than that of Russians before the death of Stalin. This ignorance is exceeded only by their lack of interest. In my three weeks in China, only one person asked me about my own country or about any other country I had visited. He was a university graduate, and his question was: "Is it still possible to buy and sell Negroes in the United States?" From the Chinese point of view, they do not need to learn anything because they already know.[14]

Communications media are only a part of the control of the mind and spirit used by the Party. Group activities also control a man's life. In the true Communist pattern there is no use for the individual but only for groups or classes. Men and women study together, work together, play together, and talk together. Nonconformity is regarded with horror and group activity is the denominator of conformity. There are numerous mass organizations designed to sop up the time and energy left over from work. In these activities—trade groups, factory groups, study groups and schools, youth organizations, women's organizations, communal groups—men can realize a kind of individuality, release their desires, and be a part of something. Far more than in Confucian China, here in the Communist regime everyone knows his place. There is no other place, no room to hide.

In such a system hypocrisy may be expected. There is no other way to explain why, in the initial years of the system, educated men who knew better made the most incredible public statements. Had they not made them, they would have been alienated from Chinese society. Yet for years, outside observers, viewing this physical and intellectual regimentation, fatally underestimated the attraction of the Chinese Communists. A deep, passionate nationalism is the greatest asset Peking has. It is this, at the bottom, that enables the regime to call for the most enormous sacrifices from the population. To oppose the Party is to oppose China. To be a Chinese is to be Communist. Critics failed to see that Peking was building the most efficient administration in modern Chinese history or that face, graft, and favor were swept away. Nor did they see that the youth, while gullible from a Western standpoint, were being motivated by a tremendous sense of purpose; tens of thousands of them were living on bare subsistence and working at all kinds of jobs in a dedicated manner, with the vision of a new life and a new society to be built on the sacrifices of their generation. The new pattern had little if any place for the family. Children were turned against their parents and husbands and wives separated, in the best interests of the state.

In the creative arts and especially literature, Lenin's position that "Literature must become Party literature" was taken. When the Party took power it began to exercise direct controls over creativity in the arts, insisting on "national forms" and the end of the Western tradition in literature; for not only did Mao enjoy the popular Chinese literature, but literature was to assist the Party in getting rid of the middle-class mentality, which looked to the West for models of reform.

Beginning in 1964 the most rigid cultural orthodoxy, the purpose of which was to make Chinese culture self-sufficient on Maoist principles, was placed in effect. Translations of Western literature were removed from bookstores, foreign films were barred from being shown, and the works of the writers of the May Fourth Movement were not republished. Originality in literature was forbidden and writers were instructed that any fiction not consonant with the thought of Chairman Mao was evil, for there was no middle ground between what was evil and the thought of Chairman Mao. Writers who resisted were disgraced and their reputations destroyed.

> The remainder manufactured literature. As time passes literature becomes propaganda written by a generation grown up without the knowledge of individual creativity who dutifully manufacture propaganda simply because it is physically less taxing and materially more rewarding. . . .[15]

A doctrinaire attitude is also taken toward the sweep of the past. There was an early tendency to denigrate achievements of the past as "reactionary" or "feudal" and to insist on a brand new culture that would be "modern" and "scientific." While it was admitted that there were some socially valuable things from the past, they could not be permitted to exist side by side with the present if the masses were to be culturally homogenized. This is one reason why artists and intellectuals were to toil with their hands while workers and peasants were to be encouraged as poets and artists wherever they had the capacity. In 1960 this attitude was modified and more discriminating attention was paid to the past, for it was realized that it is awkward for a fervent nationalism to divorce itself from its own past. In the material past, such as with archeology, great care is taken in the recovery and display of artifacts. In literature, art, and music, however, creativity is still judged by the standards of "socialist realism."

THE PEOPLE'S LIVELIHOOD

The machine is my husband
The factory is my family

> *The fruits of my labor are my children*
> *The Party is my father and mother.*
> —A Communal Slogan

The Economic Mobilization of China

The Chinese Communist Party recognized the primacy of economic reconstruction and industrial development.

> The effect, good or bad, great or small, of the policy of practice
> of any Chinese political party on the Chinese people depends
> in the last analysis on whether and how much it helps to develop
> their productive forces, and whether it fetters or liberates their
> productive forces.[16]

Its goal was the attainment of a socialist economy through a "step by step" era of transition, during which the privately owned sector of the economy was to be slowly "remolded." Its hidden problem was whether a revolutionary party in arms could do the day-to-day job of building a complex modern economy; if doctrine were permitted to rule economic development, the results could be ruinous. The results of the first fifteen years of industrialization can be divided into, roughly, three periods: (1) an initial period of caution (to 1952); (2) a period of rapid moves to collectivization in industry and agriculture (1952-58), continuing into communalization and an intense mobilization of labor (1958-61); and (3) a period of recovery from the mistakes and disasters of the second period.

THE PERIOD OF RECONSTRUCTION

In October, 1949, China was a land ruined by war, inflation, and misgovernment. In her litany of poverty there were not enough land, tools, animals, fertilizer, machines, steel, power, roads, capital, transport, factories, or money. There was too much labor and too much hunger. It could be easily seen that needs would have to be met through the extensification, industrialization, and cooperation of agriculture, which would permit an annual rise of 4.3 per cent and enough forced savings to provide the capital to invest in light and heavy industry. Initial steps planned by the Party were the total mobilization of agriculture, whose increased production would not, it was hoped, be consumed by a rise in population, and the investment of the surplus of this agricultural production in heavy industry, aiming at an annual increase of 15 per cent. The heaviest industry (steel, power machine tools) was chosen as an emblem of power, in an unfortunate emulation of the Soviet experience. In addition, the Party believed it impossible to achieve industrialization without totalitarian methods. It was easy to take over control of existing industry, for 66 per cent of it had belonged to Japan and 9 per cent to other foreign owners, all of which had been taken by the Kuomintang as spoils of war and turned over to state corporations in 1946. Thus, the Chinese Communists inherited an almost totally state-owned heavy economy. What was not state owned was directly expropriated or harassed out of existence, with the exception of a small, privately owned segment, which was permitted to remain until 1951, when it, too, was driven out of business.

The urban labor force was as easily taken over. A strike ban and compulsory arbitration were put into effect, along with such disciplinary measures as labor passports, which froze men and women to their jobs. Wage rates were placed on the stretch-out-speed-up system, where workers who achieved the high norms of production got the highest pay. Trade unions were encouraged, but simply as arms of the state for labor discipline. Communal facilities (toilets, kitchens, and baths) were provided as an amelioration for workers in a country too poor to provide them on any other basis, and a rationing system was introduced to maintain at least a fair minimal living for all. As depressing as this might seem to workers in more advanced countries, the hard labor and meager supply of Chinese industrial workers attracted the hundreds of thousands of impoverished countrymen who were coming into the cities. It was certainly better than that which they had left behind.

Management was in the hands of bureaucrats, which posed a real danger to development, for state managers are responsible not to the market but to the state; and while the market signals failure rapidly, by the time the state discovers that something is wrong the damage is often irreparable.

From 1949 to 1954 China was administered in seven large regions. Then, with the first Five Year Plan it was decided to treat China as an economic unit. In 1957 the trend toward economic centralization was stopped because of the great variations in local standards and outputs, and it was decided to treat China as a series of cooperating economic zones. China today is composed of twenty-two provinces (2,200 hsien), two autonomous regions, and two metropolitan areas (Peking and Shanghai). Economic policy itself was planned by the State Council and administered by its four technical commissions: State Planning, National Economy, State Capital Construction, Scientific and Technological. The State Economic Commission was established in 1956 to handle planning and execution on an annual basis, while the other commissions were concerned with long-range planning and investment.

Until 1953, the emphasis was on patching up the economy and getting started, and very substantial achievements were made in construction of dams, power plants, railroads, steel and machine factories and in the production of heavy industrial materials. The first Five Year Plan (1953-57) was initiated with relatively modest objectives but with emphasis on labor intensive methods—that is, methods that use a great amount of human labor, as opposed to machine labor—and on irrigation; more food was needed, which meant a remaking of agriculture both technically and with regard to the social structure of the peasantry.

LAND REFORM AND COLLECTIVIZATION

The formal history of Chinese Communist land theories and policies goes back to the 1927 period of the attempted Soviets. The initial Kiangsi policy had been to dispossess the landlords and redistribute their land among the poor peasants while winning over the "middle" peasants. This was done on a trial-and-error basis; and though little is known of the period, the Party did learn that simple redistribution was not the answer. Rather, the answer was increased production through modernization. With the opening of the struggle against Japan in 1937, confiscations were halted in order to win the broadest possible support among all rural Chinese, and in those areas that the Party controlled, the emphasis was on the control of rents and interest rates.

The leaders of the Party were not peasants, and their interests in the villages were ideological, but in the 1930's and 1940's they learned a great deal about the government of villages, rural organization, and propaganda in the countryside. They cherished, however, the delusion that there did exist in China an elite rural "feudal" landlord class such as had, in fact, once existed in Russia and in Europe. And they were, as Liu Shao-ch'i stated, committed to land reform as a measure of class war:

> The basic aim of agrarian reform is not purely to relieve the impoverished peasant. It is to free the rural productive forces from the shackles of the feudal system of land ownership by the landlord class, in order to develop agricultural production and thus pave the way for the New China's industrialization.[17]

Since they classified as "landlords" about 12,000,000 people with their dependents, they proposed to eliminate an entire social class. Actually, the Party had to instruct the peasants in how to recognize a landlord, for where there were no landlords they were created by Party definition. If a "rich" peasant drew more than 25 per cent of his income from rents then he was a "landlord." But the real problem was not that 50 per cent of China's arable land was owned by 4 per cent of her families who lived among and were, generally, indistinguishable from their tenants. The real problem was the monopolization of the rural money and credit supply by a mass of moneylenders and usurers.

Observers were puzzled by the 1950-51 expropriations of land when about 70 per cent of the peasantry became owners of, on an average, only one acre per family, a unit so small as to condemn China eternally to low productivity and to deprive the state of the food it needed for the army, for the urban groups, and for industrialization. Observers did not understand that this expropriation was just the first step in the class struggle. It was the beginning of a controlled terror designed as a school of revolution for the rurality. The rural ruling class was to be knocked out and the peasants shown how to organize. Land reform was

planned as a political school combining reform with rural education, literacy programs, health programs, the interconnection
of the countryside by roads and telegraph, and the teaching of
agricultural technology. In other words, the Party saw land reform as part of a massive attempt to upgrade the political sense
of the peasant, to give him self-respect and a comprehension of
what was going on. By bringing into being a new class of literate
agrotechnical workers, the Party would have bound to itself the
most important force in China.

Land reform, as it began in 1950, was undertaken quite cautiously. Landlords and moneylenders were forced to make resti-
tution for their previous oppressions and, in large numbers, were
tried and sentenced to death or imprisonment or deprived of all
power and privilege. This met with general approval among the
peasantry, but since, as has been pointed out, there was in China
no small and easily identifiable landlord class but rather a mass
of millions of people whose destruction, however satisfying or
just, threatened to disrupt agriculture, the Party soon exempted
"rich" peasants from trial and confiscation.

In 1951, it was announced that within three years land reform
would be completed. This was correct insofar as the old order
of sharecropping and usury had been destroyed. But the problem in 1951-52 was no longer landlords but production. There
were more Chinese eating more food and there was a large army
and a large city population demanding more food. The forced
deliveries of grain were inadequate to the need.

The next move was to establish agricultural cooperatives. This
took the form of "mutual aid teams" and "producers' cooperatives." In the "elementary" cooperative each member retained
the plot of land given him by reform. In the "advanced" or
"higher" cooperative he yielded his land to the cooperative but
retained his own garden plot. In the elementary cooperative
each member received a share according to what he put into
the organization in the way of land, labor, and tools. In the advanced cooperative each member received according to his labor
input and was to be reimbursed in the future for his capital investment of land and tools. A member could withdraw—he still
held title to his land—but this was inadvisable since only the

cooperatives got fertilizer, seed, credit, and new ploughs. Also, the state was now the only marketing agency; nothing could be bought or sold in the countryside save through an official organization. The unorganized could not exist. Again, as with expropriation, the results were intended to be more than economic.

It was imperative to break up that rival to the Party—the family. The individuals who made up the family had been forced to identify themselves with the Party and the state. Land reform had involved the classification of everyone as a landlord, rich peasant, middle peasant, poor peasant. The villages had been commanded to hold "speak bitterness" meetings against selected individuals and families in which the selected received penalties ranging from ostracism to death. The consequent disruption of families and clans broke the structure of rural and family government and helped to atomize the peasantry.

Now, by ending the ancient family ownership, the Party-directed cooperative replaced the family as the economic-social unit of the Chinese village. With the end of the family as a power came the end of parental stultification of the economic and emotional destiny of young Chinese, and a great freedom of movement and vertical social mobility were established for the individual while, for the state, the integration of cooperatives brought about the first centrally directed national structure in Chinese history. But the need for more food and more agricultural taxes for investment capital worried Peking. Production, at the least, had to be kept level with the rising population, but the cooperatives failed their quotas, and there was resistance from the peasants. In 1954 and 1955 there were poor harvests. In many cases peasants worked hard but seemingly only to become capitalists themselves. There was still much rural unemployment, and, as a result of the agricultural imbalance, industry was suffering.

The economic transformation that had been proceeding slowly and cautiously now took a different path. In 1955 a sudden move to labor and agricultural collectivization was ordered. This decision, contrary to Soviet advice and to the warnings of Chinese economic experts, was evidently made because of the Party's belief that the Chinese people should be directed toward desired ends and that China was now ready for the great struggle against nature. Within eight days of the announcement, it was stated that millions of peasants had spontaneously given their land to the collective. Whether true or not, the collectivization of agriculture was completed by fiat and by force within a year.

Collectives are not farms per se. They are large-scale enterprises that demand advanced techniques, managerial skill, and the application of electric power. The farmer becomes a salaried employee, and his title in land is voided. The stripping away of the cherished and long-fought-for individual holding in the land was a blow to the relations between Peking and the peasant. Until collectivization, the peasantry had stood with the new regime and had accepted the leadership of the Party. Between May and December, 1955, this seemingly indestructible link between village and Party was, if not broken, badly corroded. By taking away the peasant's land the Communist government resembled any previous government. The state had created a new landlord class—itself.

However, there was economic improvement. The agricultural tax was based on the normal annual yield of the income-producing land, payable in cash, grain, or other crops, with provision for surtaxing or remission, depending upon the actual yield. It was honestly collected. By throwing out middlemen, improving roads and canals, controlling price fluctuations, and establishing rural credit, the marketing of crops was enormously improved, although the state, by controlling the market, did in effect levy a hidden additional tax when it set a low market price. The pace of collectivization was hard, but harder still was the fact that grain collections still tended to remain static while population rose, and much rural labor was underdeveloped. Evidently further steps were needed.

The Great Leap Forward

"The Great Leap Forward"—the mass mobilization of Chinese to raise industrial and agricultural production—got under way in the fall of 1957. Dizzy with political success, convinced the masses could do the job without incentives, and utterly disregarding the limitations of China's resources, the Party embarked on the total rural and urban communalization of China.

THE COMMUNES

The commune was defined by the Party as "the basic unit of Communist society." There was no single kind of commune, nor were they restricted to the countryside. There were city communes and industrial communes as well as agricultural communes. A commune was a tripartite organization. At its base was the production team, consisting of twenty to thirty neighboring families at work on their common land (the number would vary with the density of population, local habits, terrain, and crops). Eight to ten teams, sometimes an entire village, formed a production brigade, and an aggregate of twenty to forty brigades, managing great amounts of land, made up the commune itself. The production team shared out of its net annual proceeds according to the individual's labor input during the year, and the brigade set the crop programs for the teams and allocated land. Land management, water conservation, and heavy construction were planned and managed overall by the commune. Each member of the commune (whether rural or urban) labored all year at whatever task was at hand, and there being no slack season, he worked hard. He turned everything he possessed over to the commune—bedding, savings, clothes, utensils—and in return the commune guaranteed him food, shelter, clothing, medical care, and burial. He could not leave the commune, for no one else would feed or employ him.

Communalization of China was instituted hastily and ruthlessly, and although officials reported it as being a great success, the inception of true Communism, resistance began almost at once. There were a significant number of Party cadres who sympathized with the peasant dislike of communalism, but not enough to balance the fanatic drive of most of the cadres, who were made responsible for the success of the teams, brigades, and communes. The following year, the Party encouraged criticism from within the communes and received a mountain of complaints, directed at the abuse of power by bureaucrats, at the unreasonable demands made upon the workers, and indeed at the whole communal idea. The Party responded by blunting the intolerance of the cadres and permitting a bit of grass-roots democracy in the countryside, but at the same time an attack on "Rightists" was launched. The fact was, as the Party Central Committee itself stated, the peasant and the worker were being driven beyond endurance. Twelve-hour days with only two rest days a month were grinding down an underfed people.

At first the communes paid monthly wages, but they were not always paid on time and not always fairly paid. So a system of "work points" was put into operation whereby one was paid according to the quantity and the quality of his work, and a sharing-out of profits, based on the accumulation of these points, was made twice a year. The points were based on "norms," and in large communes there were hundreds of norms, for everything from fabricating clothes to hauling manure. The same was true in the cities, where industries and crafts, and repair and maintenance were communalized, with each factory or shop having its dormitories, nurseries, and mess halls. Unlike the country, where society was one big commune, the cities were aggregates of communes. But the cities lacked the discipline, naïveté, and homogeneity of the countryside. They were big and complex, with shifting masses of people and with a level of sophistication that knew how to ignore or short-circuit street and ward Party leadership.

In 1958 urban communalization was, in effect, stopped because it was not working. But the Great Leap Forward did not slacken. Every possible device was used to train labor, to use the unemployed, and to disperse production. Great efforts were put into small-scale projects, like "backyard" steel, made within a smelter that could be built cheaply of local materials within a week. Although the unit production of such a smelter would be small, the aggregate production of tens of thousands of these smelters, it was hoped, would enable China to surpass Great Britain in steel production. Unfortunately the results were inferior steel, which no amount of exhortation or sweat could make into good steel.

The substantial increases in techniques, number of engineers, and heavy industry that had been so marked up until 1956 had depended, to a degree unrealized by the Chinese, on Soviet aid. The impressive growth of industrial complexes in Manchuria and North China, the tripling of railway mileage, the five-fold increase in coal tonnage, the control of inflation, and the rebuilding of the cities had been due to the utmost marshalling of China's resources and to Soviet aid. In 1959 the strain told. Factories began to close down, the steel output dropped considerably below capacity, textile mills laid off workers and sent them to join their relatives in the countryside, and trains moved slowly, while miles of cars lay on sidings for lack of parts. Coal production dropped, too, and with it, power production. Everything dependent on coal power, from river steamers to locomotive plants, slowed to a halt. Workers were exhausted trying to attain impossible production targets. Good Chinese engineers were shunted aside by the slogan "Let politics rule the factories," and the Russians began to go home. In the countryside, where all of Peking's hopes had been based, natural disasters—floods, storms, insect plagues, droughts, and frosts—struck for three straight years at half of China's croplands, destroying one-sixth. The great water conservation projects, designed to reclaim and serve the land, had been built on a crash basis without adequate planning.

The only means that Peking had of measuring the Great Leap lay in the government statistical system. This proved unreliable and short-handed for the task, and it was discovered too late that the cadres' passion for results had led to the falsification of figures. The result was an inordinate lag between failure and Peking's comprehension of it. For example, in April, 1958, Chou En-lai had announced a spectacular and continuing rise in grain production. In August of that same year it was announced that these rises were nonexistent and that future crop estimates would have to be cut by one half. Disaster and mismanagement brought hunger. In 1960 stringent food controls were put into effect. The following year Peking began buying great quantities of wheat from Australia and Canada; flour and grain from France, Argentina, and West Germany; sugar from the Soviet

Union; and powdered milk from New Zealand and the United Kingdom. Payment for these was made in gold, severely upsetting China's balance of payments, depleting her small reserves, and curtailing her ability to buy in the world market materials, machines, and parts for her industry. In 1959-61 agricultural exports from China declined drastically, while agricultural imports rose. The per capita consumption of food during the years 1958-61 is unknown, as well as how much food was produced. All that is known for certain is that the Great Leap failed.

In September, 1959, there was a dismissal of influential men who had, apparently, opposed the Great Leap. Among these were General Huang Ko-cheng, Vice-Minister of Defense, and Marshall P'eng Tei-huai, Minister of Defense, who had pressed for modernization of the People's Liberation Army and had branded the commune policy a blunder.

RETREAT

In June, 1961, the Central Committee of the Party ended the Great Leap, an open affirmation of what it had privately decided the previous year when priority was given to agriculture over industry. The years of experiment had brought home the realization that the limit of industrial development was determined by the quantity of agricultural surplus available for capital and that this quantity depended upon actual production, not upon quotas imposed by the state. Thereafter the quantity of production was played down and a new program planned that called for a more realistic progression in agriculture and in consumer goods. The failure of the Great Leap was blamed on the cadres and the weather. ". . . Marxism-Leninism cannot replace research in every specific branch of science," the *Peking Review* announced in 1961. The Party now began to repair its relations with the people in order to gain credit for recovery and reconstruction. The fundamental unit of agricultural production, again, was the team, while the production brigade remained the basic unit of ownership, whose crops the team planned and distributed.

Heavy construction was practically abandoned in 1961 under

the slogan "Agriculture first," as the Party admitted, by implication, that the right doctrine alone was not sufficient to lift the country up by its own bootstraps, for a heritage of poverty dragged at the ambitions of China.

How much hatred exists among the Chinese for the sufferings they endured in the Great Leap can be at best only conjectured, but there is no doubt of the official hatred for the Soviet Union, which was accused of abandoning China in her crisis. A sense of isolation from the Communist world was evident even in the early 1960's. Coupled with this was China's realistic concession that the triumph of Communism might take ten or more generations and even then not be inevitable without constant watch over the intellectuals.

In 1963 three mass movements, with slogans, were launched reminding the Chinese people that they were on their own in the world: "Re-education in the class struggle," "All cadres to the production front," and "All intellectuals to science." The following year the Party issued a nation-wide call for the heirs and successors of the revolution. The older men in power, knowing they could not live much longer, had begun to worry about the loss of revolutionary fervor among their potential younger successors. Such men might tend to be "bourgeoisie" or revert to "capitalism," as in the U.S.S.R., or make the Party a career end in itself. They desired to pass on their inheritance to true revolutionaries, even though it was the obsession with revolutionary doctrines and mass propaganda that brought on the disasters of 1958-61.

The Recovery

The most significant fact about China's economy in the 1960's was not that an enormous depression had been caused by the Great Leap and natural calamities, but that, by 1963, China had emerged from that depression. In agriculture there had been improvement in crops, especially with the good wheat crops of 1963-65 (raised on 6 per cent more land than in previous years). Enormous efforts had gone into covering the countryside with irrigation pumps to serve against drought, transport facilities were improved and expanded, and the urban food supply had returned to adequate levels. Yet deep strains remained in the agricultural sector. The problems of rural employment seemed insoluble. Peasants tried moving into the cities to get jobs, but this way was soon closed off. In 1966 the government permitted production teams to contract labor to industry for specific periods of time. These contracts ranged from the simple processing of farm goods on the farm to the use of entire production teams in mining or milling for terms up to seven years.

In 1965 a Japanese study of China's agricultural economy projected an average growth rate of 5 to 7.5 per cent per year, which would, given an average annual population increase of 2 per cent, yield China an average individual income equivalent to that of the U.S.S.R. in 1935. A Soviet study of 1966 placed agricultural and industrial output at the 1957 level. The great problem was to keep the peasant productively employed, for agriculture, far from providing the export capital that Chinese industry needed, had to be supported by taking away resources from industry. The village and not the commune became the basic production unit. Yet, despite their failure as economic units, the communes achieved an enduring social change, marking the end of the traditional Chinese family farm. The introduction of work points and wages industrialized agriculture and made the countryside a net of conruralities working the land, under political direction, for wages. The rise to power of young people and the communal care of the institutional needs have tended to westernize the family. It is apparent that the great social-familial changes that began early in the twentieth century have been truly effected.

In 1963 the National People's Congress heard the Party leadership give them a moderately optimistic economic report in which it was implied that the excesses of 1957-61 would not be repeated. In 1964 the Party announced that though China was still poor and technically backward, it had achieved a modest increase in steel and fertilizer production and, in the international market, was exhibiting a large range of consumer and heavy goods for sale. But the most dramatic industrial achievement of all was the detonation of a nuclear device in 1964 at Lop-nor. China's first reactor, built by the U.S.S.R., went into service in 1958 near Peking. By 1965 other reactors were in operation at Mukden, Chungking, Sian, and Paotow. In 1957 the U.S.S.R. had secretly agreed to help China with the construction of an atom bomb but backed out of this agreement the next year. The Chinese then proceeded on their own with building and testing. The most remarkable thing about the first Chinese explosion was that the fissile material was not plutonium, which can be derived rather easily from standard nuclear reactors, but Uranium 235, a rare isotope whose production demands a complex series of processes and machinery that consumes heavy amounts of electric power. The presence of the gaseous diffusion plant at Lanchow for the production of U-235 demonstrated that China had the industrial and scientific capacity, even if she had to channel all of it into producing a single product, to achieve what the West had thought impossible for her.

However, whether this industrial potential meant that life would get appreciably better for all Chinese still depended upon politics. The economy continued to play second fiddle to the deep puritanism, the love of austerity, the passion for struggle, and rampant nationalism—and this was emphasized by the *Liberation Army Daily* in June, 1966, when it stated that "We should constantly endeavour to improve the people's material and cultural life. But the most important thing is to heighten the people's proletarian consciousness by bringing politics to the fore and stepping up politico-ideological work." The third Five Year Plan began in January, 1966, but its targets were not announced. Despite the announced plan of a balanced economy, rational economic projections remained subordinate to ideology, as was demonstrated in December, 1966, when Mao Tse-tung invited young political cadres to interfere with the work of the factories and mines. There were signs of hardening as the material incentives restored after the Great Leap were withdrawn. The Party has given the Chinese people much pride and public splendor. The Chinese are working harder and living longer than ever before

and enjoy great institutional care. But whether politics can prevent them from overrunning their resources only time can tell, for
the root problem of China's economy is her population growth.

The annual growth of China's population is inexorable, but
the actual rate of growth and the total population is not known
with certainty. In 1947 an inexact census gave a count of 457,-
000,000 people; in 1953, 582,600,000 people; in 1957, 640,000,000
people. While all the figures are only approximate, experts calculated an annual population growth rate ranging from 1.6 to
4 per cent per year, with a Japanese study of 1965 setting the
probable rate at 2.3 per cent per year. This means that if food
production increased at the optimistic rate of 2 per cent per year
and if the human population grew at the rate of 14,000,000 per
year, even superb harvests would be inadequate; and, in fact, the
harvest of 1966 was poor. Through better health, with infanticide
gone and heavy mortality rates reduced, prostitution and con-
cubinage outlawed, and women liberated from traditional mis-
use, most of the old bonds on population growth have been
removed. When one adds to these factors the traditional Marxian disbelief in Malthusian economics, it becomes apparent
that the rise in population lies at the core of all the great problems faced by a modern China whose ultimate fate might be
to drown in a sea of human beings.

THE PEOPLE'S NATIONALISM

The Principles of War and Peace

> *Independence is armed force, freedom is armed force,*
> *equality is armed force.*
> —People's Daily, *June 23, 1964*

Though barred from participation in the major organs of international relations and communications, the Peking regime is
far from isolated in the real world of international power and
politics. It deals, overtly and covertly, with many of the nations
of the world. It is the chief force for revolutionary change in
Asia, and it is the dominant power affecting the fate of East,

South, and Southeast Asia. Because of their extent and complexity, Chinese foreign relations will be dealt with under three separate headings: China and Asia, China and the United States, China and the Soviet Union.

The principles of war and peace held by the Chinese are a blend of force and diplomacy, of logic and irrationality, largely conditioned by practical considerations of their own weaknesses and the strengths of their major opponent, the United States. Their primary military weaknesses are vulnerability to air and naval power and inability to mount sustained logistic support for their armed forces. Their strength lies in their geographic location, their knowledge of land warfare, and the formidable attraction they hold for other, weaker Asians.

The armed forces of China are very large. The People's Liberation Army consists of 2,800,000 men, the People's Navy 150,000, and the People's Air Force 250,000. Neither the Navy nor the Air Force is very powerful. The Navy is basically a coast defense force, while the Air Force is largely equipped with outmoded planes and has short supplies of jet fuel. The Army, however, is not only large but able. After sustaining a million casualties in Korea, it was transformed from an armed horde into a flexible fighting force, with a logistic setup, artillery and armor, and a communications service. The officer corps is trained in one or another of sixty-seven military academies, and the body of the Army has been filled since 1955 by a conscription wherein all males over eighteen years of age are drafted for four years of service. The armed forces are politically and professionally controlled by the Party through the Military Affairs Committee, which dictates to the Ministry of National Defense. It can be assumed to be a courageous army, well disciplined, well trained, heavily indoctrinated by its political officers, and capable of manufacturing all infantry weapons, although it has difficulty securing tanks, dependable electronic equipment, and planes. Chinese military doctrine still rests on the use of manpower rather than machines for the simple reason that manpower is the primary strength of the People's Liberation Army.

The turns of China's foreign policy depend upon the consensus of the top Party leadership. Significantly, most of the men who make up this leadership are intellectually isolated; with very few exceptions they have not even traveled in Asia, and even fewer of them have seen the industrialized West. Thus, their ability to calculate the events of the outside world is questionable. Foreign affairs are directed by highly placed Party men like Chou En-lai or Chen Yi. The Foreign Ministry has a reasonable degree of autonomy and flexibility, since it contains the only Chinese who are expert in the art of dealing with the non-Chinese world. But the Ministry is always responsible to the will of the Party, and the Party tends to judge the whole world by its own standards, often refusing to accept the evidence of direct observation. Since the Party operates in an atmosphere of doctrinal confusion, in foreign affairs it is, as one expert points out, apt to be "irrationally sincere." That is, through deliberate campaigns of hate and misrepresentation, Chinese Communists themselves have come to believe in the Western or non-Communist countries as "warlike" and the world as a place in which peace can be had only through "people's movements." They are against war save when they choose to call one a "national liberation movement," a device that enables them to denounce "imperialistic and warlike powers" while justifying their private wars against India, Korea, and Tibet. This same delusion by stereotype gave them, until 1959, an uncritical reverence for the U.S.S.R. Since Marx declares that a Socialist state cannot act like an imperialist state, they could not believe that the U.S.S.R., under Stalin, was in fact a colonial power, nor could they conceive of their own aggressive actions toward their neighbors as imperialistic. Since 1959 they have dispelled their illusions about the Soviet Union, and their policy has become less doctrinaire, although their neighbors see a long-term danger in the chauvinistic desire for expansion that has always marked the beginnings of periods of unity and strength in China. For their part the Chinese will no doubt pursue, as a matter of justice, not only their old hegemonies in Asia but a position in the world. To the world, of whom they constitute one-fourth of the population, they are a people who can be neither ignored nor wished away.

China and Asia

China's policy toward her neighbors in Asia has two aims: to recreate the old Empire, at least to the extent of reasserting Chinese hegemony over the great borderlands, and to make China the good friend and protector of weaker Asian peoples. Corollary to these aims is the intention of driving out every vestige of non-Asian influence, including Russian, and to this end China seeks to render all other Asian Communist parties neutral or committed to China.

From the outset Peking felt that they had two substantial appeals to the people of Asia. One was the long and intimate relationship of China with the peoples on her borders. The other was the call to the masses of Asia to rise against their reactionary governments and against "imperialism" and "feudalism." Yet Peking's initial hostile manner of pursuing her Asian policy showed that her fundamental drive was her belief in the use of violence to mold history. The reassertion of the old dominion over Tibet, Burma, Annam, Central Asia, and Korea, although based on official agreements of mutual aid and respect, was evidenced in covert actions that aroused considerable suspicion in South and Southeast Asia. Until 1954 China was hostile even to such friends as India.

In October, 1950, the People's Liberation Army entered the ancient theocracy of Tibet, claiming that it was "an integral part of Chinese territory." India's protest was rebuffed with the statement that "the problem of Tibet is entirely a domestic problem of China." It was not until 1954 that a Sino-Indian agreement was worked out whereby India acceded to China's claim. But almost immediately a dispute began between the two countries over the immensely long, ancient, and ill-defined Himalayan frontier, a problem aggravated after 1950 by several attempts of the Tibetans to revolt against their new masters. In October, 1959, coincident with the Great Leap, came severe clashes between Indian and Chinese troops in Ladakh and in the Northwest Frontier Agency, in which the Sino-Indian pact was revealed to be a mere façade for Chinese ambitions, demonstrated again in September, 1962, in a clash of Indian and Chi-

nese troops in the Chipchap valley of Ladakh. Five years later
the border is still unsettled. Since both Chinese and Indians regard the controversy as a matter of principle, and the Chinese, in
addition, are vitally interested in connecting Sinkiang to China
proper by a road system through Tibet, it seems unlikely to be
settled by peaceful means. A similar situation had been enacted
on the Burmese frontier, where the Chinese claimed territory in
1951, but the dispute was settled in 1960 with a mutual exchange
of border territories. However, in 1966 a covert struggle was
under way between China and Burma for control of the northwest frontier of Burma.

In 1955 the Party line began to change from advocating immediate revolution to promoting the solidarity of the Asian
(and African) peoples against imperialism. At Bandung, Indonesia, in that year, Burma, India, Indonesia, Ceylon, and Pakistan called a conference of all Asian and all independent African
powers save for North Korea, South Korea, Formosa, and
South Africa. This conference of quite diverse nations was
united in its condemnations of colonialism and its hopes for
freedom, equality, and peace. At Bandung the Chinese were
peaceful and pleasant, agreeing on the need for the peaceful
solution of international problems. They had been equally
agreeable at the Geneva conference the previous year, called
to determine some solution of the war in Indochina between
the French and the Annamese. Nevertheless, in 1957, parallel
with the supreme confidence evidenced in the Great Leap
Forward, came a new and forceful demonstration of Chinese
foreign policy. This included the invasion of the Himalayan
areas of India, threats against Annam, and the claim to leadership within the "peace zone" of Asia. It seemed as though the
Chinese had decided to match their domestic aims with territorial expansion—a Great Leap of disciplined masses toward
goals dictated by Chinese nationalism and animated by revolutionary confidence. The motivating voices were not just those
of Marx and Engels, but of Tai Tsung and Ch'ien Lung.

The failure of the Great Leap with its implication that China
was to remain poor only served to convince Peking that it

should take the lead among the underdeveloped nations, for the gap between the two worlds—the haves (including the Soviet Union) and the have nots—was growing apace and creating prospects of war and revolution. In addition, by 1960 China headed a defined Asian Communist bloc directed not only against the United States but also against the Soviet Union and based on the principle that no accommodation could be tolerated with the enemy. The success of China in South and Southeast Asia stems from the heterogeneous religious, ethnic, and linguistic nature of the areas. Since these are not nations but communal groups with deep and varied antagonisms toward each other, the local Communist parties have been able to play one group off against another. As for the South and Southeast Asian Communist parties themselves, they represent neither workers nor peasants but are the manipulators of the visible regional dissatisfactions, which, while differing sharply in other respects, have in common a uniform passion against colonialism. The people these parties draw to them are not so much radical or Communist as they are merely resentful. Further, under Chinese direction the various Asian Communist parties are more Asian than Communist, and their unexpressed common slogan is "Colored workers of the world, unite."

In April, 1960, the Chinese-African Peoples' Friendship Association was formed. The following April Kwame Nkrumah of Ghana visited Peking and signed an aid agreement, and by 1964 some 60 per cent of Chinese aid was going to Africa, although many of the widely proclaimed projects were either very slow abuilding or technically unsound. In November of that same year an enormous three-day rally to support the revolution in Africa was held in Peking. The Chinese people were told that the center of the struggle between East and West now lay in Africa. Certainly most of the newly independent African states recognized Peking and not Taipei, and some of the African rebel leaders such as Pierre Mulele of the Congo had even been trained in China. A number of African presidents made their pilgrimages to Peking to be told, as

Liu Shao-ch'i told President Dabat of the Republic of the
Congo, that China supported Africa and indeed regarded such
support as their "unshakable, glorious, international duty." In
his turn, Chou En-lai had, in 1964, traveled throughout Africa
and visited Burma, Pakistan, and Ceylon. One visible fruit of
this diplomatic offensive was the French recognition of Peking
and the French intimation that a "third force" of France, China,
England, and Germany could preserve the peace.

Nor was Chinese diplomacy limited to Africa. In 1961 the
President of Brazil had visited China and concluded a trade
agreement; the mission was followed late that same year by
a similar visit from President Dorticos of Cuba. And of course
vigorous activity was continuing in Asia. On August 17, 1964,
in an Independence Day speech, President Sukarno of Indonesia threw his lot in with Peking. Engineering troops of the
People's Liberation Army were, in 1965, building roads in
Nepal and Laos, and fourteen divisions of the People's Liberation Army were stationed in the Himalayas. Moreover, the
South Vietnam Liberation Front had established a headquarters
in Peking as had the Thai Liberation Front.

By 1964 China had taken over or rendered neutral all Asian
Communist parties save those of Mongolia and Ceylon, and, in
the process, had thrown the Soviet Communist Party out of
East and South Asia. China's greatest asset in Southeast Asia
was its partnership with President Sukarno of Indonesia. Sukarno had agreed to be one jaw of a vise that was to squeeze
every vestige of Western power out of Southeast Asia. But this
vise was broken in late 1965, when an attempted seizure of
power by the Indonesian Communist Party was stopped by
the Indonesian army. Following this the army and the non-
Communist Indonesians literally exterminated the Communists,
killing along with them thousands of Chinese residents. This
coup in reverse, plus the presence of an immense United States
military force in Southeast Asia, made it improbable that the
nations of mainland Southeast Asia would have to succumb
to Chinese terms. In addition, the aggressive and self-righteous
nature of Chinese policy, the testing of nuclear weapons, the
mob actions of the Red Guard, and Peking's obvious hostility to

any world or Asian order not created in the Chinese image was blunting the very real emotional ties that many Asians held with revolutionary China. The continual threats against India and China's offer in 1962 to help form an anti-Indian confederation from among Nepal, Sikkim, Bhutan, Nagaland, and the Northeast Frontier Agency of India, the denunciation by China in 1965 of the efforts of nonaligned states to halt the Vietnamese war and the testing of nuclear weapons, had led to a considerable disillusionment. The weak nations of mainland Southeast Asia had little recourse but to watch events. The strong Asian nations, India and Japan, considered developing their own nuclear weapons. Meanwhile the Soviet Union and the United States sought to contain China.

China and the Soviet Union

From the beginning of the new Chinese regime, the relationship between Peking and Moscow was ambiguous, though based on a respect that was mutual but wary and cynical. China owed nothing to Russia, but she looked upon her as the most advanced of Communist countries, one that China ought to emulate and one that was obligated to help China. This feeling notwithstanding, the Chinese Communists received no substantial material or moral help from Russia during the years 1928-48. Indeed, in the period 1945-48, when the Soviets looted Manchuria of everything movable, they stripped to the bone the one industrial base on which the emerging Chinese Communists counted heavily.

For her part, Russia saw China as an independent Communist country with, indeed, no obligation to Moscow, but also as the most populous and potentially powerful of the Communist nations. Russia found, possibly with a surprise that was as great to her as it was to much of the world, that she was not able to dominate the Chinese Communist Party the way she had dominated other Communist parties. The Chinese Party was loyal to Mao Tse-tung, it had its own internal security arrangements and its own People's Liberation Army, and it would neither bend its will nor its ambition to Moscow.

Yet, in the dawn of the Communist victory in China, Mao

Tse-tung felt an obligation to the fraternal world order of Communism and in his *On the People's Democratic Dictatorship* he told the Chinese that there was no middle way in world policy between imperialism and socialism, that there could be no exception to this rule, and that internationally they belonged to the anti-imperialist front, headed by the Soviet Union. Therefore in February, 1950, China and Russia signed a thirty-year treaty of mutual assistance in which each pledged to come to the aid of the other in the event of an attack by a third power. In the same year the Soviets began sending technical and financial aid to China. Yet all was not too comradely, as can be seen in the Sino-Soviet agreement of 1951 on the use of the Amur River. This is a document so precise and legalistic as to indicate a great suspicion between Communist neighbors. When Joseph Stalin died in 1953, Nikita Khrushchev, the new leader of the Soviet Union moved to decrease the tensions between Russia and China, not for fraternal reasons, but because Russia needed support in an Asia where China was becoming the revolutionary magnet. Furthermore, Siberia had been so developed that the guts of the Soviet economy now lay east of the Urals and had to be protected from Siberia's greatest neighbor. Thus Soviet aid was increased substantially, ranging from building complete plants in China to sending Russian professors to teach in Chinese universities. This aid, however, was not free: in exchange, large amounts of Chinese materials and food went to Russia.

The Russians also shaded Communist doctrine to please the Chinese and placed Mao Tse-tung in the Marxist pantheon, an honor not usually accorded living heroes. But if the Russians believed that these strategies would bring the Chinese Communist Party into a subordinate relationship, they were wrong. Chinese statements on the Hungarian revolt of 1956, while supporting the Russian repressions, nevertheless demanded that all Socialist countries be independent and equal states, and in speech after speech Mao hammered on the need for *independent national Communism*. With these actions the Chinese were setting out bait intended to draw the leadership of the fragmenting Communist world into their own hands; yet, from

1953 to 1957 there was reasonable cooperation between the two countries.

Then, in 1957, that unity, which for national and ideological reasons had already become a carefully erected façade, showed its first perceptible crack, perhaps beginning with the Soviet promise to help the Chinese construct an atomic weapon. Presumably this promise, combined with the increasing industrialization of China, intoxicated Peking into believing that a swift and effective combination of strokes in domestic and foreign policies could rapidly alter the world balance of power and permit a rapid Communist takeover of Asia and Africa. For it was at this point that Peking launched both the Great Leap Forward and a bold foreign policy.

The Russians, aware that the Chinese were wrong in their belief that they could emulate the experience of the Russian Revolution, were horrified by the Great Leap. There were simply no similarities between the two countries: China had formidably large masses of people to deal with, possessed a fraction of Russia's natural resources, had nothing to approach the Tsarist industrialization, and had none of the Bolshevik comprehension of world affairs. Although Premier Khrushchev went to Peking to warn the Chinese against the perils of internal communalization and the rising dangers of a world war, his warnings were of no use. The predicted disasters came about.

In June, 1959, the Soviet Union suddenly withdrew its atomic assistance. Moreover, by 1960 whole trainloads of Soviet advisers and technicians had begun to leave China, and shipments of Soviet materials and supplies were withheld, thus damaging China's industrial recovery. In November, 1960, in their respective presses, bitterness between the two great Communist powers began to make itself apparent. Early that year the Chinese had made clear the contrast between Chinese and Soviet attitudes toward the West:

> United States imperialism, hostile to the Chinese people, has always adopted a discriminatory attitude against our country in international relations. Therefore, the Chinese government has to declare to the world that any international disarmament agreement and all other international agreements arrived at

without the formal participation of the Chinese People's Republic and the signature of its delegate cannot, of course, have any binding force on China.[18]

Since this statement was made at Warsaw at a time when the United States and the Soviet Union were engaged in disarmament talks, it was a blunt admonition to the Soviet Union.

In December, 1962, the quarrel became more open and shrill when the Chinese denounced "anti-Marxists," leaving no doubt that they meant Premier Khrushchev. A month later the Russians denounced the idea that any "minority" possessed the Communist truth. During the remainder of 1963 each side took uncompromising stands. Khrushchev warned that China seemed to be ignoring the threat that a nuclear war could obliterate it in a few hours. Mao replied (in February and again in June) that Khrushchev was splitting the world Communist movement through wrongheadedness and that the Soviet leadership ought to get rid of him. By mid-1963 there seemed little hope of reconciliation. There was a public exchange of letters in which both sides frankly stated their distaste for the other. Peking had never forgotten either Stalin's refusal to help the Chinese Communists during the twenty-year civil war or the postwar Soviet rape of Manchuria. To this they added the charge that the Russians had abandoned China in 1959, in her greatest hour of need. They made no bones about this:

During that period [the Great Leap] we also encountered an unexpected difficulty. In July 1960, the Soviet authorities actually took this opportunity to bring pressure to bear upon us and extended ideological differences between the Chinese and Soviet Communist Parties to state relations; then suddenly and unilaterally decided on a complete withdrawal of the 1,390 experts who were in China to help in our work, they tore up 343 contracts for experts and the supplements to these contracts and abolished 257 items for scientific and technical cooperation and since then, they have reduced in large numbers the supplies of complete sets of equipment and key sections of various other equipment. This has caused our construction to suffer huge losses, thereby upsetting our original plan for the development of our national economy and greatly aggravating our difficulties.[19]

On the ideological level the Chinese accused the Russians of having forsaken the Marxist-Leninist approach to war and of encouraging "illusions" that war can be abolished while imperialism exists; they said further that Russia had exaggerated the significance of nuclear weapons and that talk of nuclear war was simply blackmail. (Privately the Chinese feared that the Soviet Union might really coexist peacefully with the United States.) The Chinese went on to accuse their comrades of restoring capitalism, abandoning the dictatorship of the proletariat, supporting "racism" and colonialism around the world, and, indeed, trying to force Communist parties throughout the world to accept the unilateral decisions of Moscow. The Chinese stated these charges at great length, and the Soviet Party replied at equal length, denying each charge, placing the blame for the deterioration of relations squarely upon the Chinese, stating that they failed to understand Marxism-Leninism, war, or the world situation, and accusing them of trying to split and dominate the world Communist movement.

In November, 1963, in a desperate effort to preserve the unity of the world Communist movement, Khrushchev, who had for several years been exhorting the Chinese to conduct the argument in private, proposed a new start on adjusting differences and the acceptance of existing boundaries in Siberia and Central Asia. The Chinese responded a few months later by rejecting offers by other Communist parties to mediate in the dispute, and they refused to accept frontiers based on secret treaties in which they had not participated. They further reproached the Russians for lack of fraternity, save in their support of the Korean War (though even there the Russians, they suspected, had acted in their own interests), and finally they called for Khrushchev's removal. This last demand was met, in a move that astonished the world, when, in 1964, Khrushchev was deposed by his own party. His successors continued his efforts to come to terms with the Chinese, but, ominously, that same year the Chinese began speaking of Russian territorial aggres-

sion against them. In March Mao Tse-tung reminded Moscow
that Amuria and Sinkiang, having been torn from China by
the Tsars, might someday be "peacefully reclaimed," and on
July 10 he said to a group of Japanese newspapermen:

> The Soviet Union occupies an area of 22,000,000 square kilome-
> ters while its population is only 200,000,000. It is time to put
> an end to this allotment. Japan occupies an area of 370,000
> square kilometers and its population is 100,000,000. About one
> hundred years ago the area to the east of Baikal became Russian
> territory and since then Vladivostok, Khabarovsk, Kamchatka
> and other areas have been Soviet territory. We have not yet
> presented our account for this list.[20]

Earlier that year the two governments had exchanged notes
concerning incidents along the Kazakh-Sinkiang frontier and at
the confluence of the Amur and Ussuri Rivers.

Until 1964, the long series of exchanges had been regarded
by many neutral observers as serious but not fatal, for while
the disagreements and recriminations were bitter, they were
motivated, it was thought, by the pursuit of differing tactics
within the same ideological framework. But with the announcement of China's territorial claims against Russia it became clear
that the split was more fundamental. Then the battle moved
from party conflicts to the more serious arena of governmental
differences. In May, 1964, the official paper of the Russian
government called Communist China "racist" and a "police
state." In March, 1965, the Soviet government openly denounced the Chinese government as having instigated an attack
on a friendly embassy in Moscow (the Embassy of the United
States), of having promoted a riot in Moscow, and, in so doing,
of having engaged in what *Pravda* called "the most unfriendly
attitude." In March, 1966, there was a public exchange of
calumnious letters wherein Peking accused the U.S.S.R. of a
"series of dirty deals with the United States" and Moscow accused Peking of conducting an anti-Soviet campaign among
the Communist parties of the world. The efforts of the new
leaders of the Soviet Union to compromise relations with China
had failed, as had the previous efforts of Khrushchev, the man

whom they had, presumably, demoted for having failed to solve the bitterness between China and the U.S.S.R.

China and the United States

On February 19, 1965, the United States Secretary of Defense stated to a press conference that China was the chief adversary of the United States. China, he said, was implacably antagonistic to the United States, and in the pursuit of her aims proffered to the nations of Asia and Africa, and to a lesser extent those of Latin America, a revolutionary doctrine that "any non-Communist government of an emerging nation can be overthrown by externally supported covert armed aggression, even when that government is backed by U.S. economic and military assistance." [21] This statement marked the final stage of one of the most melancholy reversals in modern international relations. Yet for the fifteen years preceding the declaration, it had been obvious that the United States and the People's Republic of China were not only antagonistic but in a kind of war with each other.

The People's Republic felt a genuine hatred of the United States for supporting the Kuomintang in the civil war and then working actively to isolate and enfeeble Communist China. As early as 1947 and continuing to the present, the United States has been portrayed to the people of China as the main imperialist and aggressive force in the world and the greatest enemy of China. To support this image frequent "Hate America" campaigns have been held, pressure has been placed on every American position in Asia, and Peking's influence in the worldwide revolutionary movement has been directed to the destruction of the American interests.

For her part, the United States, while not conducting hate campaigns, has radically revised her former attitudes toward the Chinese. From the nineteenth century onwards, Americans had taken a sympathetic, avuncular, and largely distorted view of the people and institutions of China. While well-meaning and often supported by charitable help, this view rested on a mistaken concept that the Chinese were a great, democratic, placid mass of hard-working and exploited people, ruled by scholarly mandarins. These people were, the view held, dreadfully misgoverned and even mistreated but, given time and help, they could, if they adopted the Western forms of life and government, become remarkably like the United States and its people. Meanwhile, the United States was prepared to extend private assistance and officially admonish those other nations whose policies infringed upon the integrity and well-being of China. And with the opening of World War II in the Pacific the dreams and idle talk of three-quarters of a century materialized in the reality of fighting in China and for China.

While the propaganda of the war period portrayed China as one of the great democratic powers, the real picture was that of a ruined nation temporarily holding in abeyance a civil war until Japan could be defeated. The difficult ties of the wartime alliance and the defeat of the Nationalists came as a shock and a humiliation to the United States. Not only had she, through her ally the Kuomintang, suffered a military reversal in China immediately after her great military victories over Japan, but she found that the Communist victors disdained and distrusted her and were prepared to drive her entirely from China, if not the Asian continent. The American image of the Chinese now shifted from that of the proud, industrious, wise, and enduring people of the pre-war period to one of hard, untrustworthy fanatics. While both images were false and each in its way was to hamper United States policies, the fact remained that Communist China officially hated the United States, and the United States, if she did not officially hate Communist China, at the very least privately disliked her.

In practical terms, the presence of a hostile China was an unexpected and grave danger to the treaty commitments and national interests of the United States in the Western Pacific. By treaty, and later in actuality, the United States was obliged to undertake the military defense of Japan, the new Republic of Korea, the Republic of the Philippines, and the island of Taiwan, on which remnants of the Nationalist government had been established. When the obligations to Japan, Korea, and the Philippines were undertaken, the United States had believed that China would be a friendly or at best a neutral power. Now, confronted with a hostile, although weak, China, the United States was forced to re-examine her extensive military defenses along the rim of East Asia.

THE KOREAN WAR

Following the surrender of Japan, the United States and the Soviet Union had agreed that, for the sake of convenience, the Soviet Union would disarm and collect Japanese troops in Korea north of the Thirty-eighth Parallel and the United States would do the same south of that line. This was construed by the United States as a provision of agreement to facilitate the surrender, and there had been no intention, at least on the part of the Americans, to divide Korea arbitrarily and permanently. However, Soviet forces militarized the line, refusing even to permit postal service to cross, and proceeded toward establishing a People's Republic in North Korea, using the Korean and Manchurian Communists who had been active underground for so many years against Japanese rule in Korea and who, upon the Japanese defeat, formed People's Committees. These were recognized by the Soviets as the local governments of North Korea.

In the southern part of Korea the situation was confused. The surrender had come suddenly, and the United States had no immediate plans for the government or the occupation of Korea. American troops under General Hodge were rushed into South Korea and controlled their section of Korea through the old Japanese administration, ignoring Korean nationalist groups of every shade. Korea had since 1905 been first a protectorate, then a colony, and finally an integral part of Japan. In these forty years of bondage the Japanese had made great efforts to de-Koreanize the Koreans. The use of their mother tongue was proscribed in the schools, and their patriotic and nationalistic activities were severely repressed. They were not eligible for advanced education or positions in the civil service; they were excluded from the professions and the higher reaches of business; they were discriminated against by the police, the courts, and the credit systems; and quite often their land was expropriated for Japanese colonists. Although Korea under

Japanese rule was industrialized, the Koreans enjoyed none of the fruits but were tied to farming, and, since their agricultural economy was designed to act as a supplemental feeder for Japan, frequently, while Korea exported rice, the Koreans went hungry. One result of this brutalization was that when Korea was freed in 1948 there was no Korean administrative or executive class; few Koreans were prepared to undertake the work of self-government. With the exception of those Korean nationalists in jail or hiding, the active resistance groups had operated either from Manchuria, as had the Communists, or from exile in China, Europe, or the United States. The plight of free Korea was bad enough. Divided as she was to become, her situation was soon tragic.

Protracted negotiations with the Soviet Union, beginning in Moscow in December, 1945, and continuing throughout 1946 and 1947, failed to resolve the Korean division. While the Soviets agreed there should be a provisional government for Korea, they refused any plan for unification that did not give Korean Communists control of the government. The United States continued to negotiate but began in late 1946 to form a Korean administration in the South. In late 1947 the United States placed the whole matter before the United Nations, which agreed to supervise free elections in Korea for a Korean Congress, which in turn would then draw up a constitution. The Soviet Union refused to permit either United Nations personnel or an election in their area, so the election was held in South Korea. The election was free and honest, but unfortunately a number of non-Communist leaders and factions who were unpalatable to the United States had been forcibly eliminated from competition. In August, 1948, the Republic of Korea was established, and Syngman Rhee, an old and stubborn man but a profound Korean patriot who had been in exile for thirty years, was elected President. The United States extended economic help, and the new Korean government began an extensive and long-overdue program of economic reforms.

Whether the contrast between North and South Korea became intolerable to the Soviet Union, or whether it deemed

South Korea vulnerable enough to win without difficulty is unknown. The first conclusion might be inferred from the fact that thousands of refugees made their way from North to South. The second seemed apparent; there were no American combat troops in Korea, and the Republic of Korea forces themselves were weak and ill-equipped. Whatever the motive, on June 25, 1950, North Korean forces crossed the line and launched an attack upon South Korea. Late that same day the Security Council of the United Nations condemned the action as a breach of the peace and called upon all United Nations members "to render every assistance to the United Nations" in this matter. Immediately President Truman ordered United States naval and air forces into action to cover the retreat of the South Koreans, and a United Nations command was set up under the overall command of General Douglas MacArthur.

The summer and fall of 1950 were disastrous for United Nations forces in Korea. They were driven back and hemmed in at the southern port of Pusan. However, in September the United Nations forces launched an amphibious attack at Inchon that was spectacularly successful. Those North Korean forces which were not trapped fled back across the Thirty-eighth Parallel. The United Nations forces then moved north of this parallel in pursuit of a new goal—that of unifying Korea. This was a far broader war aim than the original United Nations resolution, which had simply aimed at repelling the armed attack on South Korea and restoring "international peace and security in that area." It was this march to the Yalu that brought the Chinese into the war.

The intervention of China, who had approved the original North Korean aggression, need not have been a surprise. Apprehensive about the danger to her own national territory if foreign forces crossed her frontier at the Yalu and Tumen Rivers, she had publicly stated that if such a move seemed imminent, she would fight. This warning, as well as the massing of Chinese troops, was, strangely, disregarded by the United Nations command.

On November 25, 1950, the United Nations had two army commands in Korea. One, the Tenth Army, was extended along the eastern coast, and the other, the Eighth Army, was extended along the western coast. Both armies were based south of the Thirty-eighth Parallel, and their leading elements were extended as far as the Chinese frontier. On the morning of November 26, a great force of Chinese "volunteers" struck between both armies, fanned out, cut off the leading elements and began to drive the remainder back. By January, 1951, these "volunteers" (China, never officially at war, sent only "volunteers") had retaken North Korea and the southern capital of Seoul. The United Nations forces under new command drove back, and after months of bitter fighting, during which very heavy losses were inflicted on the Chinese, reached and crossed the Thirty-eighth Parallel.

In July of that year the Chinese asked for truce negotiations. These took place at the village of Punmunjom and lasted for two years, during which time the war continued. The Chinese permitted it to drag on because they refused to allow the voluntary repatriation of prisoners of war. Finally, in July, 1953, an armistice, not a peace, was agreed upon.

The agreements concluded seemed detrimental to the Chinese. For one thing, the boundary line settled upon was not the Thirty-eighth Parallel but the military line north of it, held by the United Nations forces. For another, almost three-quarters of the Chinese who were prisoners of war voluntarily refused to return to China. But the enormous material and human losses sustained by Peking, and even the humiliation of seeking an armistice, were more than balanced by the tremendous nationalism and loyalty to the regime aroused through the call for "volunteers" to fight the "imperialist aggressors" and by the fact that since neither side had "won" the war, Westerners, notably the United States, were "paper tigers." Principally, the war had once again served to remind the Chinese that their pre-eminent enemy was the United States. Since that armistice the relationship between the United States and China has been one of implacable distrust and hostility, the more so on the Chinese side. The most striking demonstration of this came in September, 1965, when Defense Minister Lin Piao declared that China's support of revolutionary warfare in all of the underdeveloped countries was a long-range strategy aimed at the destruction of the United States. At the time, Marshal Lin stated that the immediate focus of this strategy was the people's war in Vietnam, which would demonstrate that the strategy of a people's war would work anywhere.

The stalemate began to loosen in March, 1966, when Vice President Humphrey spoke of "containment without isolation," a visibly flexible response to the United States Senate hearings, which were concerned with involvement of the United States in Vietnam and had been pushing toward the broader issue of China policy. Peking, however, accepted none of the inducements offered, such as the lifting of the travel ban on Americans who wished to enter China, or such proposals as the lifting of the United States trade embargo and the beginning of diplomatic relations. Normalization of relations between the two countries, Peking countered, could only begin with the removal of United States forces from Taiwan and the Straits of Taiwan. Coincidentally Peking disappointed any hopes for bringing her into the United Nations when Foreign Minister Chen Yi set as the condition for entrance the expulsion from that body of members of whom China does not approve.

CHINA IN PERSPECTIVE

The Red Guard

Article 21 of the constitution of the Chinese Communist Party states: "Every Party member may carry on within the Party and in Party meetings free and practical discussion to express his or her views on Party policy and on various issues before decisions are reached. However, when a decision is reached, it must be abided by and carried out unconditionally."

This disciplined unity had always been a characteristic of the Chinese Communist Party to a degree unknown in other Communist parties. The leadership group had, seemingly, always been able to move together on a common program. Personal and power differences, such as existed, were subordinated to a uniform agreement on ideology and program.

To an extraordinary degree the Chinese Communist Party had been free of the internal purges so marked in other Communist parties. Since 1949 only two of the high-ranking Party members had been denounced and dismissed from their office, and only once between 1949 and 1965 had the entire Party organization been shaken up. Then in the fall of 1965, and continuing through 1966 and into 1967, there began a purge of the Party, the Army, the government, and much of the intellectual class— indeed of all sectors of Chinese society save for workers and peasants, enormous in extent, all important for the future of China and singular indeed in the agents chosen to do the purging.

The Great Cultural Proletarian Revolution, as the purge was called, began in a small fashion with the Socialist Education Campaign of 1962, which stressed the need for intellectuals to perform hard physical labor and for all Chinese to think like, or to depend upon the thinking of, Mao Tse-tung. The announced purpose was to remind young people (and two-fifths of China's population is under seventeen years of age) of the hard road traveled by their revolutionary parents and thus to arm these youngsters against backsliding into bourgeois habits. This intense movement for the apotheosis of Mao Tse-tung's thoughts often took turns amusing to observers. For instance, the victory of the Chinese ping-pong team over the Japanese ping-pong team at Belgrade in 1965 was announced, in front-page headlines, as the victory of a "stubborn-minded military gymnastic battalion who had armed themselves with the spirit of Mao Tse-tung." Yet humor would be misplaced, for this was part of a massive attempt to indoctrinate a generation of youth with no personal experience of the hard revolutionary days before 1949.

The campaign intensified in the fall of 1965 with a drive to make the Army more political. This was done in direct response to Army officers, who openly preferred modernization to reliance upon the thought of Mao Tse-tung. Previous to this, in June, 1965, officers had been stripped of their ranks. The Party was determined that it would "direct the gun," and it was

having trouble in maintaining unquestioned control over techni-
cal-military aspects of the army.

By the beginning of 1966 the Socialist Education Campaign
was not having its desired effect on the educators, writers,
propagandists, and intellectuals who did not hold the faith
firmly. Therefore, if the young and those responsible for the
minds of the young could not be convinced, then the schools,
universities, and Party training headquarters would have to be
cleaned out. From Mao's point of view it must have seemed
that his whole life would be wasted unless there could be
recreated among the generations to follow him that vigorous,
ruthless, creative leadership that marked the Yenan period.

The full fury of the new revolution broke in the spring of
1966, with a special denunciation of technicians who ignored
politics as a horrible example of how China might be sub-
verted to capitalism, as, it was said, had happened in the
U.S.S.R., where economics had been placed ahead of politics. Foreign Minister Chen Yi stated that, apart from the
thought of Mao Tse-tung, the Chinese people could no longer
have faith in any other thought, and China was notified that
adherence to the thoughts of Mao Tse-tung would insure China
against the creation of any privileged group of intellectuals,
bureaucrats, or politicians.

The agents of these thoughts of Mao's were enormous bands
of adolescents styling themselves "the Red Guard," who came
into the cities of China and were given free rein to harass,
humiliate, and destroy the remnants of capitalist bourgeois culture. The Red Guard were inspired and presumably organized by Defense Minister Lin Piao, for it was at his urging and
under his guidance that the revolution, designed to "sweep
away the dust that will not go away by itself," put its brooms
into action.

As they roamed the streets, the Red Guard demanded that
all outlandish Western symbols be gotten rid of: long haircuts,
elaborate menus in restaurants, foreign stamp collections, objects of Western art, permanent waves, flower shops, Western
furniture. Homes, shops, and offices were invaded and the of-

fending objects smashed, while offenders were denounced and
paraded through the city. In many instances resistance was met,
and both Red Guards and their victims died in street fights.
The destruction was not limited to objects; place and street
names were changed at will: the Soviet Embassy found itself,
overnight, on "Struggle Against Revisionism Street," an obvious
and insulting cut at the course of Communism in Russia since
the death of Joseph Stalin. In another offensive gesture the
Red Guard closed the foreign cemetery in Peking after destroying the graves of "imperialists."

  In the mid-summer and fall of 1966 the youth of China were
called on to continue this new revolution because Mao Tse-tung
could not trust the Chinese Communist Party to do the job.
Urged on by slogans such as "Lift high the banner of the
thought of Mao Tse-tung—the bright sun that illuminates the
entire world" and "Oust those within the Party who are in power
and taking the capitalist road," these young people were ordered to act, across China, against all customs and habits regarded as bourgeois and, indeed, against any sign of a better
life. No one was exempt. Accused, attacked, and dismissed
were mayors of cities, Party secretaries, and members of the
Political Bureau, the National Defense Council, and the Central Committee. Even the revered Madame Sun Yat-sen became
a victim of vandalism and calumny, and the purge reached as
high as President Liu Shao-ch'i, once considered second only to
Mao.

  In mid-December, 1966, Marshal P'eng, former Minister of
Defense and a high-ranking member of the Political Bureau,
was arrested. Since P'eng was only vulnerable to his senior colleagues on the Political Bureau, and since he was, notoriously,
a hard-line Communist, his dismissal on the grounds of "being
out of tune with the revolution" made it difficult for outsiders
to comprehend the intricate motivations of the Great Cultural
Proletarian Revolution. For the purge extended not only to high
Party leaders and serving Party members on regional and
local levels, but to writers, to school teachers, and to small
functionaries. The charges against all these were ambiguous;

they were accused of "revisionism," of being "bourgeois" in their thinking.

Without doubt, in the interstices of the revolution a true power struggle was going on among the leadership of China. In January, 1967, a public charge was made by the Red Guard that in 1958 Mao Tse-tung had been forced out as President of China by Liu Shao-ch'i as a protest against Mao's push for rural communes. This statement, if correct, and no official denial was made, made it clear that the driving force in Chinese affairs between 1958 and 1966 had not solely been Mao Tse-tung and his followers; that there had been serious and uncompromising policy and planning splits in the higher reaches of the Party and that the Red Guard movement was, among other things, an old-fashioned power struggle in which Mao and those loyal to him were taking advantage of the Great Cultural Proletarian Revolution not only to regenerate the revolution but to trap a number of presumably loyal high officials into appearing opposed to Chairman Mao's thoughts.

There could be little doubt that the Red Guard phenomenon represented a combination of Mao's and Lin's desire for power and revenge and Mao's well-known, intense desire to fill the younger Chinese with revolutionary fervor; yet so many men of substance were dismissed and humiliated and so many highly placed men were denounced and arrested by adolescents at mass rallies that it is equally evident that formidable criticism of Mao must have existed within the Party. He had, after all, sizeable domestic and foreign failures, and no man could have remained infallible after the consequences of some of Chairman Mao's thought. In the process of cleaning China before he died Mao turned away from the Party he had built because the majority of it wanted to govern China not with revolutionary charisma but with a more pragmatic approach. The true dream of the Chinese revolution had been to create a powerful modern state and army. The Party may have seen the unlikelihood of accomplishing this simply through the thoughts of Chairman Mao; these thoughts made no provision for a shift in China's rigid international policies or for a genuine debate on matters

of resource allocation and capital accumulation. So the Party
was cleansed lest it abandon principles for policy.

By January, 1967, it became abundantly clear that two great
factions were fighting for the control of the Party and of China.
One was led by Mao Tse-tung and Marshal Lin Piao. The
other was presumably led by President Liu Shao-ch'i and Teng
Hsiao-ping, former head of the Party Secretariat. Both factions
were endeavoring to control the communications and transport
facilities of the country as chief instruments in assuming full
control of the country. While there was brawling in the streets,
the country was still far short of a civil war, but the Mao-Lin
faction was meeting stiff resistance from the workers in the
cities and from many local and regional Party secretaries, who
happened to be, at the same time, local and regional military
commanders. Ironically enough Mao had himself created this
opposition during the years when he established the absolute
rule of the Chinese Communist Party over China. At that time
the Party had given great power to regional Party bosses, and
these bosses were now using the means they commanded locally to fight for their power and for their existence. Paradoxically, they were obliged to consolidate and arm their proletariat
against the proletarian revolution.

To observers the situation was, to say the least, obscure. A
kind of madness seemed to have been loosed that not only made
intelligent analysis impossible but indicated that it would be
extremely difficult to slow down or end the new revolution.
The expansion of the revolution to the countryside, met with
resistance from peasants. Communes broke up, ate their grain
stores, and divided up their profits. Troops were sent to guard
state grain stores while the peasants were urged, with warnings of famine in Kiangsi and Anhui Provinces, to get to the
spring planting. The Red Guard, meanwhile, had gone out of
control and was alienating vast masses of people. A substantial number of provinces were under the control of the Army.
In fact, the People's Liberation Army seemed the only remaining monolith in the turbulence created by the new revolution. China was being urged to learn from the Army while
the Army, in turn, was given control of a large number of

civilian activities and Army men were placed on the Political Bureau. But in late January, 1967, even senior Army men were being denounced in the wall posters of the Red Guard, and the Army was placed directly under the Military Commission of the Party, chaired by Chen Po-ta, Mao's long time secretary, who with Madame Mao had emerged as the directors of the new cultural revolution. Thus by early 1967 no Chinese institution had escaped Mao's new revolution.

China in Proportion—1967

If China is indeed the "world's elephant," then what little hard evidence we have of China would suggest that many, if not all, of the variant descriptions of contemporary China are not accurate, and this would include those of the Chinese themselves as self-observers. China's possession of a nuclear weapon and the prospect that she may achieve the means of delivering it, her massive and expanding population, her public claims of deprivation and isolation through encirclement, and her call to all peoples to free themselves by her example and with her help, have tended to make her the embodiment of what the West fears of the future—revolution, race conflict, war, and destruction. From China's point of view, the United States is the permanent enemy that must be destroyed. Therefore, they have accepted the risk of nuclear war as a fact of life, and they have been trained to consider that their national destiny, foremost, includes the possibility of a full-scale nuclear war with the United States and possibly with the U.S.S.R. Internally, the present leaders are engaged in a desperate struggle to make the Chinese revolution permanent.

But while enmity of the world falls far short of what the Chinese believe it to be, fearful speculation inflates China's power and exaggerates her importance. Her army is large, well trained, and brave, but not modern; her navy is still almost nonexistent; and her air force is largely obsolete. Although industrial adjustment is underway, China is full of factories working below capacity. The priority given to agriculture since the Great Leap means a postponement of the accumulation of real wealth. China is trapped in the position of being a semi-industrial country forced to raise agricultural yields rapidly, a very difficult thing to achieve. While harvests have increased measurably, so has the population, and the Great Cultural Proletarian Revolution shows signs of continuing by its own inertia, even to the dreadful prospect of driving China to the edge of famine.

Peking has shown an extraordinary capacity for keeping the country going, especially demonstrated during the Great Leap period when it managed to avoid what no previous Chinese government had avoided—starvation and famine—by the central enforcement of fair shares for all.

Yet solutions to the most urgent problems seem difficult. Some alleviation of population pressure might come from the resettlement of large numbers of Chinese in thinly populated areas of the country. This plan was tried in 1956, when military colonies were established in Manchuria and Sinkiang, but the experiment was enormously expensive and at best affected a negligible number of people. Food might be increased by the introduction of new techniques, but the fertility of exhausted soil cannot be increased. Without the opening of new and fertile land or the renewal of existing land the amount of food grown will tend to run behind the population gain. As agriculture is electrified and mechanized, and as the population grows, a body of rural unemployed will also grow, which cannot be transferred to industry unless that expands at a phenomenal rate. And industry, in turn, cannot expand unless agriculture provides the surpluses needed for capital investment. One solution to the problem would be population controls lasting over a period of several generations while maintaining present levels of material consumption by planning and fair rationing. Originally the Chinese Communist Party rejected the economics of Malthus as nonsense and took the attitude that the larger the population the better. Marxism teaches that hunger and poverty are due not to population increase and food deficiency but to the nature of the economic system. Nevertheless, in 1954 the Party began a private study of birth control, followed a year later by Central Committee approval of nation-wide birth control education and clinics. This was extended in 1957 to a vigorous campaign for family planning. Two years later, for reasons unknown, the campaign was abruptly called off, the Party taking the position that all people are producers, and the more people the greater the production. In 1965 family planning was again advocated, and youth were enjoined to make late marriages. Even with moderate controls, at the present rate of growth China will have 1 billion people within her borders by 1980. Whether or not her production can be kept level with her reproduction is a question of interest not only to the Chinese but to all people on her frontiers. Yet it would be overstating the case to assume that China wants to expand her borders. Her foreign policy in Asia is committed to stabilizing her own frontiers, ridding Asia of United States power, and then communizing Asia by "wars of national liberation." This policy cares nothing for governments. The Chinese have proclaimed that no government, including that of the U.S.S.R., is representative of its people and that the peoples will have to free themselves. At the Afro-Asian Seminar in Algiers in 1964 Nan Han-chen detailed the plans for a program of political and economic warfare against the entire West by means of such "liberation struggles."

In September, 1966, China offered herself to the peoples of Asia as the base for long-term revolutionary war under the slogan "Hail People's War." It appears that the elderly men in charge of China, certainly the Mao-Lin faction, feel the need to press the revolution as far as it will go before they die. Men schooled in revolutionary warfare can hardly be expected to settle down to a conservative existence. They wish all Chinese to be schooled in the same adversity. Having appropriately rejected their own past, these men point toward a future already achieved by the West but neither know nor want to know the process by which the West became industrialized. This is a refusal to accept any other tradition, a reaching for the goals of another society without comprehension of the means. This, ironically enough, could mean a return to the statism that contributed to China's loss of technical superiority over the West, which she could boast of as late as the fifteenth century.

China must first develop every aspect of her economy if she

is to create a new society. Faith in the thoughts of Comrade Mao and the Red Guard is not sufficient. Her trade with other nations, carried on through Hong Kong, is still only 2 per cent of the world's volume. To expand it China must establish relations with the very systems she seeks to destroy. Her reliance on trade with the Communist bloc, most particularly the Soviet Union, rests on a fragile base; remittances from overseas Chinese are dropping, and foreign exchange derived from the exportation of products is neither substantial nor enduring. Thus, the development of foreign trade will be impossible as long as China remains hostile toward the United States; resents and distrusts the West generally (although with a willingness to bargain); becomes increasingly bitter toward the U.S.S.R.; and is critical of any movement or government in the "Third World" (the Afro-Asian bloc) that is not Communist or pro-Communist.

One suspects that the Chinese leadership is well aware of the needs and means for modern economic development; and yet they persist in seeing the world in their own terms. Their goal is to build Communism and accumulate power, and this they cannot achieve unless they can rationalize permanent revolution as a method of conducting public affairs. In their view, there must be generations of continuous revolutionary education, which will ultimately put "politics into command." In pursuing their faith the Chinese Communist Party has built a greater wall than that erected by Shi Huang-ti. They have isolated China not only politically but intellectually and socially from the world.

This isolation, and the possession of the bomb, may give them the time they need. Yet, tragically enough, what we would view as isolation, the Chinese must view as fulfillment, achieved through the reassertion of China's traditional cultural pride and the equally traditional rejection of alien cultures.

NOTES

1. *The Important Documents of the First Plenary Sessions of the Chinese People's Political Consultative Conference* (Peking: Foreign Languages Press, 1949), p. 29.

2. As cited in *Peking Review,* June 10, 1958.

3. Mu Fu-sheng, *The Wilting of the Hundred Flowers* (New York: Praeger, 1962), pp. 128-29.

4. Harold R. Isaacs, *The Tragedy of the Chinese Revolution* (Stanford: Stanford Univ. Press, rev. ed., 1951), pp. 312-13.

5. F. Michael, "The Role of Law in China," *The China Quarterly,* No. 9 (January-March, 1962), p. 145.

6. J. R. Levenson, *Modern China and Its Confucian Past* (Garden City, N.Y.: Doubleday Anchor, 1964), pp. 210-11.

7. This process wherein the individual knows that group loyalties are being tested against individual weaknesses and strengths has been called, in the West, "brainwashing." This term is a mistranslation of a quite common phrase that came into use in the May Fourth Movement when young people, in encouraging others to do some fresh thinking, would remark, "You ought to wash your brain."

8. Immanuel C. Y. Hsu, "The Reorganization of Higher Education in Communist China, 1949-61," *The China Quarterly,* No. 19 (July-September, 1964), p. 157.

9. *People's Daily* (Peking), March 26, 1964.

10. Dennis J. Doolin, *Communist China: The Politics of Student Opposition* (Stanford: Hoover Institution, 1964), p. 33.

11. *Ibid.,* p. 38.

12. *Ibid.,* p. 61.

13. *Ibid.,* p. 64.

14. Mervyn Jones, "Three Weeks in the Middle Kingdom," *Horizon,* Summer, 1964, p. 59.

15. C. Hsia, *Modern Chinese Fiction* (New Haven: Yale Univ. Press, 1961), p. 349.

16. Mao Tse-tung, *On Coalition Government* (Peking: Foreign Languages Press, 1960), p. 81.

17. Liu Shao-ch'i, *Report on the Agrarian Reform Problem* (Peking: Foreign Languages Press, 1950), p. 1.

18. *People's Daily,* November 13, 1960.

19. *Peking Review,* No. 49 (December 6, 1963), p. 7.

20. *Pravda,* September 2, 1964.

21. *New York Times.*

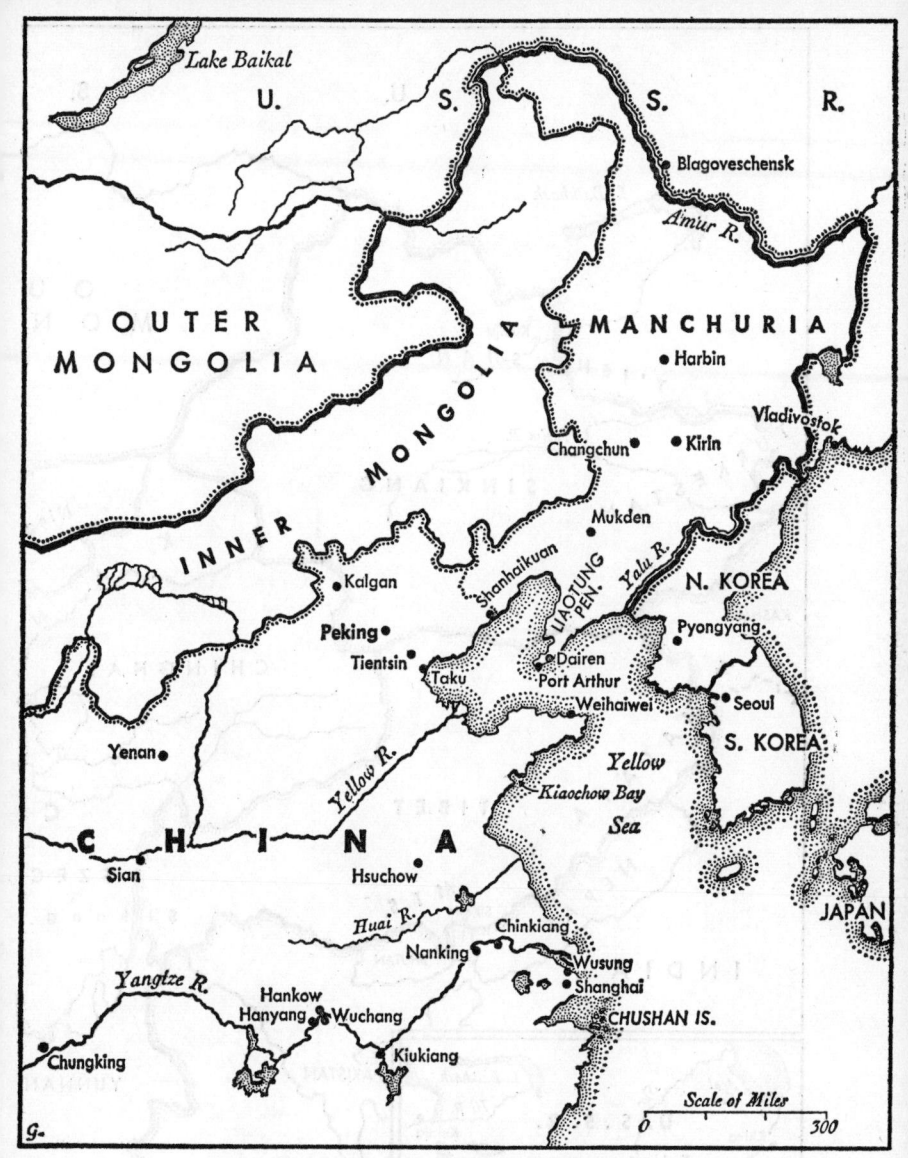

Lake Baikal

U.   S.   S.   R.

Blagoveschensk

Amur R.

OUTER
MONGOLIA

MANCHURIA

Harbin

INNER

MONGOLIA

Changchun   • Kirin

Vladivostok

Mukden

Kalgan

Shanhaikuan

LIAOTUNG
PEN.

Yalu R.

N. KOREA

Peking •

Tientsin •

Taku

Dairen
Port Arthur
Weihaiwei

Pyongyang

Seoul

S. KOREA

Yenan •

Yellow R.

Kiaochow Bay

Yellow

Sea

C   H   I   N   A

Sian

Hsuchow

JAPAN

Huai R.

Chinkiang

Nanking

Wusung
Shanghai

Yangtze R.

Hankow
Hanyang • Wuchang

CHUSHAN IS.

Chungking

Kiukiang

Scale of Miles

0   300

G-

North China and Borderlands

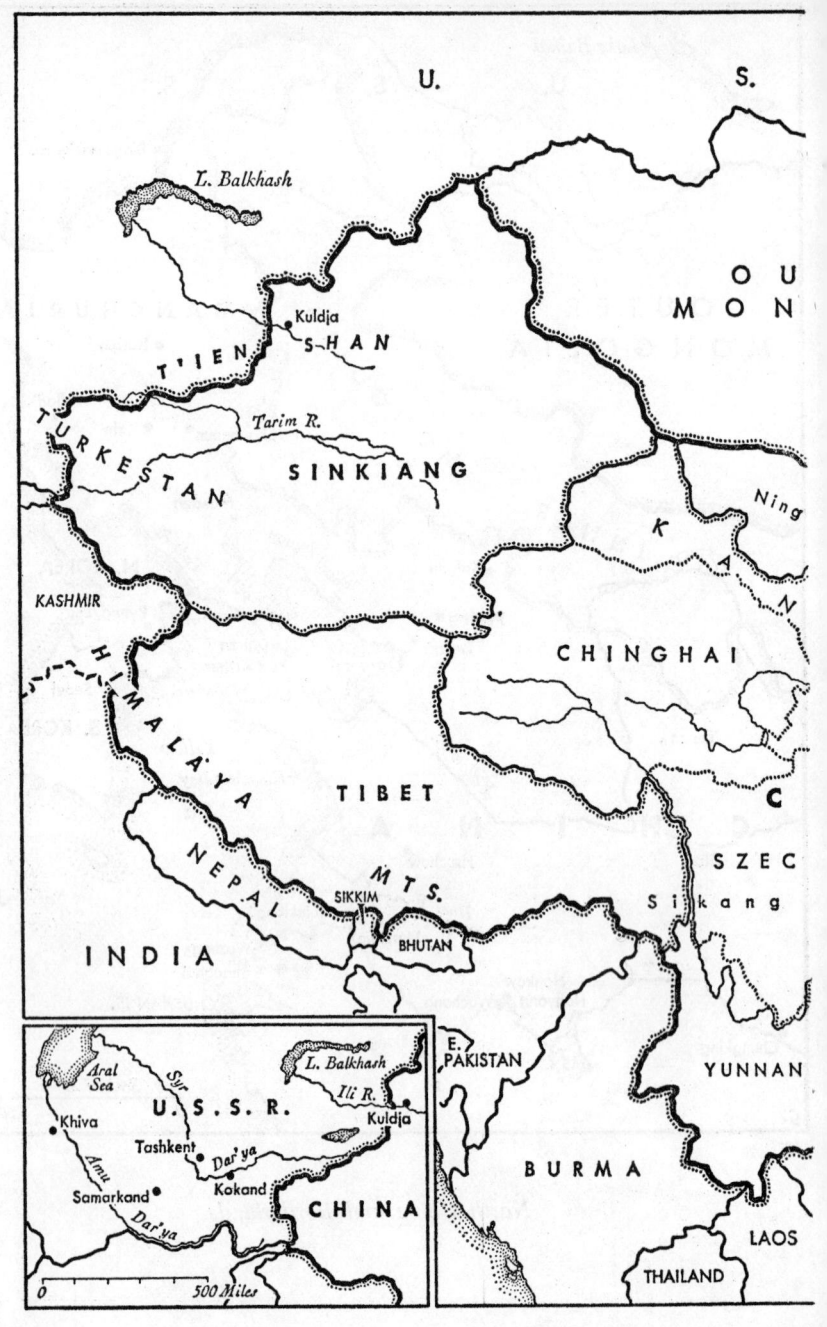

PRESENT-DAY CHINA:

Provinces, Mountains, Rivers, and Borderlands

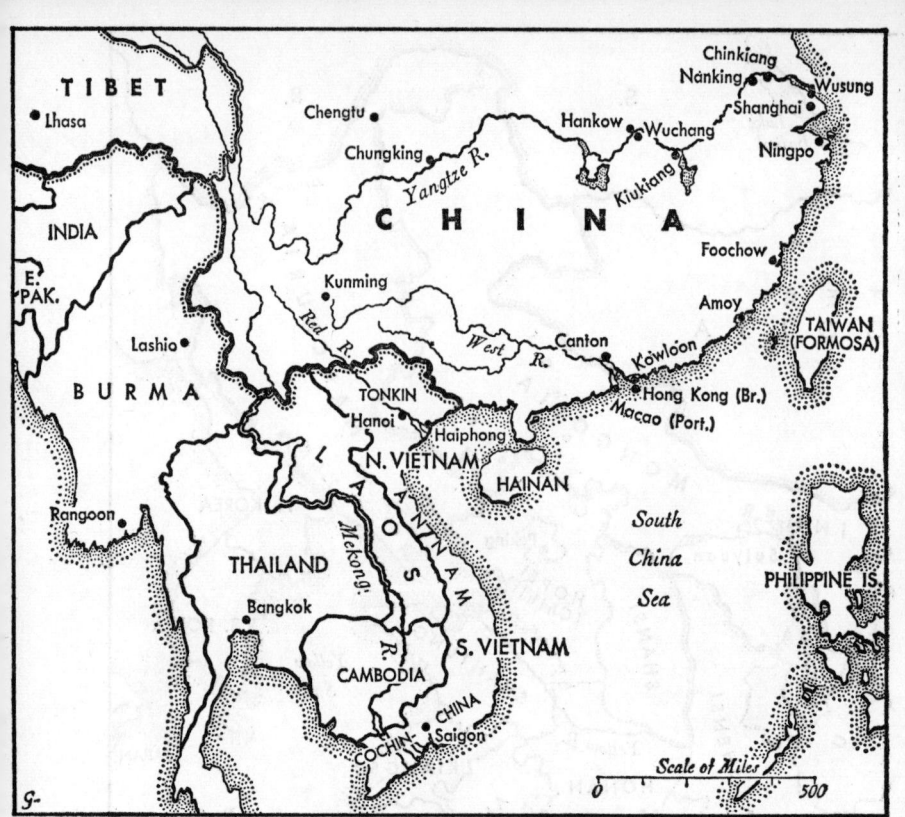

South China and Borderlands

Index

INDEX

CHINA
SINCE 1800

John A. Harrison

This informative book fills the need for a concise general history of modern China. It narrates China's "Time of Troubles" since the beginning of the nineteenth century, encompassing her encounter with foreign imperialism, her reactions to the thrust of alien cultures, the decline of her own cultural stability, and the years of political upheaval and economic ruin that set the stage for a decisive civil war. The concluding chapters present a detailed study of Communist China and bring the history of The People's Republic up to date.

China Since 1800 provides the dramatic background for the fall of the Chinese Republic and the rise of Chinese communism and puts into focus the powerful, enigmatic nation we confront today.

John A. Harrison, who is Dean of the Graduate School and Professor of History at the University of Miami, has been a student of Eastern Asia for some twenty-five years. A former director of The Association for Asian Studies, he is at present book review editor of the *Journal for Asian Studies* and the author of articles and books on the history of Eastern Asia.

An Original Harbinger Book
Harcourt, Brace & World, Inc.

Cover design by Jacqueline Schuman

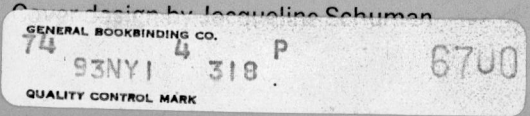
0-15-616880-4